Scribe Publications
YOU ARE NOT SPECIAL

David McCullough, Jr, taught for 16 years at Punahou School in Honolulu, and has been teaching at Wellesley High School near Boston since 2002. He lives with his wife and four children in Sudbury, Massachusetts.

You Are Not Special

and other encouragements

David McCullough, Jr

SCRIBE

Melbourne • London

Scribe Publications Pty Ltd
18–20 Edward St, Brunswick, Victoria 3056, Australia
2 John St, Clerkenwell, London, WC1N 2ES, United Kingdom

First published in the United States by Ecco, an imprint of HarperCollins Publishers,
New York, 2014

Published by Scribe 2014

Text design by Suet Yee Chong
Printed and bound by CPI Group (UK) Ltd, Croydon, CR0 4YY

National Library of Australia
Cataloguing-in-Publication data

McCullough, David, Jr., author.

You Are Not Special: and other encouragements / David McCullough Jr.

UK edition.

9781922247780 (hardback)
9781925113488 (e-book)

1. Educational sociology–21st century. 2. Education–Aims and objectives.
3. Parenting–Psychological aspects. 4. Attitude (Psychology).

306.432

scribepublications.com.au
scribepublications.co.uk

For my children . . . for everyone's

Let us, then, be up and doing. . . .
— "A Psalm of Life" by Henry Wadsworth Longfellow

Contents

★

Foreword

L ATE IN THE AFTERNOON OF JUNE 1, 2012, I GAVE A commencement speech. My audience, or so I thought, was seated there before me, the senior class of the public high school in Wellesley, a suburb west of Boston, where I teach English. I did not know the electronic world was eavesdropping, nor would I have thought anyone beyond earshot would take an interest in what I might say. Within a few days, though—thanks initially, it seems, to a line or two taken out of context—my speech and I became international headlines. Suddenly I was the "you're not special" guy.

From Berlin to Beijing, Facebook, Twitter and the blogosphere went crazy. The video, which I did not know was being shot, went viral. My e-mail in-box exploded. My voice mail overflowed. Local, national and international print reporters, radio people, television people scrambled to interview me. Pundits and provocateurs everywhere climbed onto their soapboxes to gas about the speech and me and kids today. Letters of appreciation began arriving. Long-lost students and friends checked in. Limousines appeared in my driveway. On the street strangers stopped to praise and thank me and take my picture. Sane-seeming people urged me to run for office. Far-flung rabbis, priests and ministers borrowed from and sermonized about what I'd said. It was sudden, surreal and gratifying. All because of a twelve-minute speech.

And I, a somewhat ruminative sort perfectly content with a quiet life and disinclined to opinionize, scratched my head.

My hope that afternoon—my only hope—was to be helpful to the graduates. This was simply good-bye and good luck to a group of kids I liked very much and knew pretty well, kids for whom I felt responsible. Moments after I sat down they would be done forever with high school, with childhood, and off to the rest of their lives. We were releasing them to the wild, and mine were last-minute reminders, instructions and a fond fare-thee-well.

The substance of my remarks came from a growing concern about what I've been seeing over the last several years, in my classroom, around school, across the culture, in my own household. Spurred by well-meaning but all too often micromanaging parents with resources to expend, teenagers in great number are becoming ever more preoccupied with conspicuous achievement—often at the expense of important formative experiences. Many are suffering from (or, rather, enjoying) inflated notions of themselves and regard every opportunity as theirs for the asking, every accolade their due. "We're not superior . . . ," which popular notions of equality and fairness inculcated since pre-K prohibit them from thinking, " . . . we're just special." Glowing successes, they assume, and therefore much happiness, will naturally follow. In this new cult of exceptionalism, to be average, just a regular kid—for most an unavoidable statistical fact—is to be thought inferior. To be ordinary is to be left behind.

No wonder so many of our children are having trouble recognizing what matters. No wonder so many—underprepared and anxious—are having trouble finding their way. I'm not the first, certainly, to notice what's happening, nor the first to share his concerns, but twenty-six years in a high school classroom, and the teenagers in my own house, have afforded me certain insights.

Hence this book.

In its way, though, my experience has been narrow, limited to two excellent and well-heeled suburban schools several thousand miles apart—one public, one private: Wellesley High for ten years and, before that, Punahou School in Honolulu for sixteen. In that time more than four thousand students have come through my classroom, almost all of whom have been interested and kind and cooperative and receptive to my efforts. In their company I've enjoyed innumerable satisfactions and many laughs and much fondness. I've also had supportive administrators and able, inspiring colleagues—and, but for the rare exception, parents have left me to my work with generous encouragement. I've loved every day of my teaching life and have prized every affirmation. I recognize how lucky I am in all of this. This book, then, is an expression of thanks to the educators, parents and kids, mostly the kids, who've given so very much to me . . . and of admiration for those who work wonders under conditions far less ideal.

I write in sympathy with parents, too. Janice, my wife, and I have four children—three of whom are teenagers—and we often find ourselves subject to the same temptations and cultural encouragements that can prove so problematic.

I know, then, why and whereof I write; I'm in the middle of it.

In many ways adolescents have never had it better. Opportunity, at least for some, would seem nearly limitless in scope and number and wow factor. But, for fear that left to themselves children will screw up their shot at the cultural plums, many parents have reduced to just about nil their children's latitude for independence, for pursuing an impulse to explore, for taking a risk, for enduring struggles, experiencing failure and figuring out what to do about it. We're all over them everywhere they turn—in no small measure because we see in them such quality, such potential. Or hope we do. And shouldering into fifty-pound backpacks, the kids are off to their next obligation, trying to remember what they're supposed to be thinking. Then they'll want to know if it's going to be on the test, and I won't be asking for, like, quotes, will I, and is it okay if they study with a friend, and could I just go over the, like, key points one more time, and maybe post them online, too, please, and if they, like, happen to have a bad day or something, could I allow a retest or at least, you know, scale the grades?

To question their mind-set does not occur to them. They feel neither indulged nor directed nor dependent. Nor, for that matter, fretful, naïve, self-absorbed, or soft. What they feel is *perfectly normal*—although they sense they're disapproved of by certain old people for reasons they don't quite get. Yes, they're aware of other perspectives and of people less fortunate, but the conditions under which they live set for them their norm. And what they see all around are kids a lot like themselves. In fact, put to it, many privileged teenagers would, against their better judgment, intimate with a note of envy that the disadvantaged are the real advantaged for the sympathy they enjoy, the excuses their circumstances provide, the honest pride they've earned from enduring hard knocks, their more legitimate claims to cool. With apologies to Mr. Kristofferson, nothing to lose looks to many privileged kids an awful lot like freedom. With their privilege, though, come expectations, and with expectations comes stress, and stress can be uncomfortable. Troubling to them, too, is the thought that anything they might achieve will be dismissed as just another dividend of undeserved advantage. At some level even teenagers understand you can't ride the chairlift and call yourself Edmund Hillary.

But they're just kids, of course. Works in progress. Neurologically unfinished. To expect of them far-reaching perspectives and informed objectivity, even fair-mindedness, particularly about themselves, is unreasonable. Nor did they choose the circumstances under which they're being raised. As with most other things, that was done for them.

And these are strivers with blinders on. They're trained, harnessed and directed to perform, to have answers and have them first, to earn As, score goals, play Bach, to prove themselves always and forever special. In everything they do, then, the stakes seem to them frightfully high. Any sign of a wobble and in step their parents. These are children, let's remember, whose framed ultrasound images still sit on dresser tops, whose parents' Facebook postings spill freely into the boastful, whose holiday cards are handsome, back-lit portraits of them accompanied by single-spaced missives recounting the year's triumphs. From birth plus a day or two they're strapped into the car seat and in a sense never get out—they're protected, driven and aimed in one direction. Ballyhooed from the hind end of the SUV from

"Baby on Board" to "My Child Was Student of the Month at Shady Grove Middle School" to "Amherst College," they're whisked to volleyball showcases, cello recitals, chess tournaments, speed and agility training, calculus camp, attitude tutorials, "brain training." The expectation—or ardent hope—is that every dividend will soon follow. Mothers and fathers are the strategic planners, the general managers, the CFOs, the PR and marketing departments, the chauffeurs, and, should something go awry, the troubleshooters. Should catastrophe strike—not enough playing time in the big game, a B– on the research paper, a prom dress crisis—they're the cavalry.

This isn't true for every child, of course. But it sure is for a lot of them.

And their fun, their moments of restorative repose, of recreational self-determination, of simple goofing around, have been co-opted by their parents as well. Today's teenagers are veterans of "playdates." Away from school, away from lacrosse practice and Mandarin lessons, parents chose with whom, when, where, for how long, and often at what they would play. As big kids they're no less protected, no less managed: they're driven to and from hyperorganized sporting events at which coaches yell, refs whistle and parents cheer, cry foul and instruct. With hands-on guidance from adults they backpack the Sierras, raft the wild Colorado, zip-line the Costa Rican rain forest, stroll the charming streets of Prague, build irrigation systems in Zimbabwe and photograph the picturesque Zimbabweans. They fund-raise to end diabetes, protect endangered species and stem global warming. They collect canned goods for the local food bank and tap-dance their hearts out in *Anything Goes*. Worthy endeavors all, absolutely—and gorgeous on the résumé. Meanwhile, they're packed into AP and honors courses and SAT prep sessions. They're sunscreened, water-bottled and helmeted. They're taught, tutored and coached, sometimes harangued, and if need be medicated, out of every deficiency real and imagined. They're expected, then, to thrive. To soar. For many expectation starts to feel like mandate, even inevitability. Should they not soar, though, or should our exasperation at seeing them amble or flounder or stray become too much—or the sound of our own hectoring voices blister the paint—we seek to change the rules, or lower expectations, blind ourselves to perspective and call them accomplished just the same.

And why?

Today's teenagers are, too many of them, unwitting victims of their parents' good intentions—or passive agents of their parents' vanity, or pawns to their parents' insecurities, or anxieties, or limited imaginations. They've become showpieces in an arms race to impress admissions officers, and thereby the Joneses, and perpetuate the legacy of privilege. The competition is, after all, stiff out there. And from atop the stepladder of often considerable resources, kids can look pretty tall, and absolutely the view from up there can be wonderfully enriching. Too often, though, their privileges are unwisely expended, in my view, and serve to promote, however inadvertently, swelling narcissism, assumptions of entitlement, superficial and/or robotic thinking. Empathy withers. Maturation is slowed or halted altogether. Self-reliance dies in the bud. And the anxious parent feels compelled to intercede once again.

And they're tired, teenagers are, all the time. They get half the sleep they need, an eighth of what they'd prefer. The fetish for a name-brand college is acquired, or imposed, so they play along. Like the rest of us they pick their battles, and in this one they know they're Custer. They're oversubscribed at school and overscheduled after. Even under the best of circumstances their eagerness to do homework registers down there with oral surgery, yet to them it feels like that's all they do. Late into the night they trudge with fifty French vocab words, five questions to answer on the "Robber Barons and the Gilded Age" chapter, a lab report for chemistry, a ten-problem packet for math, a five-page analysis of Iago's motivations . . . none of this is their idea of a rocking good time. A rocking good time is their idea of a rocking good time and then twelve hours of downy sleep.

But the loud demand of our schools these days is to produce high achievers in big numbers. Abetted by a laudable spirit of inclusion, concern for strugglers and impulses to innovate, this is most efficiently accomplished across the spectrum with lower standards, gentler assessments and inflated grades. Should a concerned or skeptical eyebrow go up, explain it away with earnestness, hip packaging and edu-jargon. Should intellectual acuity suffer, redefine the term. And because each school year builds on the one before it, the long-term effect is underprepared kids persuaded they're doing perfectly well and have been, probably, for as long as they can remember. And since they don't know what they don't know, and not knowing has yet to prove much of an issue, they wonder what all the fuss might be. They care about indigenous peoples and the homeless and the melting of the polar ice caps, they made second team all-league, they floss their teeth and the report card shines, so where's the problem? Chillax, they say.

And it's not just how we're assessing them. Much energy among faculties is devoted these days to concerns about "student stress" and "engaging young learners" in "student-centered experiences" to which the "whole child" can "relate," to providing opportunities in "holistic learning," in "collaborative learning," in which students develop a "skill set" and have "a personal investment" and are "empowered" to "think outside the box" and become part of a "community of lifelong learners." Yet we grade them, too. Grades don't matter, we preach ad infinitum, but what the hell is this C+? Further, schools have assumed, or have had foisted upon them, aspects of raising children formerly addressed at home. A teacher is no longer just a teacher, but a tutor, therapist, guru, nurse practitioner, Dutch uncle, minister without portfolio and cop on the beat. And for fear of appearing exclusionary or bruising a child's self-esteem, teachers will minimize risk by reducing rigor, keeping goals within easy reach and throwing ever more confetti when he or she gets there.

Of course, if one stops for just a second to consider the brutalities that daily torment good and honest people the world around, that privileged teenagers are being micro-managed and indulged to their detriment seems an issue trivial in the extreme. If this is our big worry, then, well, we're very lucky to have it. Meanwhile, worldwide more than 300 million children have no shoes . . . and the cupcakes have soccer cleats for grass and soccer cleats for turf and futsal shoes and basketball sneakers and just-knocking-around sneakers and running shoes and snowboarding boots and strappy leather sandals and Uggs and Vans and Timberlands and dressy shoes and somewhat dressy shoes and not at all dressy but, you know, fun shoes, and Hunters for the wet weather and cute little Toms in three different colors and preppy Sperrys and Merrells for the rock-climby look.

So let 'em eat quiche, one might be inclined to conclude, roll off to the country club and into fatuous, self-congratulating irrelevance. Who cares? We have, don't we, a few more pressing concerns?

Well, I'll suggest these indulged kids, our kids, could be, should be, part of the solution for a planet in sore need. With their advantages they could be, should be, leading the way. They could be, should be, each of them, among the ablest, clearest of head, best informed, best prepared, most inspired, most innovative, most empathetic, and, therefore, a great cause for hope, for confidence even, worldwide. In each is enormous promise—talent, imagination, energy, heart. This I know. We should be raising them, preparing them, with that in mind, setting our goals a little beyond sparkling lacrosse statistics, next month's report card and, fingers crossed, a golden acceptance letter. We should see the comfort and security we enjoy and the resources at our disposal as opportunities, as responsibilities, to do the planet and those who inhabit it some good, to right what wrongs we can, to shoulder our share of the load and then some. And if our children are in no position to step up because of well-meant misallocations and assorted squanderings, whose will be? Of what purpose civilization if those welcome to the best it can offer wrap themselves in selfishness and delusion?

That some of us have gone a bit awry in raising our children, then, is in my view a danger. At risk is more than just the likelihood of productive, fulfilling lives. Alarmist though this may sound, send into it enough underrealized, overmatched kids and our civilization, or what these days is passing for it, will collapse upon itself, too hollow for its weight.

MEANWHILE, THERE'S THE New Millennium technology craze . . . holy moly, is there ever . . . the breathless infatuation with hi-def, 3D, 5G, glued to the hand, glued to the ear, twenty-first-century cyber gee-whizzery. They're coming at us so fast—the gizmos, the doodads, the gimcracks, the wonderments—so ubiquitously, so overwhelmingly, we've not yet found how best to wrangle each new miracle into genuine usefulness. To great and sudden fanfare they arrive, we blink twice, open our gullets and swallow them whole. And to sit for a minute to try to make sense of the latest is to be too preoccupied for the next latest.

And first they grab the young ones.

The young ones breathe and eat and sleep and futz with their hair and think about what their friends think and say "like" eleven times a sentence and slog away at their homework and fiddle constantly with electronics. This is what they do. Neither jackhammer nor dynamite could separate them from their cell phones. And they see the e-universe not as a happy novelty, nor even a facile and convenient forum for the sharing of ideas and information, but as a parallel, and in some cases preferable, reality. Teilhard and McLuhan would turn cartwheels. Social media is all the buzz. Vapidity, egocentrism, exhibitionism, de rigueur. Today's teenagers can't remember when life was not this way, nor would they want to imagine it. Their connections to one another, their communications, feel to them neither haphazard nor tenuous nor superficial, nor, well, silly. Or do, but to them it's not an issue. "Whatever," they say with a shrug. And any time the new devices save them on a task, they waste times two on the new devices. No event, it seems, goes undigitized, no news is too trivial to report far and wide and discuss with bowed heads and flying thumbs. Reality, then, is just raw material. Electronic connectedness—in and of itself, irrespective of subject—means everything. Disconnection from most everything else appears largely immaterial. And with all the nitwittery bombarding them, good judgment, the discerning eye, a solid sense of self, of perspective, become both more important and less likely. Trying to hold on to any of the old standards, the traditional ideals, is seen as a risible form of denial.

Parents have come to rely on the gizmos, too . . . and why not? First as babysitters and pacifiers—the new plug-in drug. Sit the cherubs in front of a video game—only the highly educational, of course, slipped from a PBS tote bag—and they're quiet, they stay put. Later, we'll teach them the violin there and Italian and algebra and the migratory habits of the wildebeest. When at last their own migratory habits kick in, their cell phones serve as tracking and surveillance devices. With them we remain in constant communication, participate in every decision and respond to any dicey situation as it arises—whether reeling kids in or galloping to the rescue. We sit in their pockets wherever they go, with information updated and instructions dispensed hourly.

And they're everywhere, electronics. They've infiltrated every corner of our children's lives. It's beyond saturation. It's a redefinition of existence. Teenagers bring their devices when they go to the gym, to the movies, to the bathroom. Their phones and laptops are the first thing they see in the morning, the last thing they see at night. In between they hardly look up. They do their homework there. Recreate there. Interact there. Sit teenagers with one another in a pizza place, in a car, in a store, in a park, on a couch, at a ball game, by a tranquil mountain lake, and, in the pine-scented twilight, to the hoo-hooing of the loons, they fiddle with their devices. No, not with them, *in* them. Nor for them on their own is there any quiet, no ambient sound, no aural engagement with the (actual) universe: a pause in life's din and in go the earbuds, on go the headphones, and they wrap themselves in a cocoon of music.

And as of course they would, electronics have infiltrated school, too. They're front and center now in how students experience formalized classroom learning. Smart Boards are all the rage, websites, chat rooms, tweets, blogs, wikis and Nings.* E-books, iPads and tablets have arrived. Teachers are encouraged, sometimes at administrative sword point, to "integrate technology" into all they do, are led to believe they're stick-in-the-muds and on thin ice if they don't. New is not only good, new is better, always. And absolutely the medium is the message. Any questions or throat clearings are deemed reactionary or troglodytic.

Take paper writing, age-old staple of the high school experience, traditional meat and potatoes of English class. When I began teaching in the mid-1980s, students sat with their books and their brains and made outlines, wrote drafts of their papers in longhand, then found typewriters to peck out the finished version. Screw up and reach for the Wite-out. Screw up badly and reach for a clean sheet of paper and start over. Then along came computers and writing became "word processing." Today young writers click away, let the machine supervise their spelling, usage and grammar, then hit print. Done. Already in certain corners we're eliminating the print part, and papers never see actual paper. Soon enough, one imagines, a "paper" will become an archaic concept—so too the commitment to getting things right,

---

* I'm not entirely sure which of these words should be capitalized, but certainly the nomenclature is as suggestive of frivolousness, even inanity, as it is hurried to evolve.

the respect for permanence, that paper and ink make necessary. The written word, then, will no longer be an ideological, intellectual and aesthetic stake in the ground, but an evolving pixilated abstraction welcoming any ongoing adjustment a mood, passing thought, or the "feedback" or "input" of others might suggest. Getting things right? We'll worry about that later. Gone, too, are the inculcations of practice, of mastering fundamental skills through trial and error and repeated experience. Paper and ink, the tactile experience of making something, they'll be gone as well.

Also gone these days is sustained, uninterrupted concentration: any ping or buzz or chirp announcing a communication from a friend over the course of an evening requires of a teenager at least a cursory glimpse and, usually, a quick response. Bellow at them twenty-two times in robust volume to *please* hang up the wet towel and they don't hear you. The phone pings/buzzes/chirps once and they hear it. And if the phone isn't pinging/buzzing/chirping pretty regularly, the kid becomes distracted with concern that something must be wrong. Wtf, he or she mutters. Omg.

So, are high school students now better or even more efficient writers? No. Thinkers? No. Do they find more edification or pleasure in the process? Not that I can tell.

And the Internet has made the gathering of information like a trip to a limitless supermarket . . . only it comes to you, and instantaneously. Tutorials and "massive open online courses" abound. A quick click and Wikipedia delivers. And cheating is so easy you'd have to be a monk or George Washington to resist temptation. Type in the title of a novel, for example, and up pops a list of theses for a paper. Click on a thesis and up pops topic sentences and any quotations you might need. At little cost to their notions of integrity, overscheduled, results-oriented students see these as perfectly acceptable time-savers.

Knowing how to spell, knowing conventions of grammar and usage, are no longer necessary. In fact, *knowing* is no longer necessary. It's an outdated concept, almost quaint, like churning butter or dial-up Internet service. Technology, cuz . . . what you want are, like, skillz. Knowledge? What for? Just slows you down. Why pack your head with a bunch of bs, as a student recently asked me in reasoned tones, when in under, like, two seconds Google can find anything you'd ever want to know about anything? When you think about it, he went on, school learning's kind of a waste of time. Pretty soon we're all gonna just stay home and do it online anyway. It's a . . . a, like, paradigm shift or whatever. Dawn of a new age, dude.

I tried to hang on to the "when you think about it" and chose for self-preservation's sake to slide past "school learning." "But what about self-respect?" I asked. He dipped his head noncommittally, perhaps suspecting I might have him there but unsure how it could matter. Maybe he was just trying to get a rise out of the dinosaur. I hope so.

More egregious cheating, of course, down to and including wholesale plagiarism, is just as easy. The culture seems almost to encourage it: "If you ain't cheatin' you ain't tryin'" and so on. Performance-enhancing drugs, high-finance chicanery, political rascality, cyber theft, rampaging solipsism . . . all seem everywhere and somehow normal. As an apprehended plagiarist recently put it, "Everybody else cheats, so I'd be stupid not to, too." "Ethics are situational," explained another scholar sagely. And with a couple of quick clicks you can have yourself a thorough, polished analysis of anything from *Animal Farm* to "The Zoo Story." And with Mom or Dad or the $100-an-hour tutor "editing" the paper, a kid can get off pretty close to scot-free. But, to echo my student, who needs to know anything anyway? Besides, paper writing's a bogus exercise, five color-by-numbers paragraphs, a hoop-jumping skill irrelevant beyond the high school classroom and of value to no one but the cranky old teachers you have to please.

How soon, one wonders, before we wave off thinking, too? Or even attentive meandering? It's a pain, thinking, time-consuming and unfun. Cogito, ergo headache. Probably even, like, bad for you. A study'll come out one of these days. Can't I just do a, you know, reflection or, like, post something online instead?

Since they've had so little experience operating their noggins freely and to serious purpose, teenagers today are suspicious of their own ponderings and conjurings as too unimpressive. And impressing, of course, is the whole point. If I thought of it on my own, they reason, it's gotta be no big whoop. So, they wonder, what's the big deal about where or how they got it? It's all about results anyway, right? Who cares how you get there? Besides, didn't your boy Einstein say imagination is more important than knowledge?

With their electronic enthusiasms and cultural encouragements, teenagers today seem to be abdicating both imagination and knowledge. Express a concern about it and they'll smile sympathetically, nod earnestly, because they've learned it works out better for them if they keep the old farts happy, then they turn the corner and revert to type. For children of the "Information Age," that they're so often uninformed and absent independent thought is to them utterly unconcerning. To them repackaging received thinking is effort enough. And there's always unspoken peer pressure: none of my friends seems to know or come up with much of anything, goes the reasoning, so if I did I'd be a, like, show-off and odd.

Electronics dominate their downtime, too. Electronics are the entertainer, the default time killer. Reading? Are you kidding? Even television, pop radio and talking on the phone (actual speaking, employing the larynx, organizing and articulating cogent thoughts, listening, reasoning and responding usefully in the moment to what another might say) are the pastimes of yesteryear. Norman Rockwell could do a painting. Off their schedules, teenagers today are like wisteria off the trellis: into a limp tangle they collapse. It's hard to know what to do or why. Surface thrill, then, is entertainment, nonthinking a relief—so they blog, tweet, text, Skype, IM and Snapchat. They bob their heads to a Maroon 5 tune and chuckle at a YouTube clip of some guy in a Spiderman suit falling off his roof. They ogle anatomy in action on the naughtier websites, or achieve ultimate grand master status in the splattery disembowelment of intergalactic Nazi terrorist ninja storm trooper zombies . . . all in no small part because there are no adults there. It's *their* world, vivid and immediate, where they can indulge themselves in any enthusiasm or inanity or titillation without risk of adult judgment, adult comment.

Because adults have them everywhere else.

IMPORTANT TO NOTE here are the circumstances of my own childhood: I too grew up in privilege, as did my parents before me. Like them I knew no serious want nor impediment. I too was loved and encouraged in most everything I did. I too saw unearned opportunity. I too wasted time on inanity. I too had the confidence of mostly blue skies. That, even, I sit writing these lines has a great deal to do with the fact that I grew up in a house full of books and my father is a writer with contagious enthusiasms who always encouraged me to pursue mine. Like my parents, I went to a prestigious private secondary school and a prestigious private college. At both I fell short of expectations from time to time. I made mistakes from which I did not always extricate myself smoothly. Many of my advantages I took for granted. Some I squandered. And like my parents, Janice and I are trying to give our children the best start in life we can. Sometimes, maybe even often, this means making the most of what circumstance affords us, which our children can also take for granted. Knowing how best to proceed sometimes eludes me. Often my children will show me the way. All of this informs my thinking.

This book comes from my years as a teacher, a father, a son, a former kid, a husband and an interested observer of the species. It's for teenagers and anyone with an interest in them. I hope they find it helpful. I like to imagine them putting it down—or, I suppose, turning it off—and reaching for another book, then maybe another, and, before long, getting up, heading out, taking great happy lungfuls of air, eager to do some good.

YOU ARE
NOT SPECIAL...

and Other Encouragements

Chapter 1

Mums and Dads

A body that don't get started right when he's little ain't got no show.

—*Adventures of Huckleberry Finn* by Mark Twain

BETTER, PROBABLY, WOULD BE TWO LIVES—LEARN WITH the first, live with the second . . . live *right*. This is not a new thought. Stumble and bumble along in the initial go-round, follow your nose, explore, experiment, make your mistakes, suffer the bruises and indignities, observe, assess, take notes, calculate, strategize; then come back in the second ready to claim the landscape in long, confident strides, enjoying every success in the golden light of a warm and smiling sun.

But of course life doesn't work that way. You get—each of us gets—one shot at it. You have to learn and live with the same life. And circumstances, and the landscape, and you, are always evolving, sometimes quickly, sometimes unnervingly quickly. Then, usually on a day and for reasons beyond your control, and all too soon, it ends.

This, this precisely, is why parents can be so annoying.

To mothers and fathers—and I'm right there among them—who generally love their children to the marrow of their being, experience is their legacy, their lessons learned what they have to give. Children are the only second shot at life reality allows. Children are their parents' chance to make adjustments and get things right, to apply for beneficial effect the wisdom they've accrued, sometimes at great cost. Of this, no matter how headstrong, or unhip, or downright out to lunch we may appear, mothers and fathers are seldom unaware. And to us our children's thoughts on this subject tend to be less than germane. Parents, parents always think, know best. After all, your arrival, which to us feels like a few weeks ago, forced on us undeniable, immutable adulthood, and authority has proven necessary. And compensatory. As you might not be aware, to be a parent is an enormous, sometimes unnerving, always preoccupying responsibility. And by the way, we've been around the block a time or two and you have not, of which you've been apprised more than once. Okay, more than nine hundred seventy-three times.

So, quite deliberately—and, we're certain, perfectly reasonably—we instruct and dote upon and impose expectations. We encourage and demand and pull rank when resisted. We hover and intrude and harp (this because we love you) and tell you at every opportunity and in exhaustive detail just how it was when we were kids. The tricky waters we plied. The hardships we endured. The victories we earned through pluck and guile. How effectively we studied for tests late into the night, how heroically we manned the cash register at the grocery store, hoed the turnip patch, scrubbed the kitchen floor, trudged through a driving snow to repay a borrowed dime . . . how we spoke on the telephone, a dial telephone, black in color, affixed to the wall in the kitchen, our only privacy whatever the full stretch of the cord would allow. Of course, that you've seen pictures of us in those glorious days of yore inspires enough general hilarity to, if not invalidate entirely, certainly undermine any sense of wisdom the wrinkled presume. The hair alone. How were we not forever cracking up at the sight of one another? Yet on we bloviate, our navigational certitudes set miles and decades ago.

More telling, of course, more potent, are the I-wish-I'd-known-then-what-I-know-nows, the lessons learned with the ache of a bumped nose, the sting of a skinned knee—hence the full catalogue of enriching opportunities through which the children of privilege are so often nudged at the toe of a parental shoe. Or kicked. Parents have learned, sometimes pointedly, it's better to succeed than fail, and if they have the resources to give their kids a boost, why not?

The near-term intention for many is to impress an admissions officer on an ivied campus somewhere. There's also a little unspoken quid pro quo involved: I've done this, goes the thinking, sacrificed this, so you can get that. And that. And that. So get out there, kid, and give it your all.

At work here, too, are larger cultural phenomena. Educated people, for example, are marrying and having children later and later in life, often waiting until they're in their mid- or even late thirties. Some wait to the very tolling of the procreative bell. Often they'll explain to others and themselves they want to be "ready" before they settle down and start having children. By this they mean more than just achieving economic traction: they want to ease by degrees into a parental mind-set knowing they "did" their twenties "right." The hedonist is sated, or depleted, the career rolling, the deadline looming. Some I think are just waiting to feel fully adult: at some point, they hypothesize, a nesting instinct will kick in and they'll want the minivan, the labradoodle, the whole burbs-and-babies thing. So they wait—and avoiding commitment starts to feel like savvy strategy. By the time their children have become teenagers, then, many parents in the tonier demographics are well into middle age, well into their careers and have abundant experience and connections and resources from which to draw. And what better, more natural investment than their children's ascent?

Meanwhile there's this: the growing suspicion among

certain parents that his or her work, the purpose to which he or she has dedicated him- or herself for twenty years or more, is a flimsy peg on which to hang self-worth. While George Babbitt or Willy Loman will assert the what-I-do-for-a-living malaise is nothing new, it has a decidedly contemporary feel. Slaves to necessity, many middle-agers today, even those with the luxury of options, have, from my observation, little passion for, or gut-level belief in, what they do for a living. The idealism and bounce of youth is gone. Realities have been confronted. And ceilings. Ghastly signs of aging are appearing in the mirror. Years of toil have yielded little beyond what the bank statement attests. Commitment to a particular enterprise or organization is often inches-deep and short-lived: income earners first, folks move around to move up. And it's climb or perish. Produce or hit the bricks. The price for all this is an ever-greater distance from the earth. And, often, the family hearth. For all the remuneration, then, they can feel frazzled, a bit insubstantial and distant from the satisfactions that really matter.

Which children witness. And the lesson they learn is do what you do for the material reward. Do this to get that. Hold your nose, grit your teeth, bleed if you have to, leave happiness on the sidewalk if you must, even peace of mind, but earn, baby, earn. Get yours. In high school this translates to an almost mercenary yen for grades and accolades. They're the contemporary teenager's net worth.

And worse by far than not a lot of fun—which many can well be—too many occupations in the mapless new economy defy more time-honored notions of productivity; too many seem, well, a bit nebulous, precarious, morally suspect even . . . in pursuit of, as Nick Carraway calls it, nonolfactory money—banking, finance, investments— abstract money, however green and copious, idiosyncratic of a vastly complex, nontactile, quasitheoretical, tenuous economy, generated coincidentally like heat by a robust machine busy doing other things. Promissory money that never quite fulfills.

For some fathers this can be particularly confounding as it runs counter to, even offends, traditional definitions of masculinity: callused, muscled, capable, principled. Certainly, the bottom line can be impressive—and attendant anxieties severe—but one wonders if in an unguarded moment even the slickest plutocrat will admit bottom lines matter maybe not so much after all, will look at his day's toil and wonder to what it really amounted. Or a social situation will require him to explain just what it is he does for a living, and the longer he has to go to put the right spin on it, the more contorted the semantics, the tinnier he sounds even to himself. "Well, actually," he tries, "I'm a partner in a firm that handles individual and corporate sheltered annuities in a nonstructured . . ." and already he'll know he's lost you. Enough of it and he starts to lose himself.

Farther down the food chain and without the mollifying net worth, this happens more frequently. "Systems analyst" or "account manager" or "regional sales director" ain't exactly the stuff of he-man legend. Clint Eastwood would not have played one in the movie. Consequently, many parents, many dads, turn to their kids for a little surrogate affirmation, for simple reassurance: I may sit in a cubicle from dark to dark and nudge figures around a computer screen, my ascent may be confounded by some lunch-meat MBA, my waistline may be expanding, my eyesight failing, my gums and hairline vying to see which can recede faster, my marriage settling into a contrapuntal rhythm of ennui and annoyance, Eva Mendes will never know I exist, but try to tell me my kid ain't an absolute champ. In the classroom, on the diamond, on the stage, take your pick. In the child, then, love and pride conflate, from which rises meaning; and many a father then sees in his high-achieving child great soaring affirmation, and in himself something of the quiet hero, the buzzards feasting regularly on his innards so his child might work wonders in the light.

And let's remember all of this is happening in a world fraught with subprime mortgage swaps and Madoffs and Katrinas and pedophile priests and bankruptcy and collapse and unemployment and bailouts and Occupy Wall Streets and BP oil platforms and deficits and Tea Parties and Sanduskys and Auroras and fiscal cliffs and shutdowns.

Whither, then, ideals, substance, integrity, civility, principles, progress? Civilization itself? One's children, humanity anew, comes the ready answer. The next generation is our great hope. Watch them soar.

So there's that.

Then there's today's mothers, legions of whom are out there in the workplace, too, shoulder to shoulder with the men, as or better educated, every bit as capable, or more so, every bit as busy, or more so, every bit as harried, or more so, but burdened, often, with expectations and a version of guilt from which fathers are almost entirely free. As appropriate, as essential, as it is to have women in the workplace—and not merely to satisfy just notions of equality, but to keep the economic engine running at home and abroad—a working mother has in her heart, to one degree or another, a constant ache. My children, she's thinking, need me at home. Assurances that she "can have it all" merely taunt. She can't and she knows it. Life has become an exercise in triage— she dashes from crisis to urgency and back again. Therefore, when circumstances allow her to turn to her children, or as necessity dictates, she compensates by ultramomming. She flings herself at it. In the orthodontist's waiting room she rehashes the layout of the quarterly report while rebraiding the little sister's hair and helping her with six times seven equals forty-two; in the car she interrogates the swim coach about schedule confusions and coordinates the carpool and

swings by to pick up the poster board for the Harriet Tub-
man presentation at History Day; she stir-fries the chicken,
broccoli and sprouts, sets up tomorrow morning's meeting
with sales and marketing, and explains to a semislack civ-
ics scholar at the kitchen table the checks and balances of
a tripartite government, tells him to sit up straight and put
away the gd phone. And if she's flying along at eighty-eight
miles an hour, her head is doing ninety-eight. A hundred
and eight. The least you, her kid, can do, for cripes' sake, is
get out there and try, try, try, and, all right, excel and smile
and be happy and clean your room.

These of course are not all mothers and fathers. Many
handle it all with an able hand and a tranquil soul however
the gales, outer and inner, might toss. In certain regions,
though, their numbers appear to be diminishing.

A different—and in my view rarer—scenario includes
another species of fish: the mother and/or father whose
work is so rewarding ("remunerative" can suit here, too,
as for slightly different reasons can "demanding") and
whose command and general spectacularness there are so
affirmed that he or she, perhaps with whiffs of compunction about putting workplace satisfactions (or challenges)
first, indulges the child for purposes of self-congratulation
(or emotional restitution). The plush times before the reces-
sion fertilized the notion. Children were showered with the
best of everything—down to the last laptop, cell phone and

graphite tennis racket—the trappings of privilege. In many of the swankier neighborhoods this continues unabated.

And kids cost, they cost big. In any neighborhood. With a kid in the house money pours in torrents out the doors, out the windows, up the chimney, out the dryer vent, between the clapboards. Children need to be fed, clothed, accoutred. A pair of sneakers here, a birthday present there, here a hockey stick, there a graphing calculator, there another graphing calculator because the first one got swiped, lab fees, team fees, piano lessons, braces, tuition, defrayments, copays. Bills, bills, bills, bills, bills. It's enough to make a strong parent weep. If you'd like to know why, sit down sometime and figure out how much you cost in a year . . . and not just the mocha latte budget, iTunes downloads and protein bars. What share is yours of the mortgage, the insurance, the heating oil, the electricity, the water, the taxes, the plumber's visit, the groceries, the vacation? And how about the four-wheeled behemoth in the driveway to accommodate you and your stuff and the dog you swore up and down you'd walk every day but haven't in seven months? And the gas? The oil change and brake job? And how about the closet light you left on for ninety-four straight hours and the fine for the overdue library book under the dust bunnies under the tangled sixty-dollar sweatpants under your unmade bed? It adds up, and it keeps adding and adding, and to be responsible for you is like sitting in the backseat of a taxi watching the meter run at warp speed.

And all of this with college looming and tuition to eat us, your loving parents, alive.

For all the expenditure, then, is it unreasonable to expect at least a little return on our investment of love and effort and hard-earned cash? And boundless hope. Is an expectation of focus and hard work on the kid's part so unreasonable? And while we're at it, some evidence of appreciation? And how about a smile? A kind word? Parents, you see, are people, subject to self-doubt, who don't always have every answer, who are doing the best they can. And we're only as happy, generally, as our least happy child, only as successful as our least successful child. We have, then, also, our own vested dispositional interest in your performance that churns both at and below the level of conscious thought. We too want very much to see your dreams and efforts rewarded. If you find us impatient, intrusive, dictatorial, erratic . . . well, sometimes we just can't help ourselves.

If you want to understand your parents all of this is A.

Here's B:

Fathers now—and I don't know where or when it began—go to ultrasound appointments and birth classes. We go—and this is huge—into the delivery room. Right there into the fray. We even participate. Okay, it's token participation, more than a little patronizing, but there the father stands, useful as a goldfish, inches from the action, scrubbed and gowned, coaching the breathing, as if that makes a difference, dabbing and kissing the maternal brow, which might help a little, and at last, gulpingly, with all its symbolic freight, manning the scissors and snipping the cord, which would get done anyway. And in a way the mother doesn't, in a way the mother can't, he witnesses the whole sweating, straining, gnashing, wrenching, shrieking, bleeding, fluidy, Technicolor process. And believe me it's vivid. And extremely, um . . . biological.

And miraculous.

And as beautiful as anything there is.

As of course it would, this from-the-outset involvement inspires in contemporary fathers a kind of automatic hands-on dedication our own fathers can find mystifying, or amusing, or dismaying. My father, who became one in the 1950s, sat comfortably in a waiting room as I arrived. From there he was, and has remained, ever a loving, dedicated father, whose children gave him, I think it safe to say, no end of pride and pleasure. But divisions of responsibility, sprung from practicality as much as from social tradition, left what was then understood to be mothering to my mother. He was working, earning a living, providing, which is what fathers did. It would have been odd, even concerning, if he did not. I'd see him at dinner. Weekends as he could he'd give over to family adventures or projects around the house. None of this is disassociated from the looks he would hoist a few decades later on seeing me burp an infant, change a toddler's diaper, supervise a visit to the playground, or, more recently, escort a teenager to a three-day soccer tournament in Orlando. Not only was I in some small but important way compromising my masculinity and squandering resources better spent elsewhere, I was indulging a watchful child to his or her detriment and surrendering to unfortunate cultural trends.

I, though, who became a father in the 1990s, ears ringing, palms sweating, eyes welling, was right there front and center to welcome each grayish, purplish, gooey, slithery little iguana into the world and felt him, then her, then him and him again, somehow and instantaneously become *everything* to me. The sun, the moon and the stars. One could weep. One could write sonnets—write books. And I saw up close what their sweet, beautiful, tough-as-nails mother went through to make it happen. How then could I not understand the ensuing responsibilities and parental drudgery as at least somewhat shared? How could I not then dive headlong into contemporary notions of a father's role?

Fathers of earlier generations—no less loving, no less devoted—defined themselves based on different expectations, different circumstances, different criteria: they were the sole breadwinners. They hammered away at the office.

Mothers stayed home, ran things there. Mothers, like mine, did ninety-nine percent of what was then widely understood to be mothering. So, more or less, had it always been, with their parents, and theirs before them, all the way back to, one presumes, a quiet watering hole somewhere in the Rift Valley. At home fathers shared tales of their forays in the wider world. They imparted wisdom and authority from on high. Father, after all, knew best. Often today's mothers—Janice, for example—work outside the home, too, and bring home with them much of the steam and managerial style of a day at the office. Often they win as much bread as, or more than, their husbands. This changes the equation in both fact and perception—the very concept of gender roles seems less relevant today, even archaic—which changes parenting, which of course changes children. Confronted by this new parental full-court press, contemporary children will often respond with a shrugging compliance, even passivity. This is the new normal. They go along to get along, as a teacher friend observed sympathetically, because it's too much trouble not to.

With so much invested in him or her, the compliant and accomplished child, the exceptional child, serves as affirmation of the parenting that produced him or her. The child's blue ribbon is therefore the parents' blue ribbon. The father or mother can then turn around and wave the science prize, the local sports page profile, the Duke acceptance letter at the neighbors, at his or her own parents, and say, "Ha! See?"

Also significant among today's realities is this: earlier generations had more children, which gives grandparents an authority and near-biblical aura their parent children lack. With more offspring under their roof, yesterday's mothers and fathers had to spread their ministrations, resources and expectations further and thinner, their attitudes by necessity more laissez-faire. And they were younger—often much younger than—new parents are now, and making do on the fly. How they treated their children would today feel like neglect, although more capably independent children tended to result. Starting in their early twenties, my parents raised five. To us that felt normal. Five was standard. Big was eight or ten. Three was small. Two was paltry, lonely, almost sad. One was definitely sad. None was tragic. Prayers were said, condolences offered. Today, though, usually with the explanation of financial concerns, sometimes with expiration dates looming, parents often stop at two, particularly if they find both genders represented. Three is a big brood. Four, which Janice and I somehow arranged for ourselves, starting in our mid-thirties, is prodigious. Five is reckless. Six and beyond is weird.

Then there's Pirandello's attendant mathematical quandary: is a parent's love and attention divided among his or her number of children, or multiplied by it? Certainly today's totals differ, as do their implications. With fewer children parents have more attention and resources to dedicate to each . . . however it might go from there.

Ma Joad and Atticus Finch notwithstanding, literature, our codified cultural philosophy, is, tellingly, more than a little rough on parents. Think the Morels, the Caulfields, the Tyrones, Willy Loman and dear old Pap Finn. The Dursleys. The poet Philip Larkin put it plainly if not bitingly: "They fuck you up your mum and dad. They may not mean to, but they do." Ask young Hamlet. Even from beyond the grave his old man is on his back, his libidinous mother slobbering all over his officious, unctuous, fatuous uncle/stepfather, whom with plenty of good reason the kid never liked in the first place. What's a poor prince to do?

One encounters a lot of this oppositional attitude about parents in one's reading life when the point of view is the child's. Yammering fuddy-duddies, dorkish tyrants, demanding, unrelenting, mums and dads do indeed, or at least can, the bad ones anyway, fuck you up. And like it or not, aware of it or not, as goes our literature, so goes, even today, much of our thinking. This in all likelihood is not entirely a bad thing: reacting against one's parents is in its way as instructive as cooperating with them—or can be, depending, of course, on the situation and who the mum and dad and kid might be. It at least forces one to exercise a little autonomy, to get out there and give life a shot on one's own and see what happens. Not always will things go smoothly. Mistakes are inevitable, but so too are they edifying. Or can be. At some point and inevitably, kids start to take charge of their own upbringing.

And as a parent myself, it's my inclination here to retract the two paragraphs above. Not so long ago—or so it feels—I was a teenager myself. This still-vivid point of view I cannot help but incorporate into nearly all of my parental thinking, my parental ministrations, which invariably includes empathy for frustrated teenagers. This I would guess is true of most mothers and fathers. Parents know better because they know more. How much breathing room this allows the teenager in their care is the question, but parents tend to know that, too.

However the scribblers have it, and for their occasional missteps, parents, it bears repeating, love their children in immeasurable dimension. We understand raising you is likely the most important thing we'll do in our brief visit to the planet. Of course this concept is easier to embrace when you're in the crib still and heart-stoppingly adorable and plump and sweet-smelling and utterly helpless and trusting and smile up at us wetly, gummily, wide eyes alight, chubby little arms flailing, when we come in to greet you in the morning. Later, when you back the car into an oak tree that has stood steadfastly beside the driveway only since the Fillmore administration, one must exhale a time or two . . . and then there again is the smile—albeit rueful and no longer gummy—and the heart swells. This is the fact of it. Even when you come down the stairs nearly six feet tall and freshly shaved and showered and dressed for the prom like James Bond himself, we can't help but see before us still that happy little butterball burbling delightedly through the bars of the crib.

Which is to say we parents are dealing with our own limitations and proclivities, balancing emotion and reason, the real and the ideal, and proceeding under an unwieldy weight of love. Getting it exactly right every time in every endeavor is not necessarily automatic. We know, too, how easily it all can go horribly wrong. Yet on we hope. On we try.

All of this is still B.

And while we're at it, I always took as amusing, if not entirely fitting, that life's most profound experience—really, the whole kit and variegated kaboodle of parenting—begins with a delicate urination. Slightly ignoble, that. Telling, too: what are we if not plumbing? Interrupted in the course of regular, even perfectly contented, life living, the suspecting mom, a bit aflutter, goes to the drugstore, buys the test kit, brings it home, goes into the bathroom, disrobes the pertinent region, sits and whizzes on the little plastic thingamajig and, with a catch of the breath, reads the results.

Things build, of course, from there.

For us, though, for Janice and me, it went with the first one a little differently. She, you have to understand, is petite and lovely and fiercely smart and leans hard on life's gas pedal. Full steam ahead, scorched earth, take no prisoners, these phrases come to mind—in a good way, mostly. Then one sunny Honolulu September, among the baking and custarding—she was in those days a pastry chef—the early morning runs, the late afternoon tennis, the evening swims, the mountain hikes, the reading on the lanai, the nights on the town, she grew a bit gray about the gills. Spirits sagged. Activity ground nearly to a halt. Her stomach, she reported, was in distress. She felt awful. A few days became five, six, with no letup. A tumor? No, an ulcer, we decided, had to be an ulcer. The trials of living with the slow-pulse likes of me. She went to the doctor.

Today the ulcer is eighteen. He's a fine kid. At his arrival Janice became instantly and thoroughly and beautifully maternal, endowed with such enormous loving ferocity her nickname among the local rank and file would soon become Mommy Tsunami. And if not evicted from her heart, certainly I found it more crowded in there—and didn't mind a bit.

And even with nine months to consider such notions, at his arrival the baby showed me in a way I'd had only a theoretical inkling of before: what . . . don't wince . . . I am for, what we are for. What fundamentally life is about. Each generation brings on and nurtures the next. This is it. The individual arrives, sees a bit of the world, does his strutting and fretting, his rosebud-gathering, his diem carpe–ing, and goes. But, if he's lucky, his progeny continues. *Life* continues. This is what we have against the cold and silence of eternal nothingness. Done right it should be enough. It has to be. What else is there? Our parents gave us life and we pass it along to our children, who will pass it along to theirs, and so on, a profound and, let's hope, perpetual succession. This hit me in the manner of a twelve-pound sledgehammer to the solar plexus as I, having been up through the night, weak-kneed witness to the full display, now suddenly a father, in love in a new and bigger way with Janice, was hoofing it up Punahou Street in the morning sun on my way home from the hospital for a shower and some rest. Right there on the sidewalk I danced a spontaneous jig, the full Gene Kelly minus the rain. Janice and I, we'd done something. A tiny new person had arrived.

"Life is an honor," Jim Harrison writes with his customary clarity, "albeit anonymously delivered." Well, Janice and I have given the world our four. While I pretend no answers on the cosmic antecedents, I do know she delivered each like a champion, a true heroine, and each marked for the universe a genuine improvement. Nothing will ever give me more pleasure and fulfillment.

I'll guess your parents feel this way, too.

That now was B.

Time for C.

Which brings us to school.

And the first thing to remember about parents and school is most of us don't know what goes on there. You leave the house in the morning, you come home in the afternoon. Hanging around the kitchen you're not exactly a bubbling font of information about what happened in between. Often it's hard to tell the difference between valid complaints and simple bellyaching. We take mostly on faith that you're on top of things, that you're trying your best and benefiting inch by inch from the experiences of your days; still, it's difficult not to look over your shoulder—this as much innocent curiosity as direct surveillance. And, frankly, no matter how we come by the information, from what we gather much of your day at school seems, well, a little dubious. Or beside the point. Or different enough from the high school we knew to wonder what gives. Movies in math class. Collages in history. Relaxation techniques in phys ed. Blogging all around. We hope your teachers are on the ball, that one or two might even be at least somewhat inspiring, but we lack enough evidence to put us at ease. Your anecdotes, such as they are, can be alarming, too, your reports of the stunts other kids pull, the messes they make, the imbecilities of which they're guilty. Sure, we have our expectations, which even we recognize can be burdensome, but how can this be unreasonable? You, after all, are the one telling us how grown up and capable you are. So step up and deliver.

We've been to the conferences, too, the Back to School

Nights. There's the odd play and science fair, and teacher reports and principal's missives. And the all-important word around town . . . parents, let's remember, talk. We also recall our own school days more vividly than you'd guess from the looks of us—and aside from the electronics, the reductions in polyester and hair magnitude, less has changed than you might imagine. We pay close attention, often covertly, to what circumstantial evidence suggests about your experiences, but as for hour-by-hour realities, we have little clue. Probably you'd find it invasive otherwise. What all this means is we have slim idea of context, of the atmosphere in the cafeteria, the hallways, the classrooms, the locker rooms, of the macro- and microcultures, and, further, how you compare with your schoolmates, how you stack up against what we too often see as the competition. (There are, after all, only so many As to go around, so many spots on the school newspaper, on the basketball team, in Northwestern's freshman class.) And at home we see you merely as the latest incarnation of the continuum from the ultrasound forward. Is it surprising, then, that we're sometimes not the most dexterous in our efforts to understand you and your life?

We witness you, too, couch-sprawled in front of the television, not quite catatonic, clicker fisted, pausing for six minutes on a documentary about Chichén Itzá, and, with a whoop and a whoosh, our wishful thinking sprouts wings and flaps it for the stratosphere. Before you know it, our imagination has you lecturing rivetingly at the University of Chicago on assorted scintillations archaeological and in your spare time brushing sand off shards of Etruscan pottery to the admiring gasps of assorted pith-helmeted flunkies. Against our better judgment at the McDermotts' little wine-and-Brie get-together on Saturday night we let slip with a savory morsel of pride that you've become interested in archaeology. And that nice Doug Schneider overhears and says his cousin's daughter's best friend's older brother had a great time last summer at a dig someplace in Arizona . . . and the next thing you know you're swatting mosquitoes under a baking July sun and grubbing for musket balls in the Yorktown dirt at Junior Archaeologist Camp. And you can substitute Chichén Itzá with Leo Tolstoy, U Chicago with Columbia, and now you're an impassioned scholar of literature, a soulful poet, a Nobel laureate, Yorktown is a half-empty prep school campus somewhere in Connecticut with open windows and buzzing cicadas, and grubbing for musket balls is sweating out three pages on a Formative Personal Experience. It's all the same. George Gershwin, Carnegie Hall, trombone, band camp. Kick a bending left-footed U-11 goal and you're starting as striker for UNC, for the LA Galaxy, for Team USA, and it's dribbling through cones on the Babson College turf at the sweatfest summer clinic, some buzz-cut East London expat screaming at you to pass to feet. Make a paper airplane and you're the first human being on Mars. Parents can't help it. We think it's because we love you and believe in you and want the best for you. What we fear we see in you is inadequate self-confidence, imagination and dedication. What our parents called gumption or, alternatively, grit. We fear that couch could be as far as you'll get. So we talk and talk and talk, to you, to the spouse, the coworker, the childhood friend, the coach, the teacher, the lady across the street and her nice sister Maud visiting from Indianapolis; some unfortunate something in us makes us believe if we read the books, peruse the websites and yak yak yak about it enough it might just happen, even if the kid in question is miles from earshot at the moment thinking exclusively about the double bacon cheeseburger with caramelized onions and barbecue sauce he's scarfing.

Which brings us back again to school. The springboard. The gateway.

For reasons largely pragmatic, school to too many parents is more about tomorrow than today, preparation, merely, for what comes next, a means to another means to another means to, eventually, an end. Elementary school is for middle school, middle school for high school, high school for college. Stepping-stones all, of no particular importance in themselves as soon as the foot alights and focus switches to the next. A high school course is not an intellectual adventure but a ritualized training exercise. Too often schools themselves will capitulate to this thinking. For example, for catalogue purposes the normative-level English classes at my own Wellesley High are called Advanced College Prep, the lower level College Prep. And AP courses are aimed without embarrassment at springtime tests. And Tuesday's class is about Friday's quiz, which is about next month's report card, which is about the year-end GPA, which is about the college application. And the prestige of the prestigious college about which your parents have been harping so much your ears are bleeding matters less in your years there, really, than in the opportunities it will create for you when you graduate.

In short, for reasons of anxiousness and ambition, the experience of the moment, however engaging, has little value in and of itself; it matters only as a step to the next step, which matters only as a step to the next. (And extra credit isn't extra and optional practices aren't optional.) Through everything, of course, performance is key, how adroitly you skip along, particularly in relation to others. It's procedural and competitive, sometimes more effectively executed if one doesn't engage too much in the moment. Get too intrigued by Spanish, say, and there goes your chemistry grade. Spend too much time on a Yeats poem and you can kiss your grade on tomorrow's math quiz good-bye. And somebody else gets into Brown. So c'mon, chop chop. And words like "interested," "inquisitive" or "receptive" tend to mean little, while "accelerated," "advanced," "elite," "gifted" and "honors" have with many parents great resonance. And while Sarah Orne Jewett's "A White Heron" might be an interesting little story and everything, it's really just some self-involved bleeding heart's encrypted symbolism about being female or coming of age, or whatever, that matters only insofar as it could be the subject of a paper you're expected to knock out of the ballpark. So get a move on. And too often the question at the dinner table, in the car on the way to gymnastics, in the drop-by before bed, is "How's it going in English?" (translation: "What's your grade in English?") and not "What are you learning?" or "So what do you think about it?" If your answer isn't quite right in substance or timbre, the parental stomach churns. Mostly it's simple reassurance we're after. Worrying about you is pleasant for neither of us.

FROM ACROSS TWO and a half decades I recall Mrs. Dithers (not her real name). I was young still and new to teaching, and Punahou was to me the high school version of heaven. At an open house one October night a compact but formidable woman planted herself in front of me and refused to suffer the hazy niceties prescribed by the occasion. She wanted to know, chapter and verse, how her son—Steven, we'll call him—was doing in my class . . . i.e., what, please, was his grade? I suspected she saw what everyone saw in young Steven, hence her concern. But I lacked then the experience to finesse the demand, or the damn-the-torpedoes candor that sometimes comes with years, to inform her the boy was a morose lump barely going through the motions—although I did see some aptitude, even intelligence, in his writing. I was also optimistic I and the many wonders of American literature could before much longer bring him around, maybe even do him some good. Conclusive assessments were in my view premature. And plain in her grip was the invisible bullwhip with which probably that very night she would be lacerating the poor kid's fundament. All but limbering up, was she, right there before me. "Oh," I said, hoping to spare him, and shame on me, "Steven's bright and capable. He's doing fine."

Harmless fib, I thought.

Well, the next few weeks saw Steven sink from morose to recalcitrant to vegetative. Mildew started growing on his shoulders. I'd ask him to come see me. He'd grunt vague assents but never show up. I called the mother. Fixated on the grade, her first play was to ask for another chance at a paper on which Steven had done poorly a week or so before. I suggested that was, in the long run, a bad idea. Sends the wrong message, I said. You step up to the plate and take your hacks. You hit the ball or you don't. Resolving to do better next time is more beneficial for a kid than trying to finagle his way into a fourth and fifth strike.

Which sent Mrs. Dithers into full nuclear . . . to impugn

my judgment, my fairness, my professionalism, my intelligence.

Thunderstruck, I sputtered explanations.

Next it was the school's fault for failing to provide the child "appropriate support." After all, Steven was bright and capable. I'd said so myself. Furthermore, he'd been tested. Extensively. His IQ was very high, very, very high. She had documentation. This was an exceptional young man. Still, I managed to hold my ground. She claimed next with no shortage of pride that she'd "been on him like a bad dream," so blame could not be hers.

Aha, I thought. Lucky Steven, I thought.

The boy sank lower still. Unfortunately for him, and for a colleague of mine, a stalwart old pro disinclined to spoon-feed in whose class Steven was doing even worse, Mrs. Dithers went on the warpath. Multipage, single-spaced letters began arriving complete with voluminous expert reports on fancy letterhead and crisp clinical findings—to the other teacher, to me, to the department chair, to the principal. After a few exchanges I was deemed too nice to be at fault, a well-meaning neophyte—to which I offered no dispute and gladly exited the fray. Meanwhile, almost an afterthought now as she blazed away, Steven curled into a figurative fetal position. Mrs. Dithers, and soon enough her lawyer, claimed that since the admissions people deemed her son worthy of enrollment, and since a member of the faculty had called him bright and capable, any fault for his woeful performance must be his teacher's. Mr. Monroe (not his name) was a tired old incompetent. His hurtful assessments cut the legs out from under the brilliant but sensitive Steven. The boy had arrived a happy, interested, conscientious student . . . now look at him. The entire school was a failure. A sham. Something should be done. She demanded satisfaction.

The top brass took the field.

From the sidelines, I watched. So, too, I'm sure, did Steven. I even extended a hand in the spirit of commiseration, but he'd have none of it. Just another cheeseball teacher trick.

Eventually, though, the whole thing fizzled. Blinking first, or simply satisfied she'd made enough noise, Mrs. Dithers turned and yanked Steven from the school, found a spot for him in another.

Steven's case and a few similar to his since have confirmed for me the counterproductiveness of the crusading parent, however well intentioned, convinced he or she is fighting the good fight for the mishandled or victimized (read: underperforming) child. Every time a parent swoops to the rescue, he or she denies the child not just the experience of advocating for himself, but, if things become really dire, a highly edifying collision with the concrete. Unless the kid is allowed to bang an elbow, or go splat entirely, that abject failure is best avoided and effort must be made will remain for him merely theoretical. He knows only the faux flying sensation. Soon enough he's wondering why he should exert himself at all when it's tiring and time-consuming and the cost is negligible if he doesn't. Mom or Dad'll fix it, so what the hell.

For the parent, though, this would be excruciating, even impossible, to sit by and watch. To those having difficulty with perspective, failing to intervene would be like watching the child wander onto the freeway to allow him an edifying encounter with a truck. It becomes, then, a matter of how and when one steps in, which can mean the difference between successful and unsuccessful parenting. The child needs to learn to deal with an unwanted outcome—wince a little, sulk if he has to—then figure out what to do about it. This is most effectively accomplished on his own. In this way he'll develop skills and habits of mind, and the successes when they come will be his.

Steven was obviously engaged in a dead-fish rebellion against his mother, or father, or me, or Monroe, or his other teachers, or adults generally, or the girl who spurned his attentions, or the pigeon that defecated on his head, or the uncaring universe . . . take your pick. I put my money on the mother. Respond to the nagging, the caterwauling, the bullwhipping, and you're suggesting such methods are within the bounds of acceptable treatment, and you're inviting more tyranny as soon as the next issue arises. Dig in your heels deep enough, though, be willing to tough it out, and eventually the tyrant will get the message. You could even call it martyrdom and deem yourself a misunderstood saint. For a kid who lacks the skill or confidence to advocate for himself, passive/aggressive has to be a tempting strategy. For the parent it can be highly frustrating—in many cases entirely the point.

In my experience a Mrs. Dithers is a rare phenomenon, but milder versions come along all the time. Not long ago, for example, a Wellesley dad tried what I'm certain he thought a nifty maneuver. His son, Carter, we'll call him, showed up in one of my senior classes a month or two after the school year had begun, having just washed out of a local private school for reasons of cannabis. Carter handed in polished papers as the assignments came along, but his in-class written work was sorry stuff—scattered, sloppy, largely witless. Reading quizzes he'd fail altogether. In discussions his contributions were slick by kid standards but light on substance. When I asked about the inconsistency, Carter dipped his head matter-of-factly. "Oh, yeah," he said, absent chagrin, "my dad edits my papers."

I called the father that afternoon, apprised him of the situation and offered what I thought he should hear: let the kid be.

"But don't you agree," he came right back at me with topspin, "parents should work with their kids?"

How I answered this question, I knew immediately, would be crucial—and immediate knowing has never been one of my strengths. Of course it can be terrifically advantageous for parents and their children to work together. The list of reasons is long, the first entry of which would be as a source of great loving joy for both. But it's a question of *how* they work together and with what goals in mind. And his leading "don't you agree" made me wary. He was looking, it seemed plain, for leeway to do what he could for the boy to ensure preferred results. There's a line—and it's pretty wide—between helping a struggling student and impeding his chances to learn. For purposes of expedience Carter's father felt compelled to cross it. He might not have even understood it was there.

I said, "Not really, no."

This he was not expecting. "But . . . but surely you can't be suggesting that a concerned parent with insights and experience to share should just stand by and . . ."

Rather than letting his momentum build, I cut in: "Let the kid handle things on his own. He's the one in school."

"Agreed, but . . ."

I kept going: "I'll be giving them a quiz on act 4 of *Hamlet* on Friday. You want to come in and 'work with him' on that, too?" Not, I'll admit, the most courteous riposte, but sometimes you grab what shows. Again, immediate knowing is not a strength.

With offended grumbles, out came his trump card: I won't malign the reputation of the fine institution of higher learning he named, but young Carter was all set there, his father informed me importantly, signed, sealed and just about delivered, as long as "his first semester grades reflected a commitment to success." Funny how a phrase will stick with you. A commitment to success. Of the whole episode, this I think is what chafed the most. He was asking me to play ball, to compromise my nitpicky little schoolmarm edicts just this once. Really, what was the big deal? Was I seriously going to jeopardize the kid's chances at _____ College? I mean, come on.

I said, "How are you defining success?"

I wonder still if he wondered what I meant.

Even at this distance I'm convinced both Carter's father and Steven's mother thought they were doing right by their sons. Both were hoping I'd set aside generally applicable classroom niceties for larger and more practical concerns. Their sons were exceptions and therefore exceptional. Bending here, accommodating there, these were not then unreasonable. They were taking measures, righting the ship, returning to equilibrium things as they should be. This to them was parenting. The easy guess is Steven and Carter were the way they were in good measure because these were the attitudes, the methods, the conditions, the personalities with which they were being raised. The die had likely been cast long before either arrived in my classroom. But I still wish I'd done both more evident good. And now that my two older children are high school students in need, now and then, of a parent's help, I hear Carter's father's voice and try to step as lightly as I can.

The theory is simple: kids need to understand their responsibilities are their own. They need enough freedom that mistakes and stumbles are a possibility. They need the latitude to screw up, even screw up royally, on endeavors significant and rigorous enough that they're invested and trying hard, but not so significant that they're eviscerated if they fall short. They should be confident enough to think that with the right effort they might succeed, but not so cocksure they assume they will. The possibility of failure must be real: failure can be, should be, instructive, even inspiring. And if it happens, it happens. The sun will rise again tomorrow. They should learn to fail and not think themselves—or be judged by others—failures. However well meaning, protective parents charging to the rescue deny their children this essential experience. And any little setback starts to look like doom.

With a child falling fast, though, the concrete ever closer, a parent can, understandably, be prone to leave this theory theoretical. This is where teachers come in . . . the sense of perspective, the empathetic ear, the reasoned voice, the extra attention.

I've been asked countless times over the years by mothers and fathers, many quite adamant, to change grades, disregard poor showings, allow rewrites, allow retests, extend deadlines, remove deadlines, to ease up in light of the big Law & Society paper due next Thursday, the dance recital Saturday afternoon, the lacrosse tourney in Maryland, the leadership conference in St. Louis, to forgive two weeks of homework for a family trip to Cancun, to Banff, to exempt a student from an assignment because "he just couldn't get into the book," to forgive a cut class because "she hasn't cut a class in five weeks . . . well, okay, four," to give an A to a chronic underperformer because he was "really very bright, actually," to pass for the year an angelic-looking, troubled little drug-dealing punk who'd done a surly version of nothing all year because we wouldn't want to "sour him on the idea of school." Always there are extenuating circumstances, many of them compelling. "He's learned his lesson," one will hear from time to time, "and that's what matters, isn't it?" Accommodation is expected. Lately some parents have even been showing up for conferences with paid "advocates" to lobby on their behalf. My first impulse is to fold the arms and shake the head; and usually that's the right response. Each case, though, is unique and must be decided according to its own particular details, because each case is not a case at all but a child. The risk, of course, is fairness to everyone and messages about the malleability of rules and protocols. In this one has to trust one's judgment.

Most parents from my observation are good parents. And, however heavy-handed, however bellicose, the parent who shoulders in on behalf of his or her child is not necessarily a bad one. Each should be aware, though—probably is aware—any intercession, even the feathery light, can come at a cost to the child's emerging sense of autonomy and the myriad benefits of fending for himself or herself. Always it's a matter of how.

So THAT's A, B and C. D through Z we'll leave for another time.

Remember, please, your parents love you very much. With the 7:38 rounding the bend they would no doubt gladly lie across the tracks for you. Day after day, they're doing the best they know how. They—we—think about you and your well-being and your possibilities all the time. Our occasional agitation and annoyance, even our ire— these to us are just surface ripples atop depths so deep and constant we cannot comprehend them ourselves. Remember, also, that whatever you're learning at home goes far beyond whatever you might learn in school in both scope and importance, and in staying power, too. And through it all, however it works out, we're just trying to be helpful.

And keep in mind that we have to learn with and raise the same set of kids. We too go this way but once.

Chapter 2

Know Thyself

There was a child that went forth every day,
　And the first object he look'd upon, that object he
　　became,
　And that object became part of him for the day or a
　　certain part of the day,
　Or for many years or stretching cycle of years.
　—"There Was a Child Went Forth" by Walt Whitman

Know thyself" said more than a few long-ago Greeks and wisely. Your life, after all, is in your charge, and will be from here to the end. Also, it's the only one you're going to get, this your first and last time through.[*]

---

[*]　With this claim I mean no disrespect to my Irish great-grandfather, who insisted he was coming back as a seagull. I have come upon no evidence to suggest he was mistaken.

To handle that responsibility well, to navigate skillfully, to make sound decisions, to enjoy fully whatever time you have and be of some use to others, you better know yourself.

First, let's remember you are not you. Like the rest of us, you're merely what has entered your head and found a place there—and anything is fair game. These numberless components of your identity have taken the form of quick-firing, low-amp electrical impulses in a few pounds of grayish gelatinous stuff riding along under your hair. It looks vaguely, I'm told, like a slimy cauliflower. Everything happens there. Everything. From a different but no less accurate perspective, you are also a temporary biodegradable commingling of inherited genetic material, emphasis on temporary. Additionally, or, rather, concurrently, you are what you eat, which you've heard a time or two before but have likely given little thought. So think about it. Notice, please—think about—everything. You think, after all, therefore you are. If you don't, you're not. That you are also unique in the entire time/space continuum—the whole variegated shebang—is an astonishment not just in its mathematical permutations, but also in the notion that you and everyone else who is, has been or ever will be, each unique as well, operate, more or less, according to the dictates of free will.

In short, there's no predicting what you'll do, or how, or even if it might matter. Not even you know; nor does anyone else. It's not possible. What time will you go to bed tonight? With whom will you chat tomorrow afternoon? Where and with whom will you be living twenty-two years from now? What will you wear to your granddaughter's wedding? Of which accomplishment will you be proudest when the music stops? And when, where, how will that happen? What will it be like? Nobody knows.

Which we all know. We have that in common. We also have in common our uniqueness, which seems paradoxical but isn't. Okay, maybe is, but we live with it untroubled, if only for peace of mind's sake.

If this isn't enough to get you squeezing the eyes and rubbing the melon, add to the mix certain hard realities of time. In a fleeting, temporal life it's all we have, the present, the moment, right now, but as far as we can comprehend it—at least without good Dr. Einstein's help—even right now exists only in the abstract and mostly theoretical. Okay, the moment does exist, it has to, but unrelentingly and without pause the second hand sweeps right past it: the moment it's a moment it's gone and already we've moved along to the next moment. And the next. Instantly, now becomes then, is becomes was. And, however proximate, what's past is forever retreating and the future will never arrive. Both the past and the future exist, then, only in the imagination, which is to say somewhere in the electrical impulses in your few pounds of gelatinous stuff, with nothing separating them but the cutting edge of the second hand, an edge so thin as to be nothing in itself. Which is where we live our lives. As George Carlin put it, "There's no present. There's only the immediate future and the recent past." If I have it right, then, the present is all we have and it doesn't exist. And I'm merely electricity.

Oy.

So what does all this mean? Well, many things. Too many, certainly, for my limited electrified gelatinous stuff to comprehend. They are realities with which we contend mostly by not thinking about them.

So let's think about them.

When he and I were in school together in London in the fall of 1978, my friend Peter informed me over pints of warm beer (the library was closed, obviously) that he and his since-kindergarten girlfriend, Beth, would be getting married right after college. They would honeymoon on Kauai. Then, he continued matter-of-factly, they would have a son—Danny they would call him—then a daughter, Nikki. They would live in Swampscott, where he and Beth had grown up. I found this certainty comical and gave him a bucket of the requisite grief. Less than two years later Peter and Beth had a very nice wedding. They honeymooned on Kauai. Soon enough a fine son arrived, Danny, and not long afterward a lovely daughter, Nikki. Beth and Peter are grandparents now. They live in Swampscott. They seem very happy. To him I still give grief as occasion demands, mostly on other subjects.

Probably the advent of you was less scripted. Probably your parents' initial awareness of, then interest in each other was a little more recent, haphazard and tenuous than sitting in the same kindergarten class circa 1963. Maybe they had all set your gender, your spot in the birth order and your name years before their marriage and your conception, but I doubt it. Life, you see, is perpetual rolls of the dice. Every step defies augury, to borrow from young Prince Hamlet. Everything that happens is a flukish alignment of happenstance. The readiness is all. Had the young lady who would become my mother declined at age eighteen an invitation to a party in far-off Pittsburgh, she would not have met the young man who would become my father, and my brothers and sisters and I would not exist, nor our children. But she went, met him, they danced all night, as the story goes, and that was that. Had Janice at age thirteen decided not to go to the beach that June afternoon, or had she decided to go a little earlier, or later; and had I, all of fourteen, not come out of the water just then and sat myself on the seawall to dry off and survey the universe for a minute or two; and had she not sashayed by and smiled back over her shoulder at me, felling me like a lightning-struck sequoia, our children might not exist. One can play this game late into the evening. And there's the biological randomness of innumerable sperm and eggs, any others of which could have united to make a person wholly different from the one who would wind up emerging and sits reading these lines. Unless you're Danny or Nikki, the unlikelihood of you, or any of us, is staggering, a little frightening even.

Yet, for the moment, here we are.

Somewhere early in childhood self-awareness begins; you start to appreciate a little of your individual significance, the scope of who you are. I remember quite vividly, for example, coming down the stairs in my Pittsburgh grandparents' house at age about eight, noticing my hand, the right, sliding along the banister and thinking about it suddenly in a way I never had before. The thought was no more profound than "Hey, that's my hand." Midway on the staircase I stopped. "However old I get, that hand will be my hand. Whatever I touch or do with that hand will be with that hand right there." I held it up, studied it, wiggled the fingers, flexed the wrist. Then, so it wouldn't feel left out, I did the same with the other hand. It wasn't like I was seeing them for the first time; I *was* seeing them for the first time. Almost half a century later those same hands—albeit a bit more leathery, scarred and gnarled—are pecking these words. Maybe I'd intuited a metaphor in the constant hand and the banister sliding by underneath. Maybe I happened just then to reach the point of neurological and/or cognitive development when untried synapses fire up for the first time and such thoughts occur, and there happened to be the hand. Maybe I just felt older, more fully formed, than the last time we visited Pittsburgh. Whatever it was, the revelation hit me like an electric jolt—in part, I suppose, because it was one—with an attendant and lasting tingle.

With a strange new objectivity, I was aware suddenly of my awareness of my personhood. Of my singularity. Of the independent uniqueness and finiteness of me. I could not have articulated this then, of course, but that's what was happening. Probably you can remember a similar moment in your childhood. Now flash forward four and a half decades and I'm at home, upstairs, walking past the bathroom, and standing there is Jesse, my youngest, at about the same age I was that time in Pittsburgh, staring at himself in the mirror. Rapt. I stopped and asked what he was doing. Without taking his eyes off himself lest he miss, it seemed, some essential detail, he said, "I just can't believe that's me."

There is in this astonishment weighty responsibility, of course. You have—each of us has—a life to conduct, a life like none before it, like none to follow, its trajectory up to you and happenstance. And, further, the factors coalescing in your "me-ness" are too many, too complex, too nebulous, too quick to evolve to understand with any useful measure of clarity, which you'll likely agree is a big part of the mystification and intrigue that is life. The whys outnumber the becauses by twenty to one easy. Fifty to one. And, really, what fun would it be if the becauses ever caught up? Knowing thyself, then, is forever elusive—but eminently worth the pursuit. If only for pleasure's sake you can sit back for hours on end and deconstruct yourself and the wide universe in which you reside. If you're lucky you'll come upon enough useful insights to keep the pragmatists off your back for idling away a perfectly good afternoon.

So let's give it a try. You, after all, are your sole lifelong companion. Moreover, you're the only you the rest of us are going to get. We too would like you to see you happy and productive and fulfilled.

CONVENTION SUGGESTS WE first break down our consideration into two categories, nature and nurture. While thinking about it in this way can be a little restrictive and simplistic—nature, after all, *is* nurture, and nurture the natural adjustments to an ever-evolving natural context—let's proceed just the same. We can call nature the genetic programming, every manifestation of which will have its influence. Tall people differ from short people in more than just height. The willowy experience life differently from the stout, the bald from the thatched. For the agile, the coordinated, gym class is a delight . . . at least the gym class of yore. For the fair and freckled, life in certain latitudes can be problematic. Melodious pipes, 20/20 eyesight, mesmerizing beauty . . . these are the luck of the draw, and you play the genes you're dealt. Science assures us assorted aptitudes and characteristics of personality can be inherited as well. (For an example, check the index under *McCullough, Janice B., tenacity of . . .*) Nurture is what starts pouring into your cerebrum as soon as it's open for business—the cozy comfort of the accommodations, Mommy's reassuring heartbeat, Haydn's Symphony no. 74 in E-flat Major if the roll of the dice gave you those kinds of parents. And nurture's biggest event, Dr. Freud and others assure us, is among the very first: birth.

While it's no springtime frolic for the birther either, birth for the birthee is one heck of an ordeal. Just brutal. Think of it: The sum total of your heretofore experience has been pretty much uninterrupted bliss, all of it, nine delightful months adrift in the amniotic fluid. That to you is existence in its entirety. Ultimate coziness. And perhaps Haydn. Then, for reasons as yet unknown, you're given the boot, shoved through a tunnel so tight it compresses your skull. This shoving and cramming and bruising and battering can go on for hours and hours. Then, at last, with a final heave-ho, out into the wide blasting cold and assaulting brightness you flop. Your arms and legs flail, they fly away; after months of snug quarters it feels like everything is flying away. You wince and thrash and scream. Even your own squawking is a new and jarring affront. Why me? you have to be wondering. What did I do wrong? And now what?

Bone twisting, skull squeezing; this, your first real experience, is trauma in the extreme. Welcome to the world, kid. How d'ya like it so far?

Before long, though, you're burbling; then, in a manner, talking; then, however wobbly, walking. Then, soon enough, you're out the door, the world your world.

DAY AFTER DAY being a kid, being a person, is an exercise in trial and error. This is learning, which is growing, which is an incremental evolution into a new person—who will continue to try and err, try and succeed, ever to evolve, right through to the end. All, then, is flux. Which can be more than a little frightening. Being a kid, even a big one, is investigation, tentative experimentation and assessment; it's looking around and trying things on to see how they fit. No matter how you phrase it, the question is always "Am I the kind of person who . . . ?" And because you haven't been yourself all that long, nor free to make your own choices, you don't know the answer, not for sure.

Still, there's much to help you along. "No one gets to be a human being unaided," said the poet John Ciardi. Books, for example, the accrued capital of the human experience, all the wealth of the human mind, books help you think bigger and better, therefore you are bigger and better. You should read, then, all the time, wherever your interests take you. It's too important not to. Read about Edith Wharton's Lily Bart, say, not just to be informed and entertained by her story, but to find in her elements you'll recognize in yourself. You'll make her, or anyone else you read about, part of you, which is to say part of your experience and larger comprehension of what it means to be a human being. A writer speaks directly to you; her thinking becomes a part of your thinking.

While invariably there is recognition in reading, which can be both helpful and reassuring, even exhilarating, more important still is discovery. In reading about Lily Bart, or Captain Yossarian or Anna Karenina or Okonkwo or Dean Moriarty or Gregor Samsa or Harry Flashman, or just about anyone else, you're adding to your own all-too-brief, all-too-limited encounter with life. Reading puts us in other people's skins. It gives the self a broader, more informed human context. Reading, then, is an expansive endeavor. And enriching, and, one hopes, ennobling. It shows us the distinction between sympathy and empathy and why it matters. If you've read her well, you feel *with* Lily, not for her. At the same time you see and feel the urgency of her situation and the conflicts with which she has to contend. Her experience becomes yours. With reading, then, you are at once within and without, and yours becomes a more comprehensive and therefore wiser consciousness.

And of course in a manner you read . . . you study . . . your friends and the other kids at school to instructive effect. You watch television, flip through magazines, explore the web, hear what your parents and siblings and aunts and uncles and grandparents and teachers and coaches have to say. You have maybe kind of an idea what things are about, enough evidence is all around you, but you don't *know*. So you investigate, maybe give them a little try. Each experience, then, is not just an experience but an experiment, a lesson in life, a lesson in identity. Am I the kind of kid who stays up until three A.M. studying for a physics test? Well, how can you know until you try it? Am I the kind of kid who wears skinny jeans and red Chuck Taylors? Try them on and see. Am I the kind of kid who gets a job after school? The kind who sings in the shower, blames everyone but myself, marches right up to a teacher and demands an explanation, posts a hundred and one pictures of myself on Facebook, lets my parents do my deciding, cannot be seen sitting by myself in the cafeteria, lies to protect a friend, watches what I eat, says screw it to a curfew and deals with the fallout when I get home, has a fantasy football team, writes poetry, gets a petition going to right an injustice, punts the homework to watch reruns of *The Big Bang Theory*, tweets my every passing thought, plays COD for four straight zoned-out hours, observes the five-second rule, takes pages and pages of detailed notes in World Civ class, refolds the T-shirts after I pull one from the bottom of the pile? Well, how can you know unless you know?

To be a kid, further, is to contend with questions, questions, questions, all the time, on every subject, and not just your own—and those are bad enough—but from everybody in your life. It's torment. Got a lot of homework tonight? How'd you do on the test? Can you keep an eye on your brother? So what colleges are you thinking about? Got any plans for the weekend? You gonna eat that? How about cleaning the fish tank? When are tryouts? Think maybe you could rinse out the cereal bowl and put it in the dishwasher next time? Is everything all right? And if they're not trying to pry you open with questions for which you have no real answers or just don't feel like dealing with at the moment, they're telling you things you don't feel like hearing. Sometimes you don't even know what they're saying and you wind up staring at a renegade eyebrow hair until they stop. And, Lord above, can they go on. Then they expect a response and you have nothing to say, not one lonely syllable . . . and then what?

Moreover, to be a teenager is to be a punching bag for unsolicited advice. Or meandering stories that might at some point arrive at advice. And if you follow anyone's advice, anyone at all, however brilliant, you're giving up being in charge of yourself. Don't follow it and, let's face it, you're probably being dumb. And where does that leave you?

Through it all, though, you're just trying to lead a life

that's supposed to be yours, and maybe, little by little, clarify an identity.

CENTRAL TO YOUR identity, inextricable from it, whatever it might be, is your gender. At your advent it was the first question everyone wanted answered, the first fact shared about you near and far. It's a girl! It's a boy! As semantics attest, before that determination was made you were merely an *it*.

Before we proceed, though, a caveat: I fully acknowledge and respect the existence of plain-as-day exceptions, important exceptions, to much of what I'll have to say on the subject of boys and girls, girls and boys. I intend no offense and apologize in advance if any is taken. I'll be playing the percentages as I see them, merely, and this with no formal training nor education beyond a sociology course in college thirty-something years ago that I found largely tedious. If you anticipate even a teaspoon of umbrage, skip this section.

Here's my first salvo: the genders differ . . . they differ so much, in fact, I sometimes wonder if there are two realities, the female and the male. After all, we live our lives within intractable gender-based ontological modalities, as a phrase-ologist feeling his oats might have it. Certainly our sex in-fluences the ways in which we think and behave more than we're aware—and, further, we live within our maleness or femaleness too completely to realize that's what's happening.

And always has. How then true self-knowledge? Reliable objectivity? How can we ascertain valid meaning, of ourselves, of the world around us? How can we pretend to know a jot about the other gender, the other half of the human experience?

So this also before I proceed: I'm male, have been all my life. Behaviors in which I've engaged since September of 1958, as a consequence of the body, mind-set and culture in which I've spent that time, attitudes I've assumed, experiences I've traversed, males and females I've observed, have all construed for me a male perspective and encouraged in me male behavior—or, rather, perspectives and behaviors more commonly found among, and associated with, males and therefore understood to be male. For example, left unsupervised, I am likelier to eat in one happy go, between meals and just in passing, a full third of a Mrs. Blake's blueberry-peach pie directly from the tin than most females with whom I'm acquainted. I'm also likelier to confess as much in a book I'm writing. For the sake of convenience I'll wipe my hands on the seat of my pants more often than I should— the same pair that I can wear for four, five, six days running without a moment's thought. I am known to lean over and drink water directly from the kitchen tap. I'm also likelier to pull on a sweatshirt and head outside on a contrived mission than to attend to, however pressing, tasks of what we might call a localized and domestic nature. "A man needs egress," my brother-in-law John once announced at a dinner table apropos of nothing, which has come back to me ever since on a somewhat daily basis. I enjoy the use of power tools. Outwardly, my tendency is to underreact. There are limits to the chittychat I can endure. I find shopping a trial. If I'm in a car I want to be the one driving it; and I'd rather be lost and late than stop and ask for directions—which I'll admit is somewhat ridiculous, but there it is. All of these I think have at least something to do with my gender.

Males delight in the freedoms of wide parameters and take pride in adventuring beyond them. While the concept might invite chicken/egg-esque debate, chassis design alone encourages a more free-ranging spirit; size, speed, strength, bladder-relief convenience, freedom from monthlies. From my observation, females find inspiring challenge in narrow parameters and take pride in thriving within them. A function, perhaps, of a superior grasp of the here and now. One might be tempted to call it pragmatism, but definitions of the term will vary. Males tend to orient themselves to what they'll call the big picture and proceed sequentially. For females it's details and simultaneity. And discussion. They don't need nor particularly want egress, generally, and instead deal as best they can with the seventeen things in front of them needing attention and six that don't. They'll call this a function of practical maturity males for whatever reason lack. Males find it nitpicky. Some of this is a holdover from our hunter-gatherer days, perhaps, when for reasons of necessity women kept the home fires burning while men pursued meat. In any case, together or apart, we tend to cover the bases and call it, as occasion allows, accord.

Today, unbidden, little girls color within the lines expertly, artfully, expressively. Creative fastidiousness is to them a surpassing virtue. They like boundaries and rules and protocols and the opportunity to shine within them. They tend to prefer things just so. To their male counterparts fastidiousness is a pain in the ass, a phrase males enjoy dispensing for its mildly transgressive effect. And rules imprison. Correctness is tyranny. That this has something to do with the rate at which fine motor skills develop is only part of it. The liberality of a good-enough ethos is as comfortable to males as a pair of old sneakers—about which, incidentally, they're capable of genuine sentiment. (To wit: I have a twenty-seven-year-old pair, battle-scarred though still reasonably serviceable, with which I cannot part despite strong encouragement from a certain female with whom I live.) Boys and girls also see one another, and all the other males and females happenstance provides, and start to identify attitudes and behaviors as at least somewhat gender-specific, and each of them gravitates in the direction he or she deems appropriate. This is not unexpected but tends to put them on rails.

From earliest childhood—from very nearly birth—

distinctions of gender have been manifest in hair length and attire and toys and modes of play. And interests and predilections and attitudes. Moreover, in classrooms since children first entered them at age four or five, teachers—mostly female, as it happens, particularly early on—have been standing before them prefacing comments with "Boys and girls . . ." and "Girls and boys . . ." What cumulative influence this has had I cannot say. I will note, though, we've not been saying, "Tall kids and short kids . . ." or "Jews and gentiles . . ." or "black kids and white kids . . ." or "slackers and grinds . . ." Yes, gender identity tends to cover more correctly the whole enchilada, but kids must be learning distinctions of gender matter in ways other distinctions do not, with attendant expectations. We even provide them separate rooms in which to attend to bodily functions. And of course our language is careful to specify gender.

In days of not-so-yore these notions quite deliberately affected curriculum: as recently as the progressive early '70s, for example, when hippies were in abundance, feminists on the march, and I in junior high, phys ed classes were segregated. In the gym we boys could hear the girls shriek and chirp at badminton or crab soccer through the retractable wall dividing us. Girls went to Home Ec to cook and sew, boys to Shop to inhale sawdust and pound nails. Those days are gone, although curious remnants persist: in most high school classrooms and cafeterias I've been in, girls, by choice, sit with girls and boys with boys—and this, let's remember, when hormones have entered a stage of what anyone would have to call spirited activity. They appreciate, it appears, the breathing room.

I'm also perfectly comfortable saying adolescent females are more attentive to and meticulous about their homework, their notebooks are neater, they take better care of their textbooks and binders, their backpacks are better stocked and organized, their handwriting more legible and aesthetically pleasing. Their posture is better, so too their efforts to be cooperative. They tend as well to be more adroit and disciplined students and therefore tend to enjoy more outward measures of success. They're more punctual, generally, quicker to verbalize, more demonstrative in shows of sympathy. They're more animated. They enjoy drama and if solely for entertainment's sake will often construe it in places invisible to the male eye. They're also savvier about the competition, real and perceived. Girls have a strategic bent boys tend to lack: their radars are always on, their inner note-taker forever busy. And they're certainly much the better maneuverers.

Then there are all the cultural appurtenances: the hair, the makeup, the jewelry, the eye on fashion, the gift to others that is an effort to look nice as the culture defines looking nice.* All fairly specific to girls, and, it bears noting, above

---

* Or in competition with others. It depends on which others we're talking about.

and beyond the call. Boys, after all, are an easy sell. From the female perspective boys are selfish, underevolved laggards and largely out to lunch—clods of wayward marl, as Shakespeare's Beatrice puts it. Still, for each, around and around repulsion and attraction cavort.

Connected to all this, the culture suggests, is a girl's looks, a point of relevance from which the lunkier gender is mostly free. For boys, to be determined "cute" or "hot" has at least something to do with inadvertence. The moment it appears he's trying, that for which he's trying tends to become more elusive. Conversely, one way or another, a girl must reconcile the expectation that she deliberately (albeit gracefully) set out to attract—attention, admiration, desire. Not so easy, sometimes, to accept or pull off.

And much, maybe even most, of what's within her control is the artifice—or certainly that's what the purveyors of fashion suggest—about which she's bombarded from every quarter. Her hair, then, her eyelids, her cheeks, lips, fingernails and toenails, none is necessarily that color. Her eyelashes aren't necessarily that thick and long. The skin on her face isn't necessarily such smooth perfection. ("God has given you one face and you make yourselves another," rails an irate Hamlet.) She doesn't necessarily smell that way. Left unattended her eyebrows could be arrayed somewhat differently, and her legs and armpits would not be entirely hairless. These days, even among high school kids, certain surgical procedures might have come into play. Clothing, too, clothing especially, is intended not just to maximize allure but to signal a flare for presentment understood to be feminine. All this can be, is, head-clouding, time-consuming and costly. And, further, tellingly, so much of what the culture deems fashionable and therefore attractive in a female diminishes her capacity to function in a physical world. Just stand there, we seem to be suggesting, or sit, or recline, and look fantastic—i.e., the stuff of fantasy . . . i.e., not real.

Curiously, to one degree or another, most girls seem to like it. They think it's fun. Boys find it all at once transfixing and mystifying and inane. For a sizable percentage of them, bathing regularly is expectation enough. Most, though, would, if they stopped to consider it, like to be thought attractive, but how that might be accomplished is impossible to know and, given the odds, not worth the trouble. Anyway, in this and, really, all things, how girls think is well beyond a boy's comprehending, which girls know and use to their advantage, which to boys seems unfair.

Boys are of course subject to their own preoccupations as well, having to do with, generally, appearing able and tough. Their own men. Independent, free-ranging, steady. Tall and jacked is good, too. Any perceived deficiencies in these areas are, or can be, a bit embarrassing. "Lone wolf" is a term to boys almost hallowed in its coolness—or mocking when you have parents and teachers and counselors and tutors telling you what to do all the time and pointing out in thorough detail your every deficiency. Also, maybe because girls seem to care so very, very much about *everything*, a certain pervading apathy is for boys a tempting disposition—to affect, if nothing else, a healthy counterbalance. They'll dress, then, many boys will, like they don't give a rip. The tying of shoelaces and pulling up of pants is often too much to ask. With whiffs of the outlaw, they'll schlump along the hallway, slouch in chairs, trash their notebooks, treat their backpacks like wastebaskets and revel in their general dishevelment. They'll also enjoy low-watt humor, and annihilating the occasional pixilated antagonist, and quoting ad infinitum *The Big Lebowski*. The Dude, after all, abides. These are assertions of a perceived masculine self in a world that leaves them precious little opportunity for such expression.

Somewhere in all of this sit understood adolescent norms against which both boys and girls measure themselves. Questions then arise of who's following what, kids or the expectations of them, real or imagined. Or their own unnamed impulses. Whatever the case, often without knowing it, girls are, or can be, complicit in their own objectification, while boys are wondering what's for lunch. This can't help but influence their sense of themselves and the other gender.

But has it not always been so? *Hamlet* was written four centuries before Revlon or Shiseido hit the shelves. Twenty-three hundred or so years before that, just as what we could call western civilization was getting up on its feet, Homer, whoever he might have been, suggested Helen knew a thing or two about turning heads and, at least indirectly, launching ships; and it appears Calypso, Circe and the sirens had little trouble getting men to hop to their designs. Even Penelope would as occasion allowed don a fetching frock. Bathsheba, Jezebel, Salome . . . they had their cards and played them. This for the powerless was power. Nor was Cleopatra, who had power, above a tactical come-hither. So it has been, one can't help but conclude, since the sensational Aphrodite stepped out of her scallop shell. Or Eve improved a rib. And when a culture suggests a girl must wait to be asked to dance, or on a date, or to the prom, or to be married, it's telling her, is it not, that a certain passivity is expected? That she should be the object of desire and await the dividends. Juliet, after all, wouldn't be hanging around in the shrubbery under Romeo's balcony, would she?

Boys, meanwhile—and Achilles and Ajax and Odysseus and Telemachus and the rest of the guys—they just want to, you know, do cool stuff. If barbecue is involved, all the better.

There are, too, even today, persistent cultural expectations, however mild, however unspoken, that in school girls gravitate toward the humanities and the arts when choosing time comes and leave math, science and engineering to the boys. Young people of both genders are aware of inequities in career opportunities and remuneration. They know sexism exists. Even this, though, muddies the waters and navigation will then take a gender-based bent, with implications at every turn. Adjustments tend to look like conciliations, and conciliations to the other gender come, it would seem, at the expense of one's own.

All of it—from the pink or blue blankets of the nursery, to the shaven or the hairy armpit, to Sylvia Plath and Virginia Woolf or binomials and the tensile strength of steel, to corporate compensation packages, to the antics of birds and bees—says pretty clearly your gender is central to who you are and what's expected of you. To the extent it's possible, how you proceed is up to you. Therefore, please, know thyself.

So there's that.

ALSO, THERE'S THE COMPANY YOU KEEP. Is there ever. Like your gender, your family was chosen for you. Friends you choose yourself. The upshot of which can be highly edifying.

Let's start here . . .

On a cool spring afternoon nine and a half years ago—a few weeks after we moved into the house in which I'm writing these lines—I was watching our oldest play baseball. Next to me stood another father watching his youngest of seven. Our boys were third-grade classmates and new pals—both sturdy little guys charging around in too-big uniforms and hats worn low enough that their ears stuck out. Tom and I got to talking, as fathers perched along a Little League fence will, and I found in him a good and solid man plentiful with the wisdom of experience times seven. On the subject of our sons tearing it up together at the Josiah Haynes School and beyond, he offered sagely, almost Greekly, "Show me your friends and I'll tell you your future." A few months ago his Michael and my Davey, whiskery now, deep of voice, great compadres still, finished their last baseball season together and graduated from the local high school. And the soothsaying to which Tom was referring lies in this simple fact: friends are the happy result of freedom of choice. As water seeks its own level, the soul selects its own society, which Ms. Dickinson reminds us. We are, then, most genuinely ourselves in our choice of friends. The essence is in the choosing. No one is steering us right nor left to optimal effect, from no one are we seeking approval in whom our soul selects, nor do friends show up on report cards or college applications in forms airbrushed or otherwise. In that sense friends are a reliable bellwether: a kid sees in his or her friends the qualities of character he or she values for themselves. Across a lifetime, at least in my experience, these tend to change almost not at all. Show me your friends, then, and I'll tell you your future. And, of course, much about who you are.

A human fact of profound significance and universal acceptance is the indispensability of friends. In friends we see ourselves reflected to instructive effect. With them we cross-pollinate ideas, we liven the hours. Sometimes the wee hours. In their company we encounter the universe and sift together through our discoveries for the gemstones, over which we then revel together. And through the rough patches we commiserate. Friends are our other half, which Plato describes. In their affection we find affirmation and from them receive, as necessary—and sometimes as unnecessary—slaps upside the head. In friendships abides our true wealth. They warm the cosmic chill. Not erroneously Nietzsche said, "In the end one experiences only oneself." To considerable effect, friendships are our attempt to do something about that. Finally, though, and like nothing else, friends are good fun, a source of simple but deep happiness. They make experience meaningful, they return in kind.

For most high school kids all this is doubly true. No, triply.

For most high school kids friendships are the primary reality, friends individuated units of the collective self. Friendships are their magnetic north, their bona fides, friends their comrades in arms. This is true for you, too, is it not? Every day duty calls, every day together you strap on your helmet, take a deep breath and go over the top, to face parents, teachers, coaches, tutors, the whole adult firing line, who expect things of you you're disinclined to give from somewhat to thoroughly. With your friends, though, you can relax, loosen the belt, indulge in a little low-stakes opinionizing, share a few laughs. With your friends you can be who in the moment you'd like to be, who in quiet moments it feels natural being. You are yourself unguarded, then, with no concern for how what you're doing or not doing will affect you or your prospects next week, next year or however many years down the road. You're simply you and that's plenty.

This is not to say, though, that your friends have to be just like you. How redundant that would be. How boring. Rather, the chemistry of a friendship is complex. Elements must contrast to attract, others must be much the same. All of this can be, usually is, in flux. Certainly proximity matters. Then again it doesn't: experience has shown me again and again one can endure a hiatus of years, whole decades even, that see wildly divergent lives, and in a snap the intervening time vanishes and, sombreros aloft, the amigos ride again. I'll guess one day Michael and Davey will also find this true. As will you. It's rejuvenating and a glorious affirmation of what and whom we hold dearest. In any of this, though, too much scrutiny is to miss the whole. You like somebody, enjoy his or her company, and that's enough. Affinity, empathy, trust—although unspoken these words apply, and they're plenty. Think of your friends. Would you agree the happy life would be impossible without them?

And sometimes you're convinced, sometimes wincingly

convinced, the happy life is impossible *with* them. Friends can drive you absolutely flipping nuts. Friends can be albatrosses around the neck, cinderblocks in the backpack, snarling red boils on the tip of the nose. They get you into trouble, sometimes huge trouble. They let you stay up late doing the physics problems while they're painting their toenails and watching another movie about lovelorn vampires, and then just before first period want a look at your homework like it's communal property. Friends can be highly, outrageously, want-to-strangle-them-ly clueless. With both hands they shove you into awkward positions. They talk about you when you're not there. Blithely they tweet or post on Facebook things you wouldn't tell a soul. They do the right thing at the wrong time, the wrong thing at the right time, the wrong thing at the wrong time—which leaves them with a .250 batting average and who needs that in the lineup? Often and almost deliberately they test the bond by being annoying, or tedious, or needy, and then act like any of these is your problem. And they won't stop texting you. They won't stop yammering about themselves. They'll impose on you advice you haven't asked for and demand from you guidance you're disinclined to offer. Then they take your suggestion, find a way to screw things up anyway, then blame you.

But through it all—or most of it—you like them just the same and they like you. Even when you don't like them you like them, which shouldn't make sense but does. The friendship sails on.

And, oh my, the influence friends wield. Secure in their amity you road-test your identity and hear out their critiques. This process is often as instructive and essential to who you'll become as anything you might experience at home or in school. The culture encourages this, too, bathing, as it does, the mythic high school experience in an aura ebullient, sexy, sentimental and teeming with friendships. *American Graffiti, Grease, Fast Times at Ridgemont High, Election, Napoleon Dynamite,* even the Harry Potter series, to name just a few of the numberless cinematic takes on adolescence in which parents are dorky, teachers absurd and kids are bonded in friendships, a too-cool-for-school world unto themselves . . . all of these influence our expectations of high school and therefore of ourselves. Consequently, everyone yearns for one version or another of a letterman's jacket and the bitchin'est car in the valley and Wolfman Jack on the radio and mild delinquency* and squealing good times. And kids are nostalgic for high school before they

---

* Or not-so-mild delinquency. The problem here is transgression in its experimental phases can have, generally, one of two outcomes: the experimenter realizes he or she has made a mistake and suffers the bruises; or he or she finds reward of one kind or another, which tends to encourage more—and often more severe—transgression, and the inevitable bruising can be, probably will be, all the worse.

even get there. At the center of all this sit friendships, both notional and real.

(Among the sometimes largely notional friendships today are those made online, where "friend" has become a verb as well, a verb of several implications, some dubious, and the noun version can be so abstract, distant and hypothetical as to be entirely meaningless. One's every move is public, potentially infinitely public, every misstep, too. Online friends can be, often are, people you've never met and would give you the willies if you did. They're also difficult to get rid of. Where this idea of friendship is taking us I cannot say. Maybe we'll have the sense to proceed cautiously.)

Nevertheless, we're a companionable species: our friendships serve as a symbolic and practical assertion against those forces that would thwart us. I think of the nameless lone trekker in Jack London's allegory "To Build a Fire." He's you. He's me. His is the human condition. The empty, frozen landscape he intends to cross on his own is the existential universe, brutally inhospitable, utterly indifferent. His only companion, a dog, cares nothing for him beyond his capacities to see to its needs. In a statement of self-reliance—really a fit of terminal hubris—the man has chosen to disregard the advice of friends and strike out alone into fifty degrees below zero. What's the big deal, he's thinking. I'll be fine. I'll show them.

But he isn't fine. He screws up a bit, and a bit is all it

takes. His only redemption lies in the slim satisfaction of "meeting death with dignity." Then the abiding cold settles in and kills him.

London's everyman makes of his isolation a point of pride, his stoicism about the dangers an exercise in courage, but there's no joy in either; nor, of course, is there much future. And one need not trudge solo across the bleak and icy Klondike to know the importance of companionship. J. D. Salinger's Holden Caulfield is tormented by his isolation, his Manhattan cityscape nearly as cold and barren for all its crowds. To your standard teenager this is obvious. Friends are the other self, the vague but certain assurance that one's "me-ness" extends beyond the limits of skin and consciousness. Not exactly immortality, this, nor even a perfect defense against existential loneliness, not every time, but a very good thing just the same. They are an avowal, friends, a bracing affirmation that one belongs.

KNOW THYSELF. THIS is essential absolutely.

Additionally, you might want to know you are mostly water and play permanent host to trillions—a few pounds' worth—of bacteria. In fact, microbes outnumber the human cells you're toting around to the tune of ten to one. You are, then, when the head count is complete, more bug than person. Worth noting, too, is that where you sit in the birth order among your siblings determines many of the finer—

and a few of the not so fine—nuances of your personality. You should also be aware you are a creature not just of habit, but of habitat as well. The sights you see, the weather to which you are subjected, the idioms in which ideas have been shared with you, the way the light falls through the window in the room in which you sleep, assorted particulars of the local culture, the smells on the breeze—these also make you you. And do not forget what is perfectly mundane to you can be highly exotic to someone else. Does a Tyrolean kid gawk at every mountain vista? Does a Mongolian marvel at a yak? Yet what would they make of the street on which you live? Who you are, then, depends at least to some degree on where you sit. Know that someone took an interest in you at an impressionable age—a loving grandparent, an attentive uncle, a nice babysitter who sent you a postcard from Yosemite—and, significantly, nudged you in one direction or another. Know, too, that you have an unchained subconscious lurking in the shadows, pacing sometimes, whispering to you all kinds of pleas and suggestions . . . to which you respond more often than you'd guess.

And know there are at the moment seven billion, give or take, other yous near and far the green globe around, with dreams and concerns and needs every bit as significant as yours.

It's a simple enough command, know thyself. The wonder is in the details.

Chapter 3

The Theory and
Practice of School

"Schoolmastering's so different, so important, don't you think? To be influencing those who are going to grow up and matter to the world . . ."

Chips said he hadn't thought of it like that—or, at least not often. He did his best; that was all anyone could do in a job.

—*Good-bye, Mr. Chips* by James Hilton

SO MUCH DEPENDS ON KNOWING, THYSELF AND ALL THE rest. What, then, of your teachers, whose purpose is to show you why and how to learn, to help you come to know yourself, and your world, too, whose influence you have felt for almost as long as you can remember and likely will the rest of your life?

Because they too are in fact human, some teachers stink, others are terrific, some true wonderments, working miracles every day. Most fall somewhere in between. You already know this. Most teachers, too, are earnest and knowledgeable about their subject. Most want very much to do well by their students. Many are coping with challenges and burdens that would buckle other knees. Many, as Henry Adams suggests, affect eternity, nor know where their influence stops. This thought thrills them. And none, it's safe to assume, went into the profession for the money.

Or the glamour. Or the status, the luxurious travel to exotic locales, the opulent digs, the cool perks, the sultry nights, the sultanic power, the sexy, pulse-thumping rat-a-tat-tat of high-stakes adult give-and-take. Teaching can be, often is, thin pay, thankless toil, numbing drudgery, cruel futility, blunt effrontery. Teaching can be, often is, a haven for mediocrities, for submediocrities in baggy khakis and frumpy shoes, for the pompous, the lazy, the petty, the obsolescent, the tedious, the squirrelly . . . and lots of them tenured. In many regions of the plutocracy to be a teacher, even an excellent one, is to be patted on the head as a service provider, politically suspect, feasting on small potatoes, as much hindering as helping young Maggie's or Matthew's ascent.

Further, an otherwise gratifying life in the classroom can be thwarted by paltry funding, myopic school boards, sluggish bureaucrats, waffling administrators, hyperventilating parents, ovine colleagues, arrogant kids, obdurate kids, impudent kids, apathetic kids, goofball kids, or any combination thereof, and in such number, sometimes, you find yourself more day care supervisor than teacher. A clanging radiator can wreck an hour, a balky copier an entire day. And, while we're at it, let's not forget the joys of grade-level meetings, department meetings, faculty meetings, and breakout sessions—nearly all trial by talk. And avalanches, thundering avalanches, of papers to read, assess, respond to. And how about that giddiest of all delights, cafeteria duty, not six minutes of which would have Horace Mann himself muttering bleakly and plotting escape.

You should know this. Maybe you already do.

Through it all, though, I am here to assert there's no better job than teaching. Sound of mind, clear of conscience, I say that humbly and without reservation. No better.

You should know this, too: while some might like to grouse, most teachers love what they do. Love their students, their subject, their school. They admire their colleagues. They believe in the classroom and efforts to enlighten.

In fact, any number of platitudes trip easily from the tongue . . . but let's leave it at this: with the success or failure of our teachers so goes the success or failure of our species. Of what other profession might this be true? Okay, one platitude: a child at a time, teachers are building the future. Good teachers feel it. Every day they see it happening right there before them. Never is there any doubt about the importance of the endeavor. And ideals matter. This by itself is ennobling. On top of which it's fun, teaching, often great fun, can't-wait-for-tomorrow fun. And unendingly gratifying. You learn so much. You feel helpful, part of the solution, your work performed in the company and for the benefit of kids of whom you quickly grow enormously fond, scores of them adding to the list, year by year, of the best people you know. Done right, there's so much to feel good about, to be proud of, to enjoy.

As for this particular teacher, I can't remember a day in twenty-six years, not one, when I haven't climbed out of bed eager to get to school and have at it. That's a true fact, as a student of mine used to say. Any success I've had springs from this.

And like it or not, and for better or worse, your teachers will have an impact on you, possibly huge. A great one can make all the difference, between inspiration and lassitude, between fulfillment and frustration, for the hour, for the semester, for the rest of your life.

You should also know, then, thy teacher.

So, then, let's put you for an hour, for a class, in your teacher's place . . . walk a bit in those frumpy shoes.

First, your job is to help your students recognize and value what's best in themselves, then to learn to build on it. Your job is to elevate, your subject merely the means by which this process is encouraged. You need, therefore, to understand, empathize with and believe in kids—sometimes not so easy. The teenager you once were has to be alive and well inside you still and offering pertinent counsel. Absent these capacities there's no need to continue.

You have to enjoy the company of young people, too, and look on them fondly, even the knuckleheads. Especially the knuckleheads, of whom there will always be plenty. You must genuinely care about kids, all kids, and their well-being, and their growth, at whatever stage you find them, and what at any moment is or is not going on in their heads. You need to know, or at least have a pretty good idea of, what's best for them, both generally and specifically. You need to understand, too, that to them you're important, even essential, although few will show it. You must be calm as well, and confident, and patient with them and with the process, too. Like farming, little in education happens quickly.

You also have to know your stuff, and be passionate about it—a term enjoying much currency lately and rightly. Want always to learn more about it. Know wherein the wisdom lies, yet be willing and able, should occasion arise, to venture in new directions to beneficial effect. There's no faking this. There's no faking any of it. Then you have to know clearly what in particular you'd like your students to learn, where you want to take them, and how, and how, generally, you'd like them to benefit along the way. All of this must square with your school's, your students' and their parents' expectations, which is perfectly reasonable. After all, you work for them.

Next, you need to find an approach that produces intended results. This could take some time, some experimentation, a few failures and retoolings. Nothing wrong with any of this. If you stink, though, if you just don't have it, nothing will save you. Nor should it. No matter what your style—which is mostly just being yourself to constructive purpose—you should be kindly and demanding. One without the other and you're sunk. You're wasting their time and yours. The example you set, the strengths of character you exhibit, your demeanor, how you speak, when and at what you laugh, the consideration you show, your ability to think on your feet, your optimism, your willingness to work hard . . . these will matter far beyond any sparkling erudition or highfalutin pedagogy or scholarly expertise. A certain stage presence matters, too, but shouldn't to you. Not visibly, anyway. You should be at least somewhat entertaining, but only under the guise of inadvertence. Funny helps . . . but you should expend no effort in trying to be liked: your students will like or dislike you irrespective of your wishes. Fittingly, most efforts to be liked, even sly ones, will backfire. Instead, you should trust yourself, your instincts—but remember, it isn't about you. Your politics, your religious beliefs, the high jinks in which you engaged in college, the hardships you endured as a child, how much you adore your basset hound Wilfred . . . these you should keep to yourself.

Through it all, enthusiasm matters most of all—for your students, for your subject, for the day ahead.

Still, there's more . . .

You have (okay, I have) five classes, each with twenty-three or twenty-four students;* two sophomore classes, two senior, and an elective on Shakespeare, who you believe was really Edward de Vere, the seventeenth Earl of Oxford. These classes meet for an hour five times in successive seven-day cycles from the beginning of September to the middle of June. (The Shakespeare elective runs through the fall semester only.) You should have a plan for and know in some detail what you'll be doing in every class all year, but not at the expense of spontaneity. You need to both guide and follow your students' interest—not so easy sometimes. By the end of the year you will have read and responded to upward of twenty-six thousand pages of teenager writing. You need to be ready for that, too. This is not possible, so brace yourself.

---

* Class size is critical in the success or failure of the enterprise. Ideal would be fourteen or fifteen. Numbers exceeding twenty-one or twenty-two and effectiveness starts to drop off; more than twenty-five or twenty-six and it plummets.

Take care to remember your students are fully dimensional human beings, blessed, as Robert Penn Warren put it, in faculty and apprehension, each of whom matters no more or less than any of the others. Each deserves your best, irrespective of his or her aptitude or attitude, from the schlumpiest to the rocket-fueled. None wants to have his or her time wasted, his or her concerns or interests or honest efforts undervalued. Each arrives for his or her hour with you hopeful things will go well, but maybe a little wary, having been disappointed (not of course in your room) often enough before. Few have an innate interest in schoolwork exceeding mild. Each arrives with a long list of responsibilities and headaches that have nothing to do with you or your class. Most are handling pretty well other responsibilities under which you'd sink without a trace. Try, for example, a little AP physics, a little BC calculus, a little fourth-year German. And they're rushing from one to another to another with hardly a breath between.

Some, too, are dealing with a huge something at home you likely know nothing about—illness, upheaval, dissension, loss. Loneliness. Worry. Some are hungry, and not just the little I'd-love-a-granola-bar-right-about-now hungry. Many are wrung out, even the seeming bushiest of tail. A few are shifty and unscrupulous, which you'd never in a thousand years guess from the doe-eyed innocence of their gaze. A few are depressed. One is diabetic, another hearing-impaired. One is giddy with new love, another newly dumped and suffering. One has a father who drinks, another a father who just rented an apartment across town. One just heard she didn't get a part in the play. Sitting three kids away from her, beaming, is the girl who did. One recently and not all that willingly lost her virginity. A few are medicated. Ethnically, racially and in matters of faith they're all over the map. Of national and world affairs they tend to know little and care less. One or two are in the throes of orientation recognition and acceptance. One used to cut herself. One cannot for the life of him stop staring at Meghan's breasts. From the mild to the heart-breaking, a good third are suffering pimple eruptions. One is overweight and silently mortified about it. All have cell phones within easy reach. One smells. Another just had his braces tightened and his teeth hurt so much his eyes won't stop watering. One tore her ACL on Saturday and fears that's it for basketball, which has been central to her identity and ardor and aspirations since the age of nine. Another trembles with nonspecific anxiety. One has worn the same Red Army fatigue hat for four hundred–plus days straight and offers the running total every time he walks through the door. Another just suffered an affront in the cafeteria and sits there seething. All have a favorite television show, a favorite singer, a best friend. All have some regard for one another, but less than you'd prefer. All have an opinion of each of their teachers, including, of course, you. All care with surreptitious ardor about their grade, which to them, while they know it shouldn't be, is pretty close to the whole point.

Each needs you. Defers to you. Waits upon you. Wants you to be wholly terrific.

Also, there's this: only if what is understood is what is heard, if what is heard is what is said, if what is said is what is meant, have you gotten through. That's a lot to get right. Each kid, however, every one of them, would love to leave that room newly informed, freshly energized, aglow with inspiration. Few think about it that way.

To know your teacher, you should know all of this.

ONCE THEY QUIET DOWN, ask a classroom full of kids, as I'm prone to, what half of eight might be, ask it with a certain leading gravitas. "Four!" comes the immediate reply, with how-flipping-stupid-do-you-think-we-are intonations and are-you-kidding-me archings of the eyebrows and can-this-guy-be-serious glances at one another. Several are thinking, "It's four! I'm right! I got it right!" Two or three are wondering what the hell math is doing in an English class. I mean, dude, isn't that, like, against the, like, Geneva Convention or something?

Unimpressed, I stare back, let them sit there until a brittle silence descends.

"That's the best you can do?" I sigh at last . . . because

narrowly correct answers are at once limited and terminal. And easy answers are deadening: thinking need not continue. With a quick and perfunctorily correct answer, the kid, assuming herself done, folds her arms and awaits her pat on the back. Antithetical to learning, this, and learning why and how to learn—which is, done right, what school is for. And kids think having right answers as often as possible is what students are for. Which can be an issue.

So, a sly smile emerging—all right, a sly, smug smile—I say back at them, "What about E, I, and half of G?"

After a perplexed blink or two at me, at one another, then, by stages, grins, they catch on. Sitting straighter, one chirps, "Or zero, the lower or upper half!"

"Or three," cries another, "the right half!"

"Or a skinnier eight! Peel it off the page and slice it really thin like they do ham at the deli."

On they go from there.

And we've jumped a wall, fresh new thinkers legging it in every direction for fertile ground. With just that we've redefined our adventure together. And Whitman's celebrations of the commonality of the human experience, or Crane's assurance that we're all in the same boat, or Fitzgerald's notion that character matters above all . . . these are no longer clunky teacher-conclusions spoon-fed to the quasi-receptive who remain alert only for a grade's sake. Instead, they've become—or will when we get there—fresh ways of seeing what's been right there all along, newly discovered hunks of gold. And long dead writers are alive again and wise. No longer are they and their work dusty lumps of information to digest and be right about come test time. And literature becomes a vital anthology of parables perfectly accessible and relevant to the contemporary teenager. And narrowly correct answers aren't the end of learning. In fact, learning, we pretty quickly come to see, is seldom about correct answers. In a class full of interested students, being intelligently wrong—or, better, another version of right in an intelligent way—is for the teacher trying to help them grow far more useful. Now we have reason to roll up our sleeves, to open things up and see what we see. Energized, inspired, the kids start to see "why" matters far more than "what." And an hour of school is worthwhile in a way it had not been before.

Or we try this . . .

I'll ask the scholars to clear off their desks and take out something to write with, always for the conscripted a throat-catching moment. Oh crapballs, they're thinking, a quiz. What homework didn't I do? Next, I'll walk around the circle (more about the circle in a moment) and give each a piece of paper. Then I'll say, "Are you a hammer or a nail?" This I admit is a bit gratingly new-agey-herbal-tea-in-a-hand-thrown-mug. For this reason alone I kind of like it. Groans, perhaps rightly, will ensue. They've endured cheese like this before. I don't care. "Are you," I continue, "a pitcher or a catcher?"

Ceilingward hands will fly for purposes of clarification. An impatient scholar, perhaps two, will simply blurt, "Whaddaya mean?" A bolder "Are you kidding me?" will hit the airwaves unbidden, so too a few stealthily acidic exhalations. I'll enjoy them but will not respond.

I'll say, "Are you a rake or a leaf?"

Then I'll say, "Fill a page with your answer. You have ten minutes."

Almost instantly quiet will settle . . . a pall as of the tomb: ten minutes is not a lot of time and this puppy could be graded.

Most self-assessors will be torn. Automatically they'll wonder which I, the grader, would prefer them to pick. The possibility of candor will occur to some, maybe even many; nonetheless, most will conclude *hammer-pitcher-rake* without a moment's introspection or impulse for veracity as it seems forceful, confident, decisive, which they understand the world values and expects from them, maybe not today exactly but soon enough. The consequences could be many. It even has a certain college-application-essayish ring, *hammer-pitcher-rake*, which some will make note to remember. Nearly all, though, will feel *nail-catcher-leaf* would be the more accurate response. Compliance, after all, is their middle name. Admitting it is another thing. Besides, some might naturally wonder, what business is it of the teacher what kind of person I am? Who's he to even ask? Still, undeniably, they get up in the morning before they want to, stagger through a gauntlet of classes they prefer only to passing kidney stones, run around through two hours of often-joyless soccer/football/field hockey/cross country practice, dance/play/concert rehearsal, tae kwon do class, SAT prep class, cello/piano/clarinet practice, drag the carcass home, through the leftover lasagna/pork chops/boneless chicken breasts endure parental interrogations about their day and protracted advice and when-I-was-a-kids and have-you-thought-abouts, then settle in for four and a half hours of homework. "I am a hammer," they will begin . . .

When the time is up I'll collect the essays, take them to the blue recycling bin by the door and toss them into it. Eyes will widen, jaws drop. "You're all nails," I'll tell them with tinctures of disdain. "Against your preference you bowed to my authority and scribbled out your essay."

With a certain sadistic pleasure I'll watch them sag.

"Not one of you said, 'No.' Not one said, 'Why don't you do it?' You did what you were told . . . how come? Respect for my professionalism? Eagerness for my approval because I have the gradebook? Because I'm the teacher and you're the student and this is school and you're trained to obey?"

This last would garner the most nods, but concern

about repercussions stops them. They all know their single-mindedness about a grade is, for the grade's sake, best kept under wraps. Loving learning and general academic esprit de corps, they've come to understand, are also criteria for a grade. So they love learning, they love one another, they love a rousing intellectual challenge. Some would lock arms and sing if they thought it would help.

Yes, this exercise is slightly mean and gimmicky and only marginally thought-provoking, which both I and they know. What they don't know because I won't tell them is it was merely a precursor for Herman Melville's "Bartleby, the Scrivener," which they'll be reading that night . . . or, rather, I've assigned as that night's reading. (Several will simply find a quick summary online. My only real protection against this is to imply the approach of a quiz, which will make a difference to a handful.)

Most will be somewhat miffed I won't be grading their essays. They endeavored. They want recompense. "Mr. Mc-Cullough, what about your feedback?" one will ask cagily.

In return I'll ask, "Are you happy with it?" Checkmate. The rest is mop-up. (This response stymies her because she knows the answer should be, "Yes," which would seal it for me. Trumping the truth for almost every kid almost every time is what the adult with the gradebook seems to want to hear. This is, of course, other than ideal.) So, with the broad exaggerations of the sycophant, the clever will say,

"Of course . . . but . . . well . . . your critiques are always *so* helpful." I'll say, "Forget it."

The hammer-nail activity is complete, and, as far as the students know—although they trust me—it seems disconnected from my larger purposes; throwaway essays, throwaway activity. Patience tried, they'll wait for whatever comes next. Good little nails are they.

They're sitting, as I mentioned, in desks arranged in a circle. I'm in one of them, too. Knights of the Round Table/League of Nations–style, the circle suggests parity and equal investment in the proceedings. That I sit there with them implies I'm just another enthusiast of learning, in my way a student, too (which better be true or I should collect my things and scurry home), with a stake in what happens no greater or less than theirs. I know it's going to be fun and rewarding, my presence there says, and I want to be part of it. Which is also true. The moment I stand up I don the mantle of authority and the dynamic changes. Seated in a circle we're all facing one another, and facing too the ideas that percolate between us. Mostly for security's sake, kids will want to sit in the same desk from class to class, to claim it as their own in perpetuity. I won't allow this. They'll also want to segregate: boys will want to sit with boys, girls with girls. I'll discourage this. With each class meeting they must sit in a new spot next to different people. So must I. Reshuffle the deck. It's all about new perspectives, I tell them, which is true. The class, all of us together around the circle, will soon enough become the operative unit, and not strung clumps of pals.

Class hours will be dedicated mostly to close readings of particular poems or passages of prose and discussions both specific and general, local and universal. I'll offer insights and explanations and ask questions. I'll try to make it plain, though, that mine are just another set of eyes, my voice just one more in the discussion. This is patently untrue and everyone knows it, but the impression matters. I'll draw observations from the students and require them to react to one another. I will show them respect. I'll try to be direct and succinct and at least somewhat articulate.

And I'll prod them. I'll encourage questions, which matter more than answers. I'll praise an eagerness to explore, and original thinking, and risky thinking, but not jump-off-the-cliff thinking. I won't expect penetrating insights, but will make clear a failure to try is unacceptable. I'll do what I can to help them understand talking and thinking are not the same thing. I'll admonish recalcitrance or boneheadedness with teasing and humor, but only lightly and benignly as they can be delicate: to many a teenager embarrassment is torment, and teasing perilously close to mocking and outright cruelty. Some skin takes a long time to thicken. Some never does. Any defensiveness and they'll shut down. I will also zap any whose attention appears to drift. I won't let the yammerers or know-it-alls dominate. I'll try to make clear one must qualify to have opinions, which can be achieved by anyone through inquiry, observation and reflection.

I'll try, too, to be patient with the abuse of the word "like." In this I will fail.

Many, particularly among the girls, will preface an observation with the tic-ish idiom "I feel like . . . ," which of course assumes an interest in how they feel. (Saying "I think . . ." or simply leaving a statement unprefaced would be too bold and could invite contradiction.) This is insecurity disguised as more generally accepted self-absorption: a feeling, however distant or fuzzy, is understood to be all the license one needs to jump right in. Really, though, she'd just like credit for contributing to the discussion—participation, after all, is part of the grade—and builds in an excuse for error, should one prove necessary, by shading the comment in vagueness and subjectivity. Besides, her friends use the phrase all the time, and commonality among friends has a way of legitimizing everything. I try to be forgiving.

When the discussion really gets going—and usually it will—I'll become the conductor of an orchestra. The music rises. Faces grow animated. With enough observations and ideas popping, a kind of heat and light will build. The room will expand. Time will fly. This is when unified exhilaration happens. And I'm very happy I'm a teacher.

ALONG HIGH SCHOOL HALLWAYS lecturing is unfashionable, and not without reason. Done badly a lecture will kill deader than last week's halibut anything interesting about a subject and can paint the lecturer an egomaniac, a windbag, a fool. You already know this. Lecturing is seen in the trade these days as blunt trauma, a force-feeding of academic cod-liver oil, the victims of which are likely to go reeling out of the room in search of a quiet place to lie down and recover. Lecturing is too "top-down," too "teacher-centered," too "informational." Instead, teachers should "facilitate learning quests" or "model growth strategies" and "promote collaborative discovery." Still, as a means of igniting heads I'll contend a lecture—a good one, that is—can be just the right concoction. It's simple, really; you tell them what they need to hear. A good lecture, a useful lecture delivered well, will energize. That's how you know it's good.

For anything manifestly edifying, teenagers tend to have the attention span of a buff-bellied hummingbird and frames of reference narrower than a Popsicle stick. Many see taking an interest in anything beyond their immediate vicinity as akin to capitulating to authority. Moreover, the intellectual passivity encouraged by their upbringing has rendered any native curiosity largely inert. Many, then, are in it for the recompense only. Absent impact on their grade, and aside from a certain open-mindedness about sitting back and being entertained, many would rather put their heads down and snooze.

The solution, experience has shown me, is storytelling. Take from the cupboard the nutritious ingredients of a lecture and with them whip up a nice story. I claim no originality here: mankind has been educating with this method only since the days of brow ridges and knuckle dragging. More than anything, teenagers—today's and, I imagine, yesterday's—are interested in people . . . or, more to the point, real-seeming individuals in whom they can see something of themselves. Give your story, then, a well-formed sympathetic protagonist. Give him or her something to want. Then bring on the interferences, the challenges, with a reward or a frustration to greet him or her at the end. Toss in some atmospheric detail and, especially in the beginning, a humanizing moment or two. Give your story some tension, a little derring-do, a splash of wit for the sophisticates, a pat-the-dog moment for the sentimental, some ribaldry for the groundlings. Be sure, too, the story delivers the didactic goods and has its place in the development of your larger purposes. Do all that and you're in business. No sweat, really. It comes down, I suppose, to how one chooses to see life, as a story or simply a series of events.

This practice will not be entirely without precedent:

with nearly every piece we read in my classes I offer a brief biographical story about the person who wrote it. Writers write what they write for reasons. In story form I try to address a few. The kids pretty quickly come to appreciate that the source from which literature flows, from which all art flows, is people, fully dimensional, unequivocally real, even regular, people, with mothers and fathers and siblings and 98.6 and familiar appetites and hopes and worries and a point of view derived from the circumstances of their experiences. They begin to understand, then, something of the commonality of the human experience and the immediate relevance of literature. They start to see, too, their own membership in the human race. Not once did it occur to any of them that Geoffrey Chaucer or Willa Cather or James Baldwin had ten fingers and ten toes and itches they scratched and a little eye crust in the morning. Neither did they imagine Ernest Hemingway's parents drove him nuts or Emily Dickinson daydreamed about sex or Victor Hugo never recovered from the drowning of his daughter.

To today's young readers—perhaps you, too—canonical writers are neither hackneyed nor musty nor all dried out nor anything else. They're less than that—just barely familiar names, if that, of dead people who wrote probably incomprehensible and definitely boring stories or poems or plays or whatever back in the day. That they're force-fed old-timey writers confirms to teenagers they're not going to like them one little bit: if a book was any good, they figure, it would have somehow found its way into their hands on its own. And in his ignorance, to the contemporary kid old and boring are closely related concepts. Dead-writer names are like fancy words you know you're supposed to know but are too embarrassed to admit you don't, but don't care enough about to bother looking up. So the hell with 'em. No loss. Moreover, a common adolescent mind-set is if you don't know something by about age sixteen, it's probably not really all that worth knowing anyway, unless you're some kind of school-loving oddball dipweed. Old people can't even work the GPS in the car, so what right do they have to judge?

This for the teacher is opportunity; and old becomes the new new.

And today's new old story is about the strange life of Herman Melville.

By the way, all of this is introductory, simple acquaintance making for young minds. Appetite whetting. The point is not to kick-start nascent Melvillians. We'll leave the nuanced explications, the fathoms-deep explorations, the stockpiling of lofty expertise and honings of profound erudition to the PhD types they'll likely encounter a few years downstream. This, remember, is high school, and these are kids.

Now to Melville. The beginning seems a good place to begin.

I'll tell them American literature's great seafaring adventurer, heroic mythic/mystic ponderer, and then forgotten nobody was born in New York City, the latest in several generations of distinction and privilege on both sides of his family. I'll set the historical context not with dates, which mean next to nothing to teenagers, but with more telling details. I'll mention, for example, that when Melville arrived the last of the founding fathers had not yet shuffled offstage, that Manhattan was still mostly woods, that ships traveled under sail. Nearly all of what I choose to tell them, contextual detail and biographical pertinences alike, should inform and make likely a better appreciation of "Bartleby, the Scrivener." It should also serve to demonstrate my credibility, my suitability, as their teacher. I owe them that, every day. For this my expertise on both the students in my charge and Melville must be rich enough to recognize what they at this stage need to know about him and what they don't.

I'll tell them of Melville's erratic, scheming merchant father's ongoing financial crises, his early death, and the family's desperate struggles. I'll tell them of young Melville leaving school, going to work and winding up on the deck of the whaler *Acushnet* under the two-fisted Vineyarder Valentine Pease. I'll share with them the line from *Moby-Dick* that the whaleship was Ishmael's Harvard, his Yale. The liberality of this notion will please them. Ah, they'll be thinking, semesters at sea, piña coladas on the lido deck, conga lines after dark.

I'll tell them of the hardships of a whaler's life.

I'll tell them, too, about the tropical splendors of far-off Hawaii and their head-swimming impact on young Melville. I'll make much of him and his pal Toby, unable to stand shipboard life any longer once they'd had a taste of assorted Polynesian delights. I'll tell them how Melville and Toby jumped overboard one starry night in the Marquesas and swam ashore to enjoy there the kind of languorous, plumeria-scented idyll for which the adventurous in spirit, young and old alike, have pined for ever since, complete with swaying palms, tranquil lagoons, pagan drums and tawny-skinned lovelies with flashing white smiles. Suddenly the vituperative puritanical rectitude of the culture they left behind, thin-lipped and frosty, looked, well, idiotic. Okay, misguided. I'll tell them then of whispers of cannibalism and skedaddling on another whaleship, and Tahiti, then another whaler, this one bound for Honolulu. I'll tell them how he vagabonded there, enlisted in the US Navy, and at last returned to New York a changed man.

Then I'll bring them through Melville trying his hand as a writer, and the thrilling successes of *Typee* and *Omoo*, fictionalized versions of his South Seas adventures and musings.

Then I'll pause. Time for the big kahuna, the leviathan, the great, the mountainous *Moby-Dick*. All of them have heard of it, know something of its reputation, suspect they should show for it a certain quiet reverence, like walking into the lofty silence of a cathedral. Some have seen perhaps a cartoon spoof of it or elsewhere a jokey reference. Maybe *The Simpsons* did an episode. None, though, has read it. None has flipped through it. None has seen the John Huston movie. (None has heard of John Huston. None has heard of Gregory Peck, for that matter. They saw him, of course, in *To Kill a Mockingbird* in the eighth grade but didn't catch the name.)

So I'll tell them about the book. About Ishmael and moody, stricken Ahab and Starbuck and Queequeg and Tashtego and Daggoo and Pip and the rest, all federated along one keel. I'll roll up the figurative sleeves and explain a few of the symbolic implications of the ship, of the ocean, of the whiteness of the whale. I'll explain something of Ahab's obsession and charismatic evil. I'll explain some of the psychological and metaphysical ruminations, insofar as it's possible, and the growing dissatisfaction with the arrogant reductiveness of conventional religions on the empty, rolling sea, under the wide and empty sky, under the vast indifference of the universe and death eternal. I'll explain, or try to, some of the narrator's frustrations with the apparent futility of human endeavor and the elusiveness of Meaning. This, after all, is the ultimate fish story—the biggest of all to get away. I'll say something, too, about all the narrator learns from his shipmates and their experiences together, how he is transformed. I'll call him Ishmael.

That I'll do all this, by the way, will be to many of the students a quiet compliment. Hey, they'll reason, McCullough thinks I'm, you know, like, into this kind of stuff. History and whatnot. I mean, how sick is that? For several this will be all the encouragement they need: being believed in is a flattering responsibility. They'll play along, and pretty soon get swept along. Soon enough they'll provide their own propulsion.

I'll explain then that the novel was on its publication a crushing critical and commercial flop. That Melville, who thought it good, even great, was poleaxed. I'll explain the novel's eventual resurrection and the esteem in which it is held today. I won't, though, overdo the esteem stuff. Instead, I'll make it as plain as I can that while all the cultural monument hoorah is important, each new reader's opinion matters far more. Reading a book makes it yours; and they haven't read it. Yet.

Some, will ask, naturally, why we aren't reading it in class. "I wish we could," I'll say, "but it's too long, too big. We have but nine months together." This is true. True also is I tried it a few times with kids long ago and they scurried around it, grabbed Cliffs Notes and whatever else they could get their hands on—this was before Al Gore invented the Internet. They found the book muddled, weighty, dull. Too many quit on it. I'll remind them they're certainly welcome to pick it up on their own. "Yeah, right," their expressions will say.

Then we move on.

I'll tell them about Melville's growing frustration with the now pretty much uniform flat reaction to his work, the poor sales, the switch to shorter pieces for magazines. I'll mention that "Bartleby, the Scrivener" was one of these.

Then I'll explain that Melville, after little more than a decade at it, gave up writing altogether. Wiped his hands, put away his pens. Imagine Mozart walking away from his pianoforte, I'll say, Rembrandt kicking the easel across the room. In middle age, at what should have been the peak of his powers, Melville stopped writing. Then some travel, protracted financial difficulties, a humdrum job, moodiness, family tragedies, obscurity, death.

I'll offer then in closing a word about *Billy Budd*, and Melville's posthumous rediscovery and ascension to the pantheon.

By now our hour is nearly up. I'll know from their faces whether I succeeded. I'll give each his or her copy of "Bartleby." I'll hand back their essays on "Where I Lived and What I Lived For." With the bell I'll send them on their way.

TEACHERS . . . GOOD TEACHERS . . . want to offer their students the insights and experiences they need to grow. Not too complicated, really. This is why they show up in the morning. The rub lies in how and by whom that need is perceived, and by what methods it's best addressed. Irrespective of aptitude, every student walks into a classroom accompanied by his or her own particular apprehensions and hopes, and those of his or her parents—and teachers, administrators, school boards, college admissions people, politicians near and far, and grandparents down in Boca. The list is long, and everyone seems to have a stake. And an opinion. And advice. With grade inflation, flights of pedagogical whimsy, initiatives laudable in spirit like No Child Left Behind, and more dubious notions like teacher compensation and retention based on student performance on standardized tests, the situation becomes both nebulous and complex. As a consequence, "hard data"—grades, test results, per-student spending, graduation rates, four-year college matriculation numbers—become the talking points. And with the talk so goes perception and with perception so goes policy—when all of us know learning defies numbers.

Learning, true learning, is about expanding comprehension and deepening wisdom. It's about joy, exhilaration. It's about enriched and fulfilling and productive lives. It's about discovering how little you know and trying to do something about it, not only for the excitement of discovery, which is of course real, but to be a responsible citizen of the planet. It's about finding where, why and how to be helpful. It's about the ability to see. GPAs and SAT scores can tell you little about any of that. Yet on we talk, pointing always, it seems, at numbers.

Meanwhile, we lay into a really great meal not for the numerical breakdown of the nutritional benefit, nor do we get together with friends with an eye on a consequent uptick in the cognitive or experiential register, nor do we laugh or kiss or sing or dance or enjoy the sun or admire a catbird or weed the garden or root, root, root for the home team because doing so will look good in life's ledger. Learning is—or should be—like that; and when education becomes a calculated exercise in putting up numbers, particularly in the student's mind, learning suffers. And child by child, a culture changes. The teacher who doesn't understand this is in for a difficult time and should be.

Studying Herman Melville—or, rather, dipping a toe into the great tossing sea of Herman Melville—or studying Cicero's orations or *The Song of Solomon* or French gerundives or differential equations or the Wilmot Proviso—matters not in the grades a high school student might achieve, nor in the information he'll retain, nor in the skills he'll hone, nor in the college or career toward which it will move him closer. It matters in his excitement at discovering what's there. He should do it—and we adults need to help him understand it this way—for the holy-mackerel-would-you-please-take-a-look-at-this moments available to anyone willing to observe and think about what he sees. When enthusiasm builds into a wildfire it's all pure joy; intellectual growth, information retention, skill honing and shiny grades will surely follow.

They'll also become almost entirely irrelevant because the student will be too busy, and having too much fun, learning. He will see what a wonderment is the world in which we live. He might even start to see and grow excited about his place in it. Aspiration will start to glow.

And when I tell my students grades matter only to the kid who's missing the point, this is what I mean. What begins in delight, said Robert Frost, ends in wisdom. Paint a watercolor, play the commodities market, haul freight, raise sugar beets, hike the Appalachian Trail, sell software, land a tarpon, fill a cavity, restore a '65 Mustang, gaze at the sunset because you enjoy and believe in the endeavor. What are kids learning when we allow them to think otherwise? How are they benefiting?

If a teacher doesn't see it this way, or can't for whatever reason pull it off, hand him his hat.

The primary purpose of grades and test scores is external: parents, guidance counselors, administrators, college admissions people can get some idea—some highly imperfect idea—of how a student has performed. For that reason grades can be helpful internally mostly along the lines of carrot and stick. That she or he has the power of the red pen gives a teacher leverage, which comes in handy from time to time. Moreover, there are—or can be—direct connections between a grade and the benefits the student has enjoyed in earning it. But is the teacher a fair and objective assessor?

Are the performances and/or skills on which the student is being assessed the most germane? Is the driven kid who aces everything necessarily a terrific student? And how are we defining terrific? Or, for that matter, student? Is another kid, the one who loves her class, can't wait to get there, can't get enough of what she's learning, has seen her life improve because of it, inspires others with her enthusiasm, but has not yet evolved into a consistent home run hitter . . . is she a poor student? By today's measure her C+ might suggest so. Passion, joy, growth: these are difficult to quantify, assess, and compare. In looking at the aggregate we're assuming, aren't we, that different but uniformly effective teachers value the same sets of skills, or even the same attitudes, and grade the same way according to the same criteria? Schools vary, too, of course, as do the cultures of the communities they serve. With so many variables, is an equitable and accurate system of objective assessment possible? Is assessment even necessary? If the teacher's purpose is to help a child grow, can he, should he, also sit in judgment, stamping or not stamping passports to future opportunities?

And, further, who's to say when the benefit of a classroom experience will bear fruit? Something your mostly forgotten sixth grade social studies teacher said in passing one drizzly February afternoon back in Doylestown might appear suddenly in your head rich and radiant twenty-three years later under a blazing Wyoming sun when for the first time you pull off the highway, stride through the sage, and see there before you a pioneer's name and a mid-nineteenth-century date carved into the granite of Independence Rock. And wham. Your fingers tingle. Was that long-ago class, then, because you got a mediocre grade on your Westward Expansion report, a wasted opportunity for the child you used to be? Isn't it possible, or even likely, that the habits of mind inspired in art class, or math, or music, will influence even decades downstream how you see or think about anything? Isn't this education?

An old friend and veteran of more than thirty-five years in the classroom, grizzled but still kicking, told me recently, "When I started I thought science really mattered, that the substance of the subject was everything. But it didn't take long to realize what I was really trying to do was make electricity. If it works, if the lights go on . . . well, that's the kid's thing."

Sure, the artful slacker can throw on a light or two if he thinks the keeper of the gradebook might be watching. He can nod knowingly, wax poetic even, and claim with a slap of the forehead thrilling epiphanies. Pull it off long enough and he could emerge from a class having learned little more than somewhat skillful baloney liberally applied can bring him what he wants. I'll suggest, though, that same kid, by different but more insidious means, can fake his way into polished essays and correct answers on tests. In fact, I don't suggest it, I assert it. It happens all the time. With the advantages available to the privileged—the Internet, tutors, prep classes, educated parents eager to help, bountiful public libraries, travel, as well as fine schools all the way along, and, while we're at it, Ritalin or Adderall—the notion that the "hard data" of grades and test scores can provide for us reliable bases on which to make important decisions seems silly, exclusionary, even reckless.

Directly connected to all of this and worth a further word is grade inflation. Paradoxically, with rigor and performances in decline, grades are improving. In the new economy we're calling mediocre work good and good work excellent. A C is now an ugly smudge on the report card and shameful. A B is pedestrian, a shrug, oatmeal; an A merely just compensation for already understood superiority. Make grades the point and this is what happens. Everyone sees it, wishes it weren't so, yet the phenomenon persists. Meanwhile, we Americans have fallen so far behind our neighbors in other parts of the developed world in standardized measures of proficiency in mathematics and science, and one wonders what else, that to presume excellence would be laughable . . . depending, of course, on how much stock you put in standardized measures of proficiency.

Protecting delicate sensibilities seems a major part of the impetus—the old self-esteem thing again. Also, the perfectly human urge to make happy in the moment a child of whom you've grown fond. Wider and easier access to the laurels is part of it, too, since laurels have come to mean so much. Also contributing is the reasonable notion that the payoff—the reward, good or bad, that is a grade—comes in the contemporary currency. Today a B is what a B looks like in today's economy, no more than a stop on a sliding scale of perception. A gallon of gas doesn't cost thirty-eight cents anymore either. An A, though—or its gilded twin, the A+—remains top of the line, end of the scale. And Fs don't really matter, since they happen so rarely these days. And it's getting crowded at the top.

Try to do something about it and you're a crotchety old ideologue tilting at windmills and doing (often) earnest kids an injustice. You can't pay yesterday's wages. What matters is common reference and wide concurrence. Whether you call them small, medium and large, or medium, large and extra-large, or large, extra-large and jumbo, the sizes, one would surmise, remain the same; but with grades everything creeps ever upward while sizes appear to be shrinking. It seems one has to produce less and less these days for better and better reward—yet grades remain our chief criteria for college admission, for general approbation, for motivation.

A fragrant pot of slumgullion, this.

It's the next day. The bell rings and back to class the scholars troop. Most have read the story . . . or read enough about it online, they hope, to survive a quiz and hum a few bars in the discussion . . . or have interrogated a friend who has. Before they even sit—as they're scouting a seat, choosing one and slinging their backpacks to the floor before it—some are already discussing that Bartleby sketchoid and wondering if he's, you know, like, really truly dead or whatever at the end. Those who did not read are stretching their ears to snag something, anything, useful should there indeed be a quiz. As they settle I'll remain affably impassive. Many of those who have done the reading would like a quiz—but fears of appearing even somewhat eager and therefore brown of nose will keep them quiet. Those who didn't quite get around to reading—128 was a parking lot coming back from the cross-country meet, Aunt Laurie and Uncle Hal came over for dinner and stayed late, *Pretty Little Liars* was on—or those who nodded off a third of the way through the story, definitely would not. Pleading for a stay of execution, though, would be to announce their unpreparedness, and silence appears almost an admission of guilt, so they affect a chatty nonchalance. Inwardly they fret.

When at last everyone is settled, and something like quiet starts to fall—or portents gather—I'll say, "Clear off your desks."

Some will groan, some collapse in despair. Some will fail to conceal panic. Others will adopt the posture of the Thoroughbred at the gate. In a timorous voice one will ask if it's going to be hard. "There's no such thing as a hard test," I'll answer rotely, smiling, "only insufficient preparation." Kids love it when I say this. So too will these.

What I'm giving them is in my view among the most important gifts a teacher can offer: accountability. Calling on spectators in discussions works much the same way. Give a child a task to perform—read a weighty story, patrol center field, shovel snow—praise her or him for a job well done, critique kindly a less than successful but sincere effort, express disappointment in an insincere effort. Do this again and again. Require of students big jobs and small, difficult and easy. Be a rock—a compromise of standards in any of this can be highly corrosive. When in a weak moment they whine, tell them what Euclid told Ptolemy: there is no royal road to geometry. They'll wonder what you mean. Let them. Accept only hemorrhaging-all-over-the-place-and-turning-deathly-pale excuses. Be conservative in both praise and criticism, lest they think you think the endeavor is about pleasing or displeasing you. This is how we nurture responsibility, aptitude and confidence.

Because they're sitting in a circle of desks I'll be sure I've made two different but comparable versions of the quiz and pass them out alternating one and the other. This will render unhelpful peeks at a neighbor's answers. More important, it will show them I've anticipated such a possibility. If when I pass them out any boy or girl looks up at me and says, "I would prefer not to," I'll take back the quiz, give him or her a pat on the back and an A in the gradebook, and move on . . . easy to say here because none will do this. Ideally, the quiz should be a breeze for the kid who has read the story and impossible for the kid who has not. This quiz—both versions— will ask the student to explain the context and significance of a few passages. I'll collect the papers when they're done. These I won't toss. Requests for on-the-spot assessments I'll deny.

Most will have found Melville's writing, well, dense. Tough going. Boring. I'll try to remind myself they lack the experience as readers to "get" much of what's suggested in the text, the "between-the-lines stuff," the "symbolism and all." In fact, without backfilling explanation, many students will think I'm just making up—pulling out of my butt, in the vernacular—for my own amusement apparently, the implied meaning of passages, the metaphors and themes. Many think interpreting a text is like lying in a field and seeing shapes in clouds, entirely subjective and fanciful. Some will accuse me of colluding with the writer somehow, or with the Holy and Secret Order of High Priests of Literature, to trick decent, hardworking kids who only want As with the least possible effort into missing the important elements so the brainiacs get to feel superior and go to a, like, awesome college. Some will wonder if I have a teacher's copy with all the "right answers" hidden in a drawer. I try to persevere through this. Happily, I'll show them my cards. Again, they're kids.

I'll start with low-stakes questions . . . about the narrator, about his tone and attitudes. I'll ask about what goes on in his Wall Street office and why. I'll ask about the preponderance of walls in the story. I'll ask about the odd, nonname names of the miserable underlings in the office. I'll direct their attention to the narrator's diction. "Imprimus," for example—what, I'll inquire, does the use of such a word suggest about our narrator? And how about the reverent mentions of John Jacob Astor?

The kids, though, will want to get straight to Bartleby. My best efforts to suggest the story is really about the narrator and his transformation from a mildly greedy, thoroughly self-satisfied but probably decent enough businessman to a caring, engaged humanist touched by the suffering of others will hardly slow them down. ("The guy goes from a Republican to a Democrat!" a boy once exclaimed.) As an examination of the hopelessness of labor in an exploitive capitalist system, or as a condemnation of the imprisoning effect of urban anonymity and toil, or as an allegorical reaction to the loneliness of existential reality, or as an obliquely autobiographical confession even after the wind I expended on our friend HM last time, the story itself will for them have not a lot of resonance. No, they're intrigued by this Bartleby dude and his weird, unexplained and slyly skillful passive rebellion. "I would prefer not to," he says again and again to every suggestion, request and demand, however reasonable. I mean, they'll say, how clutch is that?

The kids will see in the pallid copyist not just impressive stubbornness in the face of authority, and a kind of profound, subversive, nonspecific sick-of-it-all with which many quietly identify, but power . . . the power of the nail, the catcher, the leaf. The key—and here I do my best to shepherd the discussion according to the kids' interest—is the nature of Bartleby's . . . well, we can't call it a refusal. That's the thing; it's not a "No," nor even a "No thanks." While his reasons remain his own, Bartleby—the only character in the story to merit a name—simply states a preference: "I would prefer not to," he says flatly, over and over, with little or no elaboration nor any explanation.

The beauty of this simple but enigmatic statement is it requires the narrator to stop, scratch his head, and, by degrees, recognize Bartleby's humanity, to consider him as a reasoning and feeling soul. Here before him is not just an uncooperative office machine but a human being with desires, with preferences. Thus the narrator's dormant spirit of empathy awakens: " . . . there was something about Bartleby," he confesses, "that not only strangely disarmed me, but in a wonderful manner touched and disconcerted me." That Bartleby dies shows the mettle of his resolve, or the depth of his despair, or both, and its power to transform. Stopping short of death—should he, say, come to his senses at the last minute and comply, ask for a slice of bread, a glass of water—then his passive rebellion becomes merely a gesture.

But the weird little bugger rides it out to the end. Bartleby, the kids realize, is a rebel, a martyr even. The dude rocks. He has said something. "Ah Bartleby!" the narrator, a new man, cries at the end of the story. "Ah humanity!" This to the kids is revelatory. School then is revelatory. And the powerless see their power.

In here somewhere the bell will ring, the hour having flown. The scholars will get up and shoulder into their backpacks and head for the door. Before they go I'll give them the reading for next time.

Chapter 4

Look at Your Fish

The Heart's a truant; nothing does by rule;
Safe in its wisdom, is taken for a fool;
Nods through the morning on a dunce's stool;
And wakes to dream all night.
—"Scholars" by Walter de la Mare

LET ME TELL YOU ABOUT A RECENT STUDENT OF MINE. We'll call him Jack.

He's a quiet boy, our Jack, self-possessed, responsible enough generally, amply courteous, eminently likable. In my normative-level senior literature class he was attentive, receptive, but disinclined to push himself. He found a comfortable pace and stuck with it. The snarky might be tempted to condemn him as undistinguished, B-/C+, just another kid—any of these tantamount in the current climate to pretty heavy condemnation. More and more of late,

I find myself compelled to defend kids like Jack, even to other teachers, some of whom seem to hold in a museum-lit shrine an image of the Ideal Student to which they expect all those of the flesh-and-blood variety to aspire. Anything short of that is a disappointment, a personal affront, a sign, even, of a deficient character. Superlative achievement and a whole salad bar of laurels should be everyone's goal, they too seem to believe, and learning is what happens along the way. Students like Jack can become invisible. In fact, many seem to prefer it that way.

Through the year Jack ambled along at about three-quarters speed. Over the first few months I waited for signs of ignition. When he handed me a submediocre paper as the last of the autumn leaves were skittering down the street, I deemed it reason for a sit-down. We had a pleasant talk, he agreed he could be doing better, acknowledged he had it in him, said he recognized the benefits of working hard; cause enough, I thought, for a little cautious optimism. We parted pals. But nothing changed. A nudge here, a prod there, even a mild remonstration or two . . . nothing. Fair enough, I thought. Good kid, I thought, happy to amble. Fine. A student, particularly a senior, is allowed to govern his own engagement, to deem my class not his bag. As long as something is. I left him to his own recognizance.

But across a long and mild winter came evidence of

nothing from our Jack in the way of bags, no bag in any direction. Spring eased in—nary a whiff of fervor re anything.

Then in May, a new generation of leaves greening the trees, with the effect of a revelation I happened to learn reticent Jack did have a passion after all . . . happened to learn because he mentioned it. He had, as it turns out, a big bag, a let-the-world-go-on-without-me bag, a calling. I even liked that he hadn't bothered to tell me about it until our time together was almost over; it was, after all, his. And it served as far as he knew—or would at least let on—no useful purpose beyond the gratification of doing it, which he articulated poorly, which bothered him not in the least. He wasn't being coached or spurred or assessed by an adult. No competition awaited for which he was preparing. He'd had no special training for it; nor did it play even an oblique role, as far as I know, in any of his college aspirations. The pleasure and satisfactions were his alone and for themselves and more than enough.

In May I learned Jack draws.

But it's more than that: Jack draws pictures of three dimensions. He creates detailed paper models, sculptures really, with ordinary printer paper, pencils and pens, scissors and Scotch tape. He does it purely *because he enjoys it*. From the Hogwarts castle to the Statue of Liberty to a life-size, wearable baseball cap and on and on, some no bigger than a deck of cards, some as big as a collie. Something strikes his fancy, he sits down and makes a model. If it takes a week, it takes a week. If the phone rings, he lets it. If the home-work gets short shrift, so be it. And they are exquisite, these Jack originals. They are beautifully, masterfully, done. You should see them. Everyone should see them—the Fabergé eggs of paper sports cars and Millennium Falcons. On that note, though, Jack doesn't seem to care much either way. It's nice people like them, but that's not why he does it. He tells me once they're finished mostly they just crowd the floor of his room. He tries not to step on them. The fun, the satis-faction, is in the doing.

It had begun a few years earlier. His family was on vaca-tion on the Jersey shore. Time ran short at an amusement park, if I have it right, and Jack was unable to go on a ride he'd been eager to try. The family headed for the car with a crestfallen kid in tow—which, I'll point out, is a kid for you: fun all day at an amusement park and he's glum about the one ride he didn't get to go on. Well, thinks the parent, too bad. But, thinks the kid, I really, really, *really* wanted to go on that ride. Midmope, Jack gets back to wherever it is they're staying and, not knowing why, not even thinking about why, reaches for pencil and paper and creates a me-ticulously detailed drawing of the ride, a longing drawing, a demonstration of frustrated ardor. A love letter. And, he real-ized at the end, it came out great. It was fun to do. Time and the world had vanished. For a full hour or more it had been just him and the ride whirling in his head and the drawing before him as it appeared. The process was restorative, too. It charged the battery rather than drained it.

Finished, he looked at the picture. Felt a measure of pride in his handiwork. Realized sitting there the itch was not entirely scratched. Realized the ride had a left side and a right and a back . . . so he drew them, too. When he was done, there they lay on the table, four sheets of paper with drawings on them. Then he had an idea, a delighted little zing, which was good because he still didn't feel like being done: the ride doesn't lie flat on a table. It stands upright. It has three dimensions. He went for scissors and tape.

Voilà.

Bliss does not have to be big and important. Nor must it bring one accolades of any luster to matter. Bliss is more than its own reward. And while rare is the acorn that becomes an oak tree, every oak tree, every last one, began as an acorn you could pick up and put in your pocket.

Whether Jack goes on to become an artist or an architect or an engineer or anything else directly consequent to his enthusiasm for model making does not matter. He has learned something about passion, about focus, about clearing a space in his life and doing what he does purely because he loves and believes in it. He has honed a set of abilities, too, developed standards of his own measure, and sees to it that he meets them. He knows, then, the satisfactions of seeing with purpose, conceiving ideas, dedicating himself to them, and producing good work. In choosing and doing for himself, he earns his confidence and self-worth. Very good things, these, and, I hope, lifelong.

DELETE, PLEASE, ANY COMPULSION to impress people. Don't give them that power. Recognize what needs to be done, then do what you do for the satisfaction it brings you.

Construe none of this, though, as license for self-indulgence. Nor narcissism. Not even if you were the only person on the planet.

Instead, lose yourself in what you do because you enjoy and believe in it, and let the consequences, and their benefits, be what they will. Give the moment its due; trust that the future will take care of itself. Have faith in yourself. Aim high. Focus. Work hard. Work smart. Don't pretend you know more than you do. If it's distinction you want, or wealth, or love, or praise, deserve it. And be selective in whom you choose to admire. Remember your manners. "Let your conscience be your guide" isn't bad advice, either, even if the source is an insect. Nor is "Respect your elders" . . . although, really, finally the adult to whom you owe the most is the adult you'll soon become. Him or her you don't want to disappoint. Rather than as a burden and an imposition on your time, see responsibility as an opportunity to meet challenges, to refine abilities, to affirm your independence. And to grow. Make learning your mission, then derive your satisfactions from what you and your learning contribute to the greater good. And believe me, there's much to be done. Teachers, admissions officers, friends, other kids, parents and acquaintances with whom parents sense against their better judgment they're competing in the "No, I've Got the Most Impressive Kid" contest . . . these people should matter almost not at all in the who you are and what you do department. Accept their support, enjoy their encouragement, then go about your business. They'll watch and draw their own conclusions anyway. "Follow your bliss," said the mythologist Joseph Campbell, who as a young man followed his into a shack in the woods where he sat and read for five years and emerged one of the influential thinkers of his time. If at the moment you find yourself a little shy on bliss, follow your curiosity. If you're light on curiosity, slap yourself across the face three times and try again.

More than anything else, what you love defines you, and no one but you can choose it. Once you've chosen—or it chooses you, which is more often the case—and it's really love, if you don't pursue it you'll ache. And you should ache. Maybe not today, maybe not tomorrow—to pilfer a bit from the brothers Epstein—but soon and for the rest of your life. Fulfillment will come only when you've achieved your own definition of success.

Now ANOTHER BOY, another story, this one closer to home . . . this one *in* my home: Davey, the one who began as an ulcer, grew, as they do, older and bigger, and found himself at age sixteen in an AP US history class. This is a bright, happy, receptive kid, a very successful student if enjoying learning is the measure, a B+/A– guy if grades are your thing. Grinding it out over every terrain had not thus far proven a forte. Worth noting, too, is this: to walk into a history class, any history class, with his name is to invite certain expectations. Always something is said . . . heads turn, teachers quip. Then the grandfather for whom he is named shows up on television, is quoted in the newspaper, in a magazine, in a textbook. There sit a few of the grandfather's books on the teacher's shelf. There he is up on the Smart Board expounding in a documentary. Davey smiles, appreciates the compliments, makes note to pass them along, accepts the ribbings, and says in effect, "He's him, I'm me."

Then there's this: his father is a teacher at a different high school, and the course, AP US, was one of those teach-for-the-test experiences, an approach that chafes the teacher-father. And his teacher took forever, *forever*, months, to return papers, which annoyed not just the teacher-father, whose daddish grumbles would include such vocabulary as "lazy" and "unprofessional," but Davey, too. He would shrug and gape and wonder where he stood and what the teacher was "looking for" in a paper. I offered to call the man, kind of wanted to call in the spirit of delivering the spicy earful. No way, said Davey. My deal. Worse still, the course turned out to be mostly tariffs and treaties and provisos and dates and movements and isms, all in preparation for the make-or-break exam at the end of the year. "A single hour," he came home grumbling one afternoon midyear, "one measly stinking stupid hour on the whole entire Civil War, the actual war part. No Antietam, no Gettysburg, no *Monitor* and *Merrimack*. No Stonewall. No Quantrill. Dad, no Chamberlain! Now it's carpetbaggers and Reconstruction."

April became May. He studied hard—or at least what looked like hard. He logged the hours. Burned the midnight oil. At last test day arrived. That evening after baseball practice he staggered through the kitchen door, dazed but intact. Did fine, he said. What's for dinner? he said.

But the course continued. A good month of school remained. So the teacher assigned a big important-sounding research paper on a subject of the student's choosing, due the last week of school with a self-addressed, stamped envelope so the teacher could mail the graded paper back to the student. At home Davey hemmed, hawed, indulged an occasional impulse to grouse, schlumped from room to room, and procrastinated in the name of scratching around for a subject. The teacher suggested a few topics. None grabbed him. I offered a few ideas. At last, deadline looming, with a kind of who-cares spin of the dial, he took one.

And became a man possessed.

A bounding-up-the-stairs, can't-wait-to-plunge-back-into-it man possessed. "This is so cool," he kept saying when he'd appear in the kitchen for purposes of refueling and excitement sharing. The subject was Benny Goodman and his orchestra's performance of "Sing, Sing, Sing" at Carnegie Hall in January of 1938. What Davey knew going in was that jazz was peppy old-timey music and a basketball team in Salt Lake City pretty good in the Stockton-Malone era. Quickly, though, incandescently, he became an aficionado of Goodman, of Gene Krupa, of Harry James, of big band swing. He spent long happy hours at it. The house was full of music. Then he was ablaze with Louis Prima, then Louis Armstrong, then Fats Waller and Duke Ellington and Sidney Bechet and Django Reinhardt. Today, a year and some months later, he'll tell you Ella Fitzgerald is his favorite singer. His new love of jazz brought him to all things Woody Allen, who's now vying with Robert De Niro and Nomar Garciaparra for top billing in Davey's Coolest Guy Hall of Fame. And Woody Allen brought him to Barcelona and Paris and, recently, Rome, and now he walks around speaking mellifluous pretend Italian to an imagined Alessandra Mastronardi and quoting in a spot-on impersonation Woody's old stand-up routines, and I hope it doesn't end until he's a hundred and twelve.

I read the paper with considerable admiration the night before it was due. Ardor in abundance. I told him I liked it. He seemed not to hear me. With great ceremony he patted the stack of paper together on the kitchen countertop, sunk a staple through the upper left-hand corner with satisfied muscularity, and as with kid gloves placed the masterpiece in his history binder, which he slid into his backpack, which he zipped smartly. He handed in the paper the next morning.

And never saw it again.

All summer long, nothing. Day after day at the mailbox, nothing. He asked about it when school resumed in September, and the teacher fended him off with a flustered "Oh yeah . . . that. Uh, let me see if I can find it." And there it ended. However exasperated he might have been then, Davey doesn't care now. He has Benny and Louis, and Ella and Woody. Maybe even someday an Alessandra. Each and all more than enough.

And if ever I meet the teacher I won't know whether to serve up that spicy earful—or to throw an arm around his shoulder and thank him. Whether he intended to or not, he showed my son paper writing, learning, is not about the outcome, the material reward or punishment of a grade. Instead, it's about everything before the grade—the curious pleasure of head scratching, the joy of exploration, of discovery, and of organizing one's observations and ideas and articulating them usefully, elaborating, excising, fiddling, polishing, getting it right, and taking pride in what you've created and enjoying the new perspectives having done it offers. Put a grade on a paper, though, shiny or not so shiny, and the whole experience becomes an exercise in pleasing or displeasing the grade giver. And the kid could bring home an A having learned not a dang thing, or a C– having unlocked a treasure chest.

BANISH PLEASE FROM your head now and forever the idea that work and suffering are synonyms. First, there are no synonyms. Every word has its own implication. Rapid and fast have different flavors, read and peruse, dresser and bureau, slacks, trousers, pants. Second, work is in large measure— big measure? sizable measure?—what the human experience is about. Just to keep the ball rolling is work. And done right work is a great pleasure. It's what our species at its best does best. It's why we have a skeletal system, muscles, opposable thumbs. To do. The whole human mechanism, you'll note, is designed for moving forward. Recognizing a need, dedicating oneself to a worthy task, expending effort, adhering to standards, persevering through difficulties, applying usefully innovative thought, seeing progress through to its fruition, watching others benefit from one's handiwork, earning a night's rest—these are foundational pleasures codified in the DNA. You don't have to be some cheddar-eating Yankee farmer up and threshing before the rooster's crow to feel it, nor is this a bloodless sneer at the earthly delights of sprawling on the beach in any of its many forms. Work, though, is sacred. Sacrosanct. Holy. Not words one uses lightly. Not quite synonyms, either. In his beautiful elegy *A River Runs Through It*, Norman Maclean tells us "all good things . . . come by grace and grace comes by art and art does not come easy." For something to matter first you have to invest of yourself. You must commit—total focus—then work.

I think, too, of that scene in Stuart Rosenberg's terrific 1967 movie *Cool Hand Luke* when the guys on the chain gang are looking with dread at a long, blistering hot day shoveling sand onto a freshly tarred country road. Both they and the impassively sadistic guards making them do it see the enterprise as pure torture. The men are defeated before they begin. But Luke, Paul Newman, smiling, spits in his hands and flings himself at it, lays into it with everything he has. With a growly "Hooyah!" he attacks the job. At first his fellow convicts think he's nuts, tell him so and urge him to slow down. Soon enough, though, they figure it out; his example inspires them, and they too have at it with great manly spirit. All of them strain and sweat and hustle up the line. For the first time they feel a defiant sense of power. No longer are they prisoners. "You can't beat us," they're telling the guards with every tossed shovelful, enjoying themselves mightily, giving it their everything. They get the job done with hours to spare. Beaming, speechless nearly, chests heaving, they lean on their shovels and regard with great satisfaction and pride what they just did.

And I recognize the hazards in comparing by implication kids to convicts on a chain gang and teachers to sadistic prison guards, but I'll forge ahead just the same: for school to be worth your while it has to require of you long hours of good old-fashioned toil. So little in life worth accomplishing is easy, ease by itself diminishes the value of anything it might win us. Nor are skill and knowledge easily earned. School is for learning, remember, not the snagging of a diploma nor the compiling of a track record with which to impress. For the relief of an easy-breezy class, say, one loses any sense of accomplishment or, worse, of endeavoring much of anything. If you want something to matter, you have to work to earn it. It's a law of human physics, and true far beyond the brick walls of school. Certainly the acquisition of wisdom works that way. You have to persevere through setbacks, through your own disinclinations, trepidations and self-doubt, trying your best not just as a matter of principle but as a leap of faith. Process matters wholly, and there are no shortcuts. When you encounter hardship, deal with it. When you encounter a limitation, work to push through it. When things don't go your way, try again. In this way you prove yourself worthy—you prove it to yourself.

Acing the test, crushing a double off the wall, nailing the Chopin piece, these matter in themselves absolutely, but they also provide, one hopes, lessons in the value and satisfaction of hard work. Accomplishing them shows you what you can do. In the long run, then, these experiences matter irrespective of the outcome: although some of you might have worked just as hard, kids botch tests, get thrown out at second, flub Chopin pieces. Later in life you likely won't remember the test or who won the game or which Chopin piece it might have been, but notions and habits of work inculcated in your school days will have stayed with you. You'll see. "We are what we repeatedly do," said Aristotle. "Excellence, then, is not an act, but a habit." So, if there's a long, hot road ahead of you . . . fling yourself at it. The word is "commitment." No synonyms.

Which I realize is easy to say.

Easy too, I suppose, and no doubt predictable, is wheezy, old-coot rhapsodizing about the spiritual joys of work. Meanwhile anybody not stuck in the remoter boondocks of witlessness knows plenty of jobs flat-out stink, many, thousands, are just thankless drudgery or worse. Mind-numbing, backbreaking, dangerous, peanuts-paying, demeaning, exploitive, life-sapping, absurd. Many provide no satisfaction or uplift or compensatory anything from which one can take even a crumb of sustenance. There you are, a victim of circumstance, of unhappy necessity, of lousy options. Fair enough . . . and this is where one takes pride in sucking it up and persevering just the same.

Confronted by an onerous-seeming task, your standard high school kid's instinct is to turtle and hope it goes away, or to indulge in dark mutterings about whose life it is anyway, or both, or more. Or to go through the motions and hope it suffices, maybe even convince himself or herself he or she is truly laying into it. However it's spun, though, procrastination brings with it an attendant queasiness that can ruin any of the bleak pleasures of bellyaching or inertia; and merely going through the motions satisfies no one. Moreover, under the broad heading of laziness resides, often, a reluctance to confront a limitation. If I don't try, goes the thinking, I won't have to face the fact that I can't, and who wants to look like a dolt? But limitations unconfronted remain intact. Moreover, sloth—or, its cellmate, apathy—is a temptingly easy method of registering one's objection to adult authority.

Construe school as something *they* are making you do against your will and this passively resistant attitude can become quite comfortable—and we're back in Steven Dithers territory. Irritating authority figures, flabbergasting them, outraging them . . . these to many teenagers are highly desirable outcomes. Call it getting even. Indolence is also a not-so-subtle nose-thumbing at the gleeful little dingalings right and left who make you look bad by comparison, as they pant happily and leap to every task like trained poodles for the kibble parents and teachers keep in their pocket. Resist the temptation of these attitudes, or at least pay yourself the respect of thinking them through. The biggest sufferer, really the only sufferer, will be you. Rather, if for whatever reason you find a job objectionable, with a "Hooyah!" of your own, make it go away by getting it done.

IN THE CONCORD of his day, Henry David Thoreau was considered an oddball—not a term in circulation then, although the condition appears timeless. Small of stature, big of nose, prickly and proletarian of demeanor, he could not sit still, could not stay inside, had no interest in establishing or maintaining for himself enterprises consistent with the sensibilities of his neighbors. He had no wife, no children, no career, no interest in money or property or convention. He had, though, a cantankerous spirit and considerable physical strength. He looked, more than one person noted, like a woodchuck, and did everything he did because he wanted to do it. He was good with his hands, could make quickly and skillfully from anything lying around something quite useful. He thought nothing of going for five- and six-hour hikes through fields, woods, marshes and brambles with no particular destination in mind. He walked with a loping stride like, people observed, an Indian—not then considered a compliment. He disliked roads. For reasons mystifying to his neighbors, he climbed mountains, found the Bible trite and too much fidelity to it a poor substitute for thought. Ordinary features of nature—ants, tree bark, lichen, mosquitoes, rocks, dirt—were to him subjects of rapt fascination. He had principles and stuck to them. He had his opinions, too, and no compunction about sharing them in a hortatory, aphoristic manner others found annoying. He wore straw hats and, for a period, a strange neck beard—a guarantee of continuing celibacy, a female friend assured him. Birds would land on him. That as a young man he decided to switch his name from David Henry to Henry David was deemed yet another eccentricity. By any name, though, he was forever and defiantly and quite contentedly his own man. He liked to call himself a commoner but recognized precious little about him was close to common. In the Concord of today he would probably be diagnosed and medicated.

Thoreau was a teacher, too, a failed teacher by local estimation, who had such heretical ideas as a child's interest should determine the curriculum; hiking, swimming and leaf studying were worthy intellectual endeavors; flogging the wayward was a less than terrific practice. He also took great inspiration from the essays and lectures of his Concord neighbor, the venerated Ralph Waldo Emerson. Adopting Emerson as a friend and mentor, Thoreau enjoyed with him long discussions of poetry and philosophy and human nature, and lived for stretches in the great man's house, absorbing all he could. Now and then he'd grow exasperated with Emerson, too, at his patronizing manner, his patrician attitudes, his mild hypocrisies. His response would be more activity.

And in 1845 Thoreau asked if it would be all right if he built himself a cabin in some woods Emerson owned on a pond not far from town and live there for a while. Emerson said that would be fine. In March of that year Thoreau headed into the woods and got to work.

Thoreau's time at Walden is now, of course, the stuff of legend—and history and literature. And, I'll contend, education. The ideas he hatched there changed the world. He was not a hermit, a kind of Yankee ascetic, nor a grousing, cud-chewing misanthrope, nor some proto-hippie digging the vibe of nature, man. He was an easy walk from town and went there often. A stone's throw from the pond, he built himself a small (ten feet by fifteen) but sturdy and comfortable house with two windows, a fireplace, and space enough for companionable conversation. He planted a garden. He entertained visitors. He ventured into the woods and fields. He fished and swam in the pond. Keeping things simple, he liberated his mind. He read and wrote and stayed there twenty-two months. His purposes for the experience he explained in one of the great, if not concise, paragraphs in the American canon:

> *I went to the woods because I wished to live deliberately, to front only the essential facts of life, and see if I could*

> *not learn what it had to teach, and not, when I came to die, discover that I had not lived. I did not wish to live what was not life, living is so dear; nor did I wish to practice resignation, unless it was quite necessary. I wanted to live deep and suck out all the marrow of life, to live so sturdily and Spartan-like as to put to rout all that was not life, to cut a broad swath and shave close, to drive life into a corner and reduce it to its lowest terms, and, if it proved to be mean, why then to get the whole and genuine meanness of it, and publish its meanness to the world; or if it were sublime, to know it by experience, and be able to give a true account of it in my next excursion. For most men, it appears to me, are in a strange uncertainty about it, whether it is of the devil or of God, and have* some-what hastily *concluded that it is the chief end of man here to "glorify God and enjoy him forever."*

This passage is one of the big moments, maybe *the* big moment, of *Walden*, Thoreau's account of his time on the pond. The text has long since been embraced as a preeminent scientific study of nature, as the ringing manifesto of the environmental movement, as America's foremost contribution to world philosophy. Thoreau wrote it because that's where his enthusiasms took him.

For all the words, tautology, convoluted diction and negative reasoning, the much-quoted paragraph for me is a near-eye-misting assertion of the indispensability of learning, of assuming with relish the responsibility of educating oneself for the purpose of living as fully as possible one's only life. It's about filling one's head and soul where and how one chooses to live life optimally. For Thoreau it was the woods. One could, though, substitute "woods" in the first sentence with "school," or, really, anywhere else: "I went to the seashore because I wished to live deliberately . . ." "I went to the city because I wished to live deliberately . . ." "I went to the mountains . . . the desert, the savannah, the jungle, the bayou, the (yes) suburbs . . . because I wished to live deliberately . . ." Wherever one finds it the point remains the same: live deliberately (as opposed to automatically), pay attention, front the facts, come to know by experience, eschew nonsense, give true account, be wary of canned answers, know what you're for, try your best. This is wisdom.

Less than two decades later, in his family home on Concord's main street, his writing having found only limited readership, with thousands of manuscript pages unpublished, after uttering enigmatically and beautifully, "Moose . . . Indian," Henry David Thoreau, just forty-four years old, died of tuberculosis. He's buried around the corner. His ideas today are everywhere.

IN 1834—ELEVEN YEARS before Thoreau ventured into Emerson's woods, six years before young Melville boarded the

Acushnet—Richard Henry Dana, a son of privilege, soft of hands but bold of spirit, also once a student of Emerson's, dropped out of college because of problems with his eyesight (metaphors need not be literary). Dana had absented himself from Harvard once before, having been suspended for his too-visible objection to a classmate's punishment. This time, though, a case of the measles and, one surmises, a certain distaste for the narrowness and routine of his Harvard experience, left him unable to read without pain. Rather than lying around home, though, Dana decided to put to sea. The bracing air and all that.

This, though, would be no Brahmin grandee's posh and stately voyage, the elegant hotels and spas of Europe awaiting him on the other side. Rather than a passenger, idle and cosseted, Dana would go to sea as a lowly member of the crew, an ordinary deckhand, a working stiff, aboard the brig *Pilgrim* (hmm . . .), bound from Boston around the Horn for Alta California, still mostly wild then and part of Mexico, to collect cowhides for the leather market. Under the roughest conditions, exposed to the full fury of the elements and every shipboard danger, young Dana would live and work among the dregs, the optionless, the desperate, tough men doing rough work. Purely for the benefit of the experience. This kind of thing just was not done—an aristocrat voluntarily giving up the privileges and comforts of gentility for a life of privation and struggle among the lowly—a kind of precursor, it would seem, to today's kids' service trips to the third world. (The smug might point out, though, that Dana did this to get away from Harvard rather than into it.) To some who knew him, Dana's odyssey seemed a form of self-abnegation, suicide almost. To him, however, it was purely a thrilling adventure. In *Two Years Before the Mast*, his account of the experience published in 1840, he would write:

> *I made my appearance on board at twelve o'clock, in full sea-rig, and with my chest, containing an outfit for a two or three years' voyage, which I had undertaken from a determination to cure, if possible, by an entire change of life, and by a long absence from books and study, a weakness of the eyes, which had obliged me to give up my pursuits, and which no medical aid seemed likely to cure.*
>
> *The change from the tight dress coat, silk cap and kid gloves of an under-graduate at Cambridge, to the loose duck trowsers, checked shirt and tarpaulin hat of a sailor, though somewhat of a transformation, was soon made . . .*

This transformation would prove not just curative, not just educational, but profound. At first he was painfully self-conscious and mostly inept. ("There is not so helpless and pitiable an object in the world as a landsman beginning a sailor's life.") But, earnest in his efforts, the young man evolved. Blisters became calluses. He learned the ropes, literally. His eyesight improved. His health became robust, his arms and shoulders strong—so too his spirit. He was accepted, then, soon enough, respected by his shipmates. He grew fond of them, and they him, and although he always understood he had Boston and Harvard and all the aristocrat's felicities waiting for him while his new friends faced prospects far grimmer, he felt one of them, recognized their common humanity. Their concerns became his.

Together they endured not just difficult conditions but the abuse of a sadistic captain as well. Anchored off San Pedro one day Dana watched two shipmates, good men both, bound and flogged for no reason other than the captain, a Mr. Thompson, felt like it. Sickened, Dana looked on—and in him awakened a determination:

> *I thought of our situation, living under a tyranny; of the character of the country we were in; of the length of the voyage, and of the uncertainty attending our return to America; and then, if we should return, of the prospect of obtaining justice and satisfaction for these poor men; and vowed that if God should ever give me the means, I should do something to redress the grievances and relieve the sufferings of that poor class of beings, of whom I was then one.*

The something he would do to redress and relieve was, on his return, sit down and write the book. More than that, he would become a lawyer, too, and make it his life's work to advocate for that "poor class of beings," abused and powerless sailors far beyond the reach of law—clients, it's worth noting, seldom in a position to pay for his efforts. Off San Pedro a social conscience was born, and Dana soon came to recognize his class and education provided him not just the means by which to initiate change and see justice done for the exploited and abused, but the responsibility as well. "We must come down from our heights," he would write,

and leave our straight paths, for the byways and low places of life, if we would learn truths by strong contrasts; and in hovels, in forecastles, and among our own outcasts in foreign lands, see what has been wrought upon our fellow-creatures by accident, hardship, or vice.

This was no bleeding heart's redirected guilt or a nascent sense of noblesse oblige, but a frank and pragmatic reaction to injustice seen and felt firsthand. Of what value insight, of what purpose a conscience, if one does not respond? However earnest, a wringing of the hands is a pathetic abdication.

Dana returned from the sea, resumed with fiery purpose his studies at Harvard and graduated with the class of 1837.

Declining to pay the five-dollar fee for a diploma that same spring was a classmate, an independent-minded little woodchuck from up the road in Concord. "Let every sheep keep its skin," the woodchuck would write.

While their authors certainly had their differences (the name Henry, inspiring brushes with Emerson, and Harvard class of 1837 notwithstanding), *Walden* and *Two Years Before the Mast* are both adventure stories, odysseys, in which erudite young men of literary sensibilities depart the expected byways and rough it for a few years, purely for the benefit of the experience. Turning their backs on creature comforts and conventional means of ascent—on conventional everything, really—following their own spoken and unspoken inclinations, disregarding the judgments of others, they encountered wild places and rough-hewn men, not as dilettantes paying an instructive visit with an eye on commendation, but as novitiates sink-or-swim committed to a new way of life. Theirs are two of the great books of our culture, foundational books, books that inspired other great thinkers, great doers, books that, in no small irony, advocate an education beyond books. There they still sit, Dana and Thoreau, alive and well, waiting for you and me, eager to share, in books.

Ten years after Dana and Thoreau left Harvard, Louis Agassiz arrived. Neither a student, though, nor for that matter any ordinary professor, Agassiz was the scientific sensation of the era, a young genius, an international celebrity, a great, hearty, learned, charismatic spirit and naturalist par excellence.* That he agreed to join the faculty in Cambridge was headline news: Harvard had arrived on the world stage. And into his classes Professor Agassiz welcomed just about all comers, irrespective of prior training or apparent qualification, including, to wide consternation, women. Science, he believed, was for everyone. He is credited, probably erroneously, with saying, "Study nature, not books." Certainly, though, the spirit of the statement is valid: Agassiz wanted his students to take responsibility for their own discoveries, their own education, to hone their powers of observation, to study the source material at its source, that is nature, all of it, and make their own connections and draw their own conclusions from their own revelations. The insights and wisdom of books was, he felt, received insight and wisdom, too often passively accepted, and influenced, even corrupted, by the insuperable subjectivity of the author. Further, while it might be exciting for the recipient, old ideas rattling around in a new head was for the sake of science almost entirely redundant. As Agassiz's friend Emerson (him again) had written in his 1836 essay "Nature":

---

* His dispute of Charles Darwin's ideas and his ugly notions about race would later undercut his stature. Then, though, he was a star untarnished.

The foregoing generations beheld God and nature face to face; we, through their eyes. Why should not we also enjoy an original relation to the universe? Why should not we have a poetry and philosophy of insight and not of tradition, and a religion by revelation to us, and not a history of theirs? . . . The sun shines to-day also. There is more wool and flax in the fields. There are new lands, new men, new thoughts. Let us demand our own works and laws and worship.

Agassiz brought this thinking to science.

Famously, the esteemed professor would give his beginning students a long-dead fish plucked from a vat of formaldehyde and leave them to their study. That's it. No textbook, no lecture. No reading on reserve in the library. No list of leading questions to answer. No marching orders. No quiz on Thursday. No avuncular hand on the shoulder and tips on how to proceed. No sanguine poster encouraging studiousness on the wall mail-ordered from a teacher supply catalogue. Just the student, his brain and his fish, the latter inert, nasty-smelling, laying in a metal pan before him. "What do you want me to do?" invariably the perplexed student would ask. "Look at your fish," Agassiz would answer.

So, ever obedient, the student would look. Eventually,

though, his interest in a dead fish would play out, or his eagerness to fulfill the professor's expectations would get the best of him. Maybe there was something he was supposed to be seeing but wasn't. Maybe he was missing the point entirely. Maybe there'd been some instruction he had not gotten. And there could be a test or something next week. He'd ask again.

"Look at your fish," Agassiz would answer once more.

So, with perhaps a sigh, perhaps a flash of pique, the student would look again. And eventually—little by little or all at once—discoveries would happen. Mute details would yield bright little revelations. Common functionalities, intricacies of gills, say, of scales, of fins and membranes and spines, you name it, something about the mouth, the teeth . . . in each and all was a key to some larger zoological profundity. Perhaps it was the bilateral symmetry one sees in a shad one sees also in a chipmunk, in a cow, in a sparrow, in a human being. Maybe it was something else. It took some time, perhaps, but, eventually, if the student was earnest, it happened. Something would click. Suddenly he could *see*. Agassiz was eloquent in his reserve. Yours is a unique mind, he was saying without saying it, an original consciousness, with powers of observation and reason no less potent nor less credible nor less valuable than anyone else's. Take it new places. Show it new things.

Put it to work. Figure out how best you learn, then make it happen. Take responsibility. Enjoy the satisfactions and new perspectives.

This is education.

I know all this because I've read it in books. This also is education.

SURE, THERE'S A PRETTY WIDE DISTANCE between Jack's paper-and-Scotch-tape Millennium Falcon and Agassiz's student's fish, between my son's essay on Benny Goodman's "Sing, Sing, Sing" and Thoreau's *Walden* and Dana's *Two Years Before the Mast*. Which is central to the point: open up the cranium of each progenitor, no matter how disparate, and what you'll find is enthusiasm humming along almost entirely on its own. Where it might lead doesn't at the moment matter. The hum matters. From this only good things will come, however grand or less than.

And, finally, finding that hum is up to you. A teacher can't make you passionate about a subject any more than she or he can make you love chicken-fried steak and gravy, or chilled tapioca with fresh raspberries. (Okay, I've stacked the deck: what's not to love about either?) No matter how innovative or skilled or, yes, passionate, she or he might be, a teacher (or coach, or tutor, or parent, or friend) can neither coax nor drag you by the collar to inspiration. In that regard you're on your own—which ain't that tall an order, really: all you have to do is maintain an attentive mind and a willingness to engage. Do that and odds are very good soon enough you'll be off on an adventure of your own. Your world, after all, is a very rich place. Before long you too will see work become a pleasure, discovery a joy . . . and all their many not-quite-synonyms.

Chapter 5

★

The Old College Try

Teach me to hear mermaids singing,
Or to keep off envy's stinging,
   And find
   What wind
Serves to advance an honest mind.
—"Song" by John Donne

B<small>UT HERE'S THE PROBLEM: YOU CAN'T GO FROLICKING</small> after butterflies. You can't gape at fish. You're on a mission. You have a purpose: you're going to college. For that you'll need to *get into* college, and for that you'll need good grades. For the elite colleges, the crown jewels, almost mythical in their splendor, the colleges toward which your parents have been shepherding you lo these many years, the gated sanctuaries of learning at which your boldest day-dreams have you strolling, alive as you've never been before, you'll need great grades . . . spectacular grades . . . pretty close to perfect grades . . . in challenging courses . . . Honors this and AP that . . . Intensive this and Accelerated that . . . and ceiling-scraping SAT and/or ACT scores . . . plus something extra, something extraordinary. Maybe a few somethings. Remember, you're competing against the other aspirants and many are doing the same thing. Or more. So let's for the moment shelve that joy of learning stuff. You need to achieve.

Money will help, too, a pile of money.

Now absolutely there are reasonably priced, wholly worthy, wholly transformative, four-year experiences available at public universities and colleges across the country, excellent institutions by any measure. To think otherwise would be silly. The rub, though, comes with the widely held perception that while they might be excellent, others, namely the elite private colleges, are better—often with too little thought given to how we're choosing to define "better." With the demands of the new economy, and so many attending college these days—roughly seventy percent of US high school graduates do, as well as eager, able, accomplished kids in greater and greater numbers from other countries—the prestige of where you go to school seems to matter more to more people than ever. And with applicants and dollars and faculty tending to follow reputation, perception has a way of becoming reality. Which has clout: for many high school students and their parents, the prestige of a college has become pretty close to the whole point. Lately—and perhaps consequently—the number of applications is way up at the most selective colleges, records falling right and left. Since they can offer only a fixed number of spots, this means the percentage of acceptances to applications is falling. Which heightens prestige. Which means more people apply, which makes it harder to get in, and around and around we go.

Kids see all this, of course, and a kind of voluntary culling begins—those aiming for what is perceived to be the top from those who for whatever reason think they have no shot. Or have other preferences. Or don't care. This has an enormous impact on their experience of high school and therefore in their learning and growth. And among many of those aiming for college, any college, the strain is showing. For many of those aiming for the elite colleges, the strain can be severe.

And one is left to wonder what gives.

Well, let us start our consideration at the top, with Harvard . . . everybody's gold standard Harvard, founded in 1636 and preeminent ever since Harvard, loftiest of the lofty worldwide Harvard, ten thousand triumphant Harvard, which gave us Emerson, Thoreau and Dana, and the Adamses, the Holmeses, the Roosevelts, the Kennedys, Henry James, E. E. Cummings, T. S. Eliot and on and on. John

Hancock. W. E. B. Du Bois. J. Robert Oppenheimer. Leonard Bernstein. Yo-Yo Ma. Benazir Bhutto. That Harvard. Eight presidents went there, sixty-two living billionaires. Longfellow taught there, and Kissinger, and, of course, Agassiz. At this writing, a year at Harvard costs upward of $54,000. Times four and it's the better part of a quarter of a million dollars. At Princeton, it's just a few thousand less, at Yale a few thousand more. (*U.S. News & World Report*, widely—and in my view deleteriously—accepted as the final word on such matters, puts Harvard and Princeton tied for first on their list of the best universities in the country, as they seem to every year, and about which one hears little dispute.) Next year's retail price at all three will no doubt be more, and everywhere else, too. All offer financial aid, often very generous financial aid, objectively proffered based on need, but it's their perception of need, not yours; and because their costs have become so great some schools are anticipating having trouble sustaining this generosity.

No question the scintillating classes, the proximity to brilliant minds doing exciting, important things, spectacular facilities reeking lofty ideals and ancient, noble traditions, an inspiring atmosphere, heady challenges, intense focus, exhilarating work can be wonderfully inspiriting, horizon-expanding, depths-deepening, life-changing, can whisk you to a place among the stars and leave you there for life. Superlative professors, superlative students and you . . . handpicked brainpower gathered together for the purpose of expanding knowledge and understanding, of building wisdom, of igniting the imagination, of making the planet a better place and elevating the species responsible for it. How thrilling. How essential.

But all that's only part of it, of course.

For the kid in it, college, college anywhere, is also semi- to fully drunk foolishness and wondering what the heck your roommate did with the laundry detergent and seeing that auburn-haired goddess from your Comp Lit class striking a back-lit pose under the chestnut tree in the middle of the quad and trying to think of a charming-but-plausible question to go over and ask her. It's dealing with the chortling bong-monsters across the hall and napping in a quiet corner of the library and acrimonious debates about the BCS rankings and goofing around on the rock-climbing wall and between dorms a wee-hours snowball fight and Fiji night at the semiseedy frat with red plastic cups fisted and a skull-splitting "Rosalita" blasting from the speakers and sonorous coffee shop discourses on loosely understood Derrida and poststructuralist theory and tracking down your longboard that somebody swiped that night you were shooting pool in the basement of Mattison Hall and painting yourself maroon and beering up for the big hoops game and, dry-mouthed and headachy, sleeping through your nine o'clock World Civ class. For $54,496 a year. Only it's not a year.

It's about eight months. Vacations crowd on one another so tightly you can hardly find a stride between them. These days you even get an October break. So let's call it $6,812 a month. That's $1,500 a week, give or take . . . for a little over two and a half years on campus.

So . . . worth it?

Let your parents keep the money—as I propose sometimes to my students and my own children—and march into the local public library and for thirty-two months sit there and read. Sweep the shelves clean. Follow your interests. Demand much of yourself. The complete works of William Shakespeare wouldn't be a bad place to start. Or *Don Quixote*. Or Dickens. But that's me. History, science, mathematics, geography, engineering, economics, literature . . . it's all there. You do the picking. That's the point. You'll catch the fever. Your education will be entirely of your own design and take you wherever your interests lead.

Or pocket the cash and rent a room somewhere in Paris . . . or Sapporo or Mumbai. Get a job in the little shop around the corner. Learn the language, the culture. Make friends. Walk the streets. See the sights. Have a fling. Have two.

Or go become, Agassiz-style, a foremost authority on something . . . the life and times of Peter the Great, say, or Mary Cassatt, or the sinking of the *Bismarck*, or string theory, or economies of scale, or glaciers. Make it glaciers.

Why not? They worked for Agassiz. Read everything about them. Get yourself a camera and a pair of crampons and climb all over them, Alps to the Andes. Sleep on them. Listen to them. Take core samples. Post on YouTube a video of yourself expounding from an icy pile of scree. Write a blog, an article, a memoir. Title it *On Ice. Sixty Minutes* will do a piece on you. Steven Spielberg will buy the rights. You can play you.

Or take the money and buy yourself a sturdy sloop, small enough to handle on your own, big enough to ply the deep waters. Learn to sail and navigate it. Name it for your mother or your favorite seabird or Richard Henry Dana. Read about Joshua Slocum, Ernest Shackleton, Tristan Jones, Thor Heyerdahl, Krystyna Chojnowska-Liskiewicz and Nainoa Thompson. Read Nevil Shute's *Trustee from the Toolroom*. Read *The Ashley Book of Knots*. Read about Captain Bligh after the mutiny. Read Nathaniel Philbrick on the wreck of the whaleship *Essex*. Then provision fair little *Barbara Sue* or *Osprey* and on the tide and a freshening breeze, hoist mainsail and jib and make for the bounding horizon. Don't forget the sunscreen.

Or enlist. Serve your country.

Or head to Port-au-Prince and see what good your strong back, caring heart and $217,884 can do.

Would you return after thirty-two months from any of these adventures less educated than you would after thirty-two months at, say, Harvard? Or Emory or Oberlin or take your pick? Would you return a less enriched and energized person? A more useful person?

Or here's a crazy one: go to your probably excellent state school and pocket the difference. The in-state bottom line at UMass Amherst, for example, just ninety miles west of Cambridge and a terrific place, is less than half that of Harvard. You get access to a superb education and more than a hundred grand in walking-around money. Not a bad start, that.

Notions I should think worth at least a minute's ponder.

And kids generally smile at me and nod and stop themselves from patting me on the head. "Okay, pal," they seem to want to say, "you go ahead and smell the daisies. I'm dealing with reality here." Some will simply blurt, "Yeah, but what about a *job*?"

Return on investment, I want to answer. Conventional paths, conventional destinations. And, by the way . . . is college about vocational training/diploma earning/connection making? Or appeasing ambitious parents? Or bridging the blur between adolescence and adulthood with easy access to intoxicants and licentiousness and kindred spirits with whom to enjoy them? Or is it to make a point of cultivating the intellect, for one's own benefit and that of society? Anyway, whose résumé would you find more interesting, the kid who majored in Human Service Studies with a double minor in econ and poli-sci and two years as recording secretary of the We Care Club, or the kid who went to Haiti for thirty months and did what he or she could? Whose experience is more compelling? More admirable? Who demonstrated sensibilities and aptitudes you'd like to add to your team? Who learned more?

And with so many young people these days emerging from college as if from a Saturday matinee, a bit depleted, a bit dazed, blinking in the sunlight, wondering which way to turn, needing a year or two, or five, to "find themselves," is it any surprise potential employers will hesitate? Besides, no more than a cursory look confirms that what you really need for the true springboard effect, if that's what you're after, is a master's degree. College, after all, primarily for reasons cited above, is the new high school. Grad school is the new college. A consequence, too, I think, of our everslowing process of maturation. In today's economy a master's is the true leg up. A leg up? Really, these days a master's is just about compulsory. For many fields you can remove the "just about."

Still, college is a highly pleasurable, highly energizing rite of passage. It's where you take the self, still showroomshiny, out for a spin, enjoy nascent independence, make a few instructive mistakes, forge great friendships, discover and explore some interests, develop capacities for concentration and hard work, hone skills, pick up your sheepskin and head off to the rest of your life a more complete and capable person. It's a commitment to civilization, to humanity. These primarily are the reasons your parents can be so zealous.

So you'll go to college. So too no doubt will my children. You've been headed that way since preschool. Since the Haydn. And rare is the eighteen-year-old bold and able enough to sail beyond the horizon on his or her own. You'll go to college because it's the next logical step as you've been trained to see logic. You'll go to college because you've never thought you wouldn't. Because, finally, it's the smart thing to do.

And college will be more exhilarating than you can imagine. You'll learn things, see things, so exciting you'll have trouble getting to sleep. In your head ideas will pop so brightly it will be hard not to stop people on the sidewalk and rhapsodize. Study will become a great pleasure, learning an addiction. Four glorious years. Until your eyes flutter and close for good, you'll remember your time there glowing with sentiment, ever more as memory starts to blend with nostalgia for smooth-skinned youth when all your days and nights were splendors and life was a sunlit meadow stretching eternally before you. Your college pals will be lifelong. Your loyalty to the place will run forever deep. Soft of middle, white of hair, halting of step, you'll go back, wear the old colors, sing the old songs, breathe deep the wine-sweet air. You'll stoop to pick up a chestnut under the dear old chestnut tree, feel its hard smoothness in your hand, and, to the tune of a distant choir and the tolling of the tower bells, the dying sunlight golden on the spires of dear old Mattison Hall, try with a wry little smile to remember the name of that back-lit auburn-haired girl pretending to read.

Right now, though, you just want to get in.

Everybody wants you to get in . . . everybody except, probably, or so goes the fear, the admissions people. They sit somewhere, possibly robed, certainly pale, spider-veined and grouchy, waiting to get their bony fingers on your woeful little application. For sixteen unimpressed seconds they'll scan it through their horn-rims, failing to suppress dismissive snickers. These are the gatekeepers not just to college but to the rest of your life. To success. Fulfillment. Happiness. An attractive spouse. Three adorable clear-eyed children. A fine house in a fine town. The sleek import in the driveway. The trips to Alta. The shingled cottage in Chatham with pink tea roses along the picket fence. Their judgment, further, yea or nay, is a referendum not just on your academic record and the sundry extracurricular backflips you've been turning for Lord knows how long, but on your very quality as a human being. Your justification for taking up space on the planet. Theirs is a judgment, too, on how and by whom and for what you've been raised. And your teachers. Your high school. Your community. Every aspect of your nurturing, back all the way to conception, has been arranged, orchestrated and packaged for this moment. Now there you stand before them, laid bare, awaiting judgment. At least that's sure how it feels.

And you don't know what they want.

You can't know. Because, quite reasonably, their every standard is fluid. Because every qualification of every applicant matters only in relation to the qualifications of all the other applicants in this year's pool, subject to the wishes of an administration seeking a certain kind of inbound class. It all rests on how your particular combination of qualities and achievements compares with everyone else's—which for many has the unfortunate but predictable consequence of making preparation really just jockeying for position. And gearing up a flat-out arms race. A war of attrition. I'll see your 2170 and 3.8 and raise it . . . 2230, 3.9, three 5s on AP exams, Spanish Club, Relay for Life, second team all-conference. Fine; 2280, 3.95, three 5s, Pres SC, R for L, National Merit semifinalist, concert viola, Habitat for Humanity, ulcerative colitis research internship, specimen collecting in the Galápagos, and a partridge in a pear tree. It's a mad dash to stick as many feathers in the kid's cap as it'll hold—without giving away that's what you're up to. No, the kid needs to feather up as fast as he can, certainly faster than the other hell-bent cap-featherers in the vicinity, while appearing to do it purely for love of learning and God and country and serving his fellow man and woman and the transgendered and endangered species everywhere. Up with the morning sun with a song in the heart and all the extra-credit problems done, too, and some brisk calisthenics and a Pindaric ode and a little light Gordimer washed down with kiwi-strawberry Vitaminwater, and, while we're at it, a $25 Starbucks gift card for the teacher, who works so hard . . . and will be writing the recommendation.

All too often, the kid, the college aspirant, feels compelled to become downright Stepfordian—highly skilled at achieving results and appearing sincere. And gaming the system. This for many is the new reality. Adapt or perish. Gild the lily and the hooey, too. If a feather happens to be out of the kid's reach, why then Mom or Dad will swoop in and pick him up, lift him as high as he or she can. Buy him a set of stilts, a stepladder, both. Hire him a tutor, a coach, a therapist. Enroll him in a course. Send him to a retreat, a camp. Make plain good enough is never good enough. The cost? Well, whatever. If that doesn't work, plead with or snipe at the feather bestowers. Lobby, harangue, to adjust the procedures, fudge the protocols, bend the rules, to lower just this once the standards, which are really truly absolutely unfair, frankly. And this is a *very special* case. Jordan *loves* your class. Soon enough the festooned cap weighs so much young Jordan can no longer see or stand up straight. And there at the gate crowd all the other feathery-capped girls and boys, thousands of them, red of face, sweating, craning their necks, waving their hands, chanting "Choose me, choose me."

But for the admissions people it's not simply a question of feather counting, of cold analyses and dispassionate evaluations of qualifications. Of data. First, there are just too many applicants with too many feathers, legitimate, dubious, or somewhere in between. Numbers are up, way up. Admissions offices everywhere are flooded with thousands and thousands of applications. To handle the deluge many schools are hiring temps these days, more than doubling their staff in some cases. Although this is, of course, not their purpose, let me remind you from a statistical point of view it's more or less in their school's interest to turn you down: the lower the acceptance rate the more exclusive the school (after all, it's exclusive because it excludes) and the more exclusive the school, the lower the acceptance rate and, generally, the higher the yield (that is, the number of accepted applicants who choose to enroll).* And the school

---

* Edging Princeton and Yale, Harvard admits around 6 percent—the lowest in the country—of the 30,000-plus who apply, 95 percent of whom are in the top 10 percent of their high school class. Harvard's yield hovers around 80 percent, by far the highest in the country. These numbers affect prestige, of course, but also more fungible notions like alumni giving, research grants and bond ratings.

climbs the all-important *U.S. News* list. Besides, an admissions officer's job is far more mosaic making than credential assessment. He or she is looking for a wide array of qualified tiles suited to the characteristics and culture of his or her school.

Rather than a straight academic meritocracy, then, admissions people are trying, within reason, to assemble a balanced, fully dimensional, richly varied class of interesting, worthy human beings, who are also high-octane intellects, with enough chemists for the Bunsen burners, astronomers for the telescopes, field hockey players for the field hockey field, percussionists for the kettledrums, potters for the wheels, actors for the footlights, with parity, too, among the genders. They want every race, religion and creed represented, as well, in more than token numbers, and some international students, too. With very difficult decisions to make, admissions people are admitting to need, then, a need that's always evolving, and only loosely fixed to a standard or profile of a desirable applicant. Moreover, they're trying to determine—insofar as your application and recommendations allow them—if their school is right for you. They want to know if you'll flourish there. The success and reputation of the school—and them at their jobs—rises and falls with the blossoming of those they admit.

They also understand every rejection is a shot to the heart. About this they do not feel terrific.

Let's remember, too, that however you might perceive it and they spin it, you're not competing equally for a spot in a wide open class. The entry is far narrower than it appears. Let's say a college admits two thousand applicants to its freshman class—a number determined largely by available space in the dorms. Don't get the idea that you have an open shot at any of the two thousand spots. Recruited athletes, underrepresented minorities (Hispanic, Native American, Pacific Islander and African American), legacies, children or grandchildren of major donors, children of faculty and staff, geographic exotics, accomplished visual and performing artists, compelling human interest stories . . . they have an advantage, from slim to pronounced. The admissions office's tolerance for less-than-superlative grades and/or test scores tends to be expended on these applicants—which means it's that much tougher for everyone else. At many schools there are the early decision kids, too, at others the early action kids, whose odds of getting in—for reasons of élan if not qualification (but often it's qualification, too)—are far greater than those who apply at the regular deadline.

So there go half the available spots or more.

Your stiffest competition, the most relevant competition, comes from anyone who on paper might look a little like you . . . your gender, social demographic, ethnicity, religion or absence thereof, the region from which you come, the particulars of your résumé, your academic record, your avowed interests. In addition to first-rate smarts, the admissions people want each of you to bring something to the party and it can't all be the same thing. You're applying, then, really, for one of only a handful of spots. And with the ease of the electronic common applications, many kids today from every corner are applying to twenty or more colleges apiece—which can have the effect of cornering acceptances, leaving fewer spots for other applicants.

Through it all, the most important criterion for admission is your grades—an unavoidable reality. Which even the admissions people will agree can be a nebulous, subjective and inconclusive measure. How, for example, is an A at a richly endowed prep school in any way like an A at a public high school in an impoverished rural or urban community? At any school is an A in remedial algebra the same as an A in BC Calc? An A from that nice Miss "Group Hug" Crabtree can't mean the same as one from chalk-dusty old Snodgrass the Annihilator, even though they teach the same course at the same end of the hall of the same school. I know at Punahou and Wellesley High, and elsewhere I'm sure, no teacher teaches in the same way, nor with the same expectations and rigor, nor to the same effect, nor prizes precisely the same qualities in his or her assessments. Moreover, some capitulate to weepers, wheedlers, and/or rampaging and/or sycophantic parents, while others stand their ground.

Generally, all this is known.

To no surprise, then, among the wilier college aspirants much strategizing and fancy footwork is devoted to course selection and schedule making to optimize results. Anything at which a kid suspects he or she might not soar is pretty much automatically out. Prospects of learning something are secondary. All wonder if an A in a normative-level class is worth less than a B in an accelerated class. And if I take regular French 3 instead of French 3 Honors, goes the thinking, I'll get a better grade, and it meets in the morning Monday, Wednesday and Friday, which means I'm likelier to get dear old Corky Corkindale for Bio fifth period and everybody knows he hands out As like Skittles at Halloween. But his section meets right after lunch, and if I have a free block there I can get my AP Psych homework done right before class so it'll be fresh in my head and Muckerhyde gives sixteen tons of reading and, like, homicidal quizzes, but everybody knows come May her kids get more fours and fives on the test; so there's that. But Bleakworth is just old and bitter and picks his yellow teeth with the bones of his victims and his class meets after lunch and if I have a free there they could stick me with him and I'd rather drink two quarts of toad mucus. And you better hope you get "Call Me Ben" Argyle the Metrodude for English last period (Steph says he has tats in, like, Chinese or whatever down the middle of his back, about inner harmony or something) and not Death-by-Boredom Gulch, because Argyle, Ben, just wants you to trust your chi and attend poetry slams and, you know, access your core, and homework for you tends to mean grading for him so, like, two nights a week you just blog a little whatever and chill, and besides his wife just had a baby, which he'll rhapsodize about for, like, fifteen straight minutes every class. Seriously. Half an hour if you act interested.

This is how it always goes.

Parents will get into it, too. Usually on other pretexts. But into the jungle they wade, swinging a machete like Balboa crossing the Isthmus, clearing a path for the little darling who's following along behind . . . Snapchatting. And with many high schools offering parents electronic access to their kids' grades at any moment along the way, stalking is almost encouraged, and at the first B– on a ten-minute vocab quiz in September the alarmists are blowing the bugle and charging into battle. "This isn't about the grade . . ." they always begin, which means it's about the grade. It's pretty much always about the grade. Which is fun for no one and counterproductive for most.

The numerical result of all these experiences, what you're left with when the smoke clears, your GPA, will have in all likelihood more to do with your admission to or rejection by a highly selective college than any other factor. What relation any of this bears to your growth as a student, as a human being, as a lover of learning, a blossoming intellect, is coincidental. All that's up to you anyway and always has been. Even with everything you've been through, your aptitude remains largely theoretical. What you can or can't do in what truly matters to you has likely never been tested.

In every class, no matter which, each student lives with relentless pressure to figure out the teacher's expectations and perform to them. And shine above the competition. One little screwup . . . a botched Latin recitation, a pedestrian *The Things They Carried* essay, a useless partner on the big psychology project, an orchestra performance the night before the biology test, a friend in crisis . . . and you're toast. And while an A in an elegant private school or a well-heeled suburban high school might be more difficult to achieve in some senses, at least in such places you're swimming with the current and helpful hands are delighted to push you along. In an overburdened, underfunded inner city school, though, or in a windswept rural school, or, really, in any school contending with the ordinary limitations reality tends to impose, the situation, the challenges are likely wildly different and that A could suggest in its way a far grander achievement.

And unless it's visible in your essay or your recommenders mention it, what ardor or wisdom you might have accumulated at any school is another question and, practically speaking, less germane.

In fact, inequities abound. In addition to the many built-in resources at the better secondary schools, from concerned and able college counselors to drop-in extra help centers to excellent libraries, there are professional tutors of every stripe . . . for a specific subject, for an aspect of a specific subject, for skill honing, for SAT and/or ACT preparation. You name it. Seventy-five, eighty, a hundred dollars an hour will get you whatever kind of help you or your parents think you might need. Or benefit slightly from. There are, too, thick books and DVDs galore—long shelves of them—and no end of elaborate websites. In the summer or after school or on weekends, or all three, you can take a Kaplan or a host of other very thorough test-prep tutorials. Take them twice if you'd like. All of these yield results, potentially hundreds of points' worth. If after two or three tries you still don't like your scores on the SAT, take the ACT. Take them both. Take them three or four times. Why not? Because you can cherry-pick your best numbers—"super scoring" they call it—many kids plan from the start to take the SATs multiple times, focusing their study on just one section at a time and then sending along to the colleges a patchwork of the scores with which they're happiest. All perfectly legit. With a diagnosis you can take the tests untimed. Have a problem with the test date—a religious holiday, say, a pressing family event, calamitous illness—and you can buy yourself extra study time and take it when it's more convenient. For many, then, aptitude tests aren't so much about aptitude, but canny strategizing, access to study help, and the resources to pay for it.

Adderall gets results, too. Snorted, I understand, works best.

And the essay, the admissions officer's best glimpse at the real kid, has been run through a succession of sanders and polishers: parents, teachers, tutors and the nice alum down the street.

Delivering in a big way, also, are professional college application consultants, who can amount to a kid's very own PR and marketing departments. Often these are former admissions people, high-caliber experts, seasoned pros, who have hopped the fence and hung out a shingle. Or novices with chutzpah. For fees that can run upward of twenty, thirty, forty thousand dollars, an able counselor will take an aspirant by the hand and coach and polish him or her to a high gloss, supervise every aspect of his or her application, to the last and tiniest detail, and in the end present a very attractively packaged applicant. For the parents it's one-stop shopping. These consultants charge what they charge, one presumes, because they get results. And they're multinational: a friend of mine in the biz has a long list of clients from Europe, the Middle East and Asia who want in to the same colleges you do.

And the admissions people don't necessarily know which applicant has enjoyed such boosts and which have not. While one can hope they have what Hemingway called a built-in bullshit detector, one suspects a good deal of the bovine product slips past them dressed as ice cream just the same—and the applicants, or their parents, or tutors, or counselors, run the risk of believing it themselves. Certainly with the application from the applicant point of view the understanding is rather than presenting an accurate portrait of themselves at their best, they're advertising a version of themselves exaggerated to the last limit of plausibility—quite a different proposition—and a measure of outright hogwash is expected if not necessary. And why not, goes the thinking among many; everyone else is not just doing it, they're being rewarded for it. I'll be at a disadvantage if I don't, too.

In short, most everything tends to run in favor of those with money and a willingness to spend. Scant compunction about self-aggrandizing helps, too. The psychic toll, the impact on notions of integrity, of what education is for, of simple fairness . . . well, one has to wonder.

And lest we forget, these are, many of them, the same turbocharged hyperachievers who, in addition to whisking through the best pre-K, elementary, middle and secondary schools taxes or tuition can buy, have built the by-now-familiar community centers in Ecuador, raised money for Cystic Fibrosis Awareness, taken a six-week summer seminar on the Lake Poets at Balliol, scored two goals last June at the regional semifinals outside Portland, written with fresh-squeezed European squid ink and a bamboo-handled horsehair brush on hand-pressed rice paper a volume of original haikus on the subject of greater concern for one's carbon footprint. They're nice kids, too, earnest and courteous. They do their homework faithfully and well. And their application sits right there with yours, and the calculus/physics/violin/chess champion's, and the gifted artiste's, and the three-time all-state power forward's.

And everyone expects justice.

So, IT'S "THE season." Mid- to late winter. The admissions person (neither, as it turns out, robed, pale, spider-veined nor grouchy) sits himself with his (electronic) stack of applications. The squirt he has dropped off at daycare. The morning hellos he has said along the hallway. On his desk before him steams the mug of joe. The phone he has put on silent. The desk lamp he has adjusted. Fresh in his onion is the mandate from the dean about what kind of incoming class the brass would like to see assembled this year. With a tidy exhale, into the pile he dives. His day's allotment.

And he finds there the easy admits . . . let's be generous and call it five percent. The easy rejects . . . forty-five, fifty percent. Which means half the pile or less requires consideration of any duration not exceeding five minutes. All right, let's be optimistic and call it ten.

Now it's your turn: he clicks open your application, looks it over. He purses his lips. Rubs his chin.

He measures strengths, eyes weaknesses. Weighs your grades against your test scores, casts an eye at the kinds of classes you took. Reminds himself of the reputation of your high school. Reads again your essay about your summer internship, your admiration of your grandmother, your love of travel, your passion for lacrosse, and the short one about why you want to go to his school, how it's where you always pictured yourself, your dream come true. The right fit. Any indecision about any of it and he simply reverts to the numbers. Grades and test scores. Test scores and grades. They're accepted as objective and close enough to theoretically valid and are therefore safer and easier criteria on which to make and defend difficult judgments. (Imagine the blizzards of phone calls and e-mails that come howling at deans of admission about nine seconds after the rejections arrive.)

There's your ten minutes. He puts you in the Maybe pile. You've survived the first read.

After the second go-through, and after lunch—tuna on wheat, chips, carrot sticks, tall can of ice tea with a southwestern motif—our guy and his colleagues gather around the conference table, each with his or her Maybe pile, and they confer. Files are swapped. Opinions shared. Some advocate. Some snipe. Some like your essay. Others do not. Some raise an eyebrow at your junior year chemistry grade. Others like your enthusiasm for West African dance. Someone comments on your high school's relative mediocrity, which another disputes. Someone points out your reading comprehension score is less than impressive, that your numbers are only slightly above the median. Someone else quotes a paragraph from a teacher's letter of recommendation in which she praises your heartfelt journal entries and your refreshing insights into *The House on Mango Street*. Another points out the number of kids from your area they've already admitted. Someone confesses a gut feeling in your favor. Others shake their head. Someone points to your transformative service trip to Bolivia. Another notes your sportsmanship award in volleyball. Your B in Pre Calc comes up. The slouchy young ideologue, lingering at dear old alma mater for a pleasant year or two before graduate school—maybe law, maybe business, he hasn't decided—will cross an insouciant leg, entwine his fingers behind his head, and wonder aloud if the school intends to be a meritocracy or an aristocracy. Do we, he'll ask, do we really prize diversity? Or is that just for the brochures?

And around it goes until your time is up. Consensus is reached, a yea or nay decided.

So goes your fate.

BEFORE *THIS SIDE OF PARADISE* there was *Stover at Yale*, an uncomplicated popular novel about an uncomplicated popular prepster eager to achieve gridiron and social glory at, you guessed it, Yale. He does, which pleases him . . . the end. The novel was intended, however, said its author, Owen Johnson, as an indictment of the college experience as he saw it being practiced: students, and the colleges themselves, were missing the point. ("Four glorious years," thinks Dink Stover as he steps onto the hallowed campus for the first time, "good times, good fellows, and a free and open fight to be among the leaders and leave a name on the roll of fame.") Important intellectual opportunities were being squandered. "The thing I see," Johnson told the *New York Times*, "is the rapidly growing tendency of our colleges to become not great institutions of learning, but mere social clearing houses." This was in 1912.

Eight years after the publication of *Stover at Yale*, kindly Max Perkins and Scribner's took a chance on a third go at a first novel by a young man of poetic sensibilities who'd been mediocre at pretty much everything he'd tried to that point. Who'd read Johnson's novel and found it inspiring. And, however uneven, Scott Fitzgerald's *This Side of Paradise* redefined notions of youth, fashion and college life that resonate still, for better or worse, nine decades later.

You see it on the websites and in the brochures and booklets and posters admissions offices send out. Probably they're out there putting stamps on a whole new batch right now. The crisp fall day. The perfect smiles. The sweaters. The books under the arm. The golden-hazy gothic backdrop. It's as universal and real as a dream can be, almost palpable. I sure feel it, and so, I imagine, will you when you find yourself strolling a quiet campus somewhere, ivied or otherwise, the late afternoon sunlight slanting through the treetops and a cool bite in the air, happy young people strolling this way and that, heads whirring. It's magical.

Fitzgerald felt it, too. For example, this: In a moment's respite from all the patrician drollery, he sends his protagonist out into the campus not on a brilliant October afternoon, but on a cool spring night, misty and moonlit. To the tolling of a distant bell, Amory Blaine lies down on the damp grass of an unnamed quad and considers for a moment the architecture all about him, the "gray walls and gothic peaks" and "all they symbolized as warehouses of dead ages." Soon he's struck by the "transiency and unimportance" of the current crop of students except as "holders of the apostolic succession" of scholarship, of the exhilarations of a life of the mind. He begins to take personally the "upward trend" of the campus architecture. Inspired, renewed, feeling it in a way he never had before, the lackadaisical bon vivant Amory resolves to get to work, to make an effort to learn a thing or two, to be a student, one who actually, as the word implies, studies. The impulse lasts only briefly. With the next thought he realizes "effort would make him aware of his own impotency and insufficiency." And we can't have that.

But, in the meantime, in between time, ain't we got fun?

Today's holders of the apostolic succession are still having fun, most of them, and what sourpuss would begrudge them that? Cakes and ale, the chimes at midnight, sis boom bah, and so on. I sure had my share in the late 1970s; so too, I hope, did all the thousands of young people I've seen off to college through the decades of my teaching life. And with the view from the high foothills of middle age, and as a kind of ten-cent apostle by trade, I understand far better now something I read for the first time my senior year at Lafayette College, in a hammock I strung between the columns of my fraternity. While I can almost picture the professor who assigned it, I remember neither his name nor anything of his class except that I enjoyed it. The book was thin, a paperback, a play called *Antigone* by Sophocles, of which I'd heard, of course, but never would have picked up unprompted. It was, the professor informed us, more than two thousand years old, and he left it to us to sort out the larger implications of that weighty fact. I recall admiring the play, but not as much as I wanted to. The people in it paid with lots of operatic dying just to learn what common sense should have been shouting at them all along. But what the heck . . . the thing was two thousand years old.

I recall, too, noting a line at the end of the play—with South College there before me catching the last of the April sunlight, and off to the left the marble stateliness of Kirby Hall, with the trees just starting to leaf out in pale green, and scholars strolling the little road that wound through that part of campus, with the chilly first breath of twilight settling in and somebody playing Pure Prairie League's "Amie" out an unseen dorm window, with pals trundling up the smooth stone steps for dinner and an early start on homework and then the evening's revelries, with graduation less than two months distant—and, stopping in my figurative tracks, I remember nodding a little nod and thinking, "Hey, cool line."

Wisdom is far the chief element in happiness.

Although the book is now long lost, I must have underlined the sentence, which was by then—and remains—my habit. Wisdom is far the chief element in happiness. That's wisdom, I realized with a chuckle, wisdom regarding wisdom, from long ago and far away. Now it's mine. Then, happier— although until then I'd been perfectly happy—I closed old Sophocles. With frattish laughter spilling from the open windows, I took a moment, breathed a time or two, enjoyed this new and improved state, then rolled out of the hammock and went inside to see what was cooking.

ON THE TABLETOP inches from where I'm typing these words sits a mug. It was given to me a few years ago by a former student home from college for Christmas break—a fine kid, bright, funny, genuine—as a token of gratitude for the recommendations I'd written for him, and, I think, as a kind of symbolic acknowledgment that he too was now, happily, proudly, a holder of Amory Blaine's apostolic succession. It's white, the mug, and in it stand some pens. *Georgetown*, it says on the side in blue letters, with the school seal in Confederate gray and Union blue. It's a handsome mug. Great school, Georgetown, the young man told me. He loved it. His classes were tough and all, but really great. He was having a great time. Lots of great kids. Definitely the right fit. Then half a year later I heard he was transferring. Great school and everything, he explained when I bumped into him at a baseball game, really great, just not the right fit.

A few months ago, casting a shadow over the same mug as it sat on my desk at Wellesley High, stood another fine kid, who'd come to report in a quavering voice that admissions offices had left him 0 for the Ivies. Dartmouth, Harvard, Columbia, Penn, Yale, I think, they'd all turned him down. This was an astute, engaged, highly accomplished young man, as nice as they come, paragon of the achieving student in most ways that matter, about which he was always meticulously vigilant. Well, okay, he clarified, Harvard put him on the wait-list, but they have, like, the highest yield of any school in the country, so forget Harvard, too. He'd have to settle, he sighed, for his safety school.

"Which is?" I asked.

"Georgetown," he said. Then he forced a little sunshine into his voice. "I know it's a really great school and everything, really great, I mean amazing . . . but . . . I . . . well . . . I'm just not so sure it'll be the right fit."

"Georgetown is a fantastic place," I assured him. "You'll love it. You should be proud of yourself. Besides, college, any college anywhere, is what you make it. You know that."

"Yeah," he said with an unconvincing smile and a nod. "Sure."

But, lo and behold, a few weeks later Harvard came through, where he is today, presumably the right fit.

Meanwhile, among the freshmen at Georgetown this fall are two terrific kids, both former and much-admired students of mine, smart, capable, hardworking, interested, unbowed survivors of all the protracted college anxieties, and thrilled when last we spoke to be headed there, excited about all the opportunities awaiting, the worlds soon to open to them. I'll guess that *U.S. News & World Report* ranks Georgetown twenty-first among national universities matters little to them one way or the other. (That, though, full sticker there this year is $56,502 must be somewhat significant to their parents.) And I hope sometime, maybe in the spring, they too will find a few minutes to stretch out full length on the damp grass—or in a hammock—and appreciate the gray walls and gothic spires, that they too will feel deeply, personally, exhilaratingly, the glow of the late-burning scholastic light, and the chief element, and find college, *their* college, an exciting, an enriching, a wholly sublime place to be.

Chapter 6

Rah, Rah

We never know how high we are
Till we are called to rise;
And then, if we are true to plan,
Our statures touch the skies—
—"We never know how high we are (1176)"
by Emily Dickinson

THE ONLY REAL DISTINCTION I EVER ACHIEVED ON A football field came with my graduation speech of a few months ago. This is not for lack of trying: from sixth grade through my first year of college, I donned the armor, once-more-into-the-breached with assorted bands of brothers, ran around, smashed into people, got smashed into myself, usually the latter, often by large people intent on mayhem, enjoying it all mightily. Most of it, anyway. I bore the bruises, made great friends, learned important lessons, had good fun, liked wearing for a time the football player identity. I did not, though, win the Heisman, nor get my picture in the paper, nor walk into the cool of the twilight, bloodied but unbowed, hand in hand with a cheerleader, lissome or otherwise. Okay . . . but . . . but had I not one October afternoon against the University of Pennsylvania disengaged my right arm from the shoulder with which it was accustomed to operate, I would have played a few more years and so we'll never know.

From earliest memory I have loved sports. In the household in which I grew up I was alone in this, but for a younger brother whose enthusiasm for basketball petered out somewhere in high school. And while he was patient with my ardor (how fondly I remember those backyard games of catch, however schmaltzy that might sound), my much-revered father always made plain his own disinterest in sports, his head happily occupied elsewhere. Now I'm the father of not one but four enthusiasts—which is for the contemporary parent fairly close to a full-time job. Of this my father is unsubtle in his disapproval. Nonetheless, between the football, soccer, basketball and baseball, Janice and I have traveled tens of thousands of miles, have spent tens of thousands of dollars. Gladly. All of it gladly. In full support of every endeavor.

Okay, mostly full support. Four kids, four, six, sometimes eight concurrent schedules, practices, games, tournaments, injuries, smelly heaps of laundry, fees, gas, tolls, airline tickets, rental cars, hotels, restaurants. Week after week, all year long. It adds up. And have you priced a measly pair of cleats lately? A baseball glove? Still, off we go to another gym, another field, another diamond. To wit: after a football walk-through yesterday and before an evening soccer game, Janice went ten miles in one direction for an afternoon soccer game, I ninety miles in the other for a football game. This afternoon I'll be going to another: Ethan, our third, is a linebacker and a pretty good one as local standards for eighth-grade line-backers go. He and his pals will be taking the field at 1:30. After the football game he's off to a baseball clinic. I'm transportation. Our other three have their commitments, too. So it goes, day after day, week after week, throughout the years. A clear day on the calendar is so rare we hardly know what to do with ourselves. But, as one of Leah's coaches likes to say, you're on the train or you're off. We're on the train.

So when I sermonize about what's happening today with youth sports, I do so as something of an expert, or a hypocrite, or both.

ACROSS THE STREET from our bungalow on the campus of Punahou School was a playground with swing sets and a giant banyan tree and a wide sloping field and a glorious view of Diamond Head and Waikiki and the blue, blue Pacific beyond. With all the other *keiki*, our own little ones, from the time they could walk, spent many a blissful barefoot hour there charging around in the sunshine and Manoa mist. Leah, our second, charged just a little faster and more agilely than the rest. Plain to even the objective eye. When she was five she informed us some of her friends in Kumu Nu'uhiwa's class had signed up for soccer and she'd like to give it a try, too. Janice signed her up. I drove down to the sports store and bought her one of those matching cleats, shin pads and ball sets. When the appointed morning arrived, we got her into the gear and drove her over to Kapiolani Park for the first game. Talking into the rearview mirror, I explained about not touching the ball with her hands, trying to kick it into the other team's goal, and not letting them kick it into hers. It should be fun, I said. She listened to the back of my head no more attentively than car-seated five-year-olds do.

Across a sea of bright colors we found the red and black of the Ladybugs and introduced Leah. We helped her into her jersey, gave her the final dollop of sunscreen, regathered the ponytail, wished her well and sent her onto the field. It was three-versus-three, six tiny girls, with little crescent goals set up about forty yards apart. At the whistle to begin play Leah pounced, took the ball, raced down the field, and scored. Just like that. I cheered. Janice cheered. Everyone cheered. Leah beamed. The ref dug the ball out of the net, brought it to midfield, got the girls set up, blew the whistle again. Leah jumped in, stole the ball, flew down the field again, and once more scored. We were maybe thirty seconds into the game. At her fourth goal I stopped cheering. At her eighth I stopped counting.

She's sixteen now, a junior in high school, and a lovely kid. And a soccer player. She plays with her high school team five or six days a week from the end of August to early November. With her club team she plays three or four days a week from early November straight through the snowy months and April showers and May flowers to the full heat of July; and one night a week in the winter she plays on a coed indoor team. She has played in twenty states. College coaches now ring the fields at tournaments big and not so big. Many have contacted her to express their interest, some regularly. Certainly these experiences, this way of life, have precluded others. They have required sacrifices. But she loves soccer, loves it intensely—more so, it seems, every year—and all of it has been from her parents' point of view very good for her. The sport has strengthened her strengths and helped shape who she is, who she's becoming. She understands she's lucky for the experience. She values what she has learned.

And for me, the father, denizen of many a sideline, to share any of this smacks in today's idioms of something like boastfulness. To gloss it over or not mention it is to risk in certain circles assumptions of false modesty or secretiveness. I also understand our time and money could be spent in more imaginative and socially—and maybe even personally—beneficial ways. I recognize, too, that in the name of support of the athleteic child, parents can perpetrate all kinds of ridiculousness. In fact, I said as much last June at dinner with some other soccer parents at a steak-and-burger-and-televisions-everywhere restaurant next to our hotel, between the freeway and the strip mall, near Waukegan, Illinois, where we'd convened for the Elite Club National League finals. Our daughters had been playing together for years. We'd sat in numberless restaurants just like it, from sea to shining sea. It had been over a hundred degrees that day and would be the next. Leah had wrenched her knee. The team had tied. "Why are we doing this?" I said at last.

As if a cherry bomb had gone off, all conviviality at the table ceased. The other parents blinked at me and my heresy. The entire restaurant had stopped suddenly to gape at me, too, or so it felt—patrons, waitstaff, talking heads on the televisions. At last, with a how-stupid-are-you but maybe slightly defensive tone in his voice, another dad, a sideline pal, said, "Because our girls *can*!"

In a convergence of supportive parents willing to spend, young people with athletic interest and ability ranging from considerable to middling, entrepreneurial and corporate/mercantile types recognizing markets to exploit, a culture-wide near-religious mania with tribal antecedents for all things sports, college coaches whose precarious lives are made simpler and whose yank with admissions offices can be considerable and who have scholarships to offer, we have seen of late an explosion of the club sport phenomenon. What a friend somewhat jokingly calls the soccer/industrial complex is just a fraction: pretty much any sport you can think of has been privatized, sucking in young athletes with aspirations and from their parents Matterhorns of cash. It seems nearly every sport these days has a sharply expensive, multitiered, somewhat Byzantine, ever-evolving, pyramidal travel team universe. And camps. And clinics. And tutorials. And ancillary training sessions. Parents pay and children (from ten or so years of age through high school) play, week after week, month after month, often all over the country, often to the exclusion of other sports, other interests. It's part and parcel of the arms race. Beyond the fun of playing and improving at the game, the goal, the almost universal goal, usually unstated, is a spot on a roster at an impressive college. The holy grail is a D1 scholarship from a big-time program. Membership in the elite. Or simply an easing of the cost of college.

And in a kind of hedging of bets, many kids are doubling up, tripling, on club sports, often concurrently, racing from one practice to the next, one sport to the next, changing in the car, chasing their dream. Or their parents'. Many, too, attend hugely pricey private schools for purposes of sports. Or move to other school districts, other towns, other states, with better opportunities. The ankle hurts, the knee hurts, the elbow hurts, the back hurts, the noggin hurts, the homework is being neglected, friendships are being neglected, other interests are being neglected, any sense of freedom is gone, low-stakes fun is gone, and the young athlete sucks it up. Or breaks down. But the dream shines on and the young athlete and his or her parents follow.

The club sport phenomenon started in this country with junior hockey creeping down from our friends to the north and the tennis academies from the warmer climes, Nick Bollettieri's et al. Europe, too—where sports are generally kept separate from school—has seen a long tradition of sports academies—soccer, gymnastics, tennis, skiing— focused and intense boarding schools to which promising children often quite young, are sent for the full menu. However limiting in the breadth of a child's experience, this pipelining produces at the far end of a Darwinian process a superbly trained competitor. Or so goes the thinking. What the child has given up and how those sacrifices will play out over a lifetime one can only guess.

For several sports these days, maybe even most, taking the field with the high school nine, or five, or eleven, is no longer the apex of the kid athletic experience. Rah, rah for Jack Armstrong's dear ol' Hudson High has become a sweetly old-fashioned notion, moth-eaten now, like Granddad's letterman's sweater. Many athletes are encouraged to skip high school sports altogether as an injury risk and a dulling of skills among lesser talent. High school sports, one is told these days with open disdain, are more about tie-dying T-shirts at the pregame pasta party and dressing up for spirit day at school than forging true athletes and fielding competitive teams.

This in my view represents a gross blowing-out-of-proportion and a net loss, and the consequences are many. With club sports comes disconnection from community, from the hometown. The travel-team teammates are not the young athlete's school chums. Practices and games are not after school on the field out back. Home games are not a hometown event. The young athlete is not bused—chatting, singing, yukking it up—with her pals to and from away games, games no more distant than other towns just up the road. Her team's wins are not celebrated nor losses mourned along the hallways at school or in the local newspaper. She does not see her team's photo hanging in the local sub shop, nor does the whole community turn out for the big season-ender against the dreaded Pemberton Marauders. For the schools, the communities, this turning away is a loss as well.

Now, instead, after school she sits silently in the car with her mom or dad and stares out the window or chips away at the homework until they arrive for practice at the big soccer complex forty minutes away. Or more: on Leah's team a few girls are driven to practice from other states, some from as far away as two hours. This is not unusual. Home games are wherever the scheduler can find a field. Away games can be in Phoenix. Because they're transportation, mothers or fathers tend to hang around during practice, run errands or, in at least one father's case, sit in the car and grade papers or go for a run if his legs are willing and his spirit needs cleansing. Most, though, just stand there and watch, assess, comment.

What message, I wonder, does this send the child?

But on the field of play the soccer is the best there is. Or the basketball. Or lacrosse. Or hockey. Or baseball. Or tennis. Or just about you name it. Fencing. Rowing. Figure skating. Gymnastics. Swimming. Volleyball. Cheerleading. Martial arts. The coaching, the competition, the drum-tight physical fitness, the forged-by-fire equanimity under pressure, the passion rewarded, the common spirit of making the best of what you have through unrelenting dedication to and hard work at something you love, the comrade-in-arms friendships with kids from all over the map, the lessons in self-discipline and staying on top of things—all are in most senses terrific.

Neither mine, though, nor any of the others enjoy sport unencumbered by a scrutinizing parent or two, with expectations, aspirations and opinions to share. And cripes alive, do you run into some doozies. Mothers, fathers, either, both. Wild-eyed, chittering, hyperkinetic wingnuts. Too often, too easily, parents forget they're supposed to be the adults. And their children are watching.

These club sport parents have so much invested—love, money, time, ambition, envy, urgency, their own unrealized childhood dreams, insufficiently subsumed senses of insignificance, guilt over other responsibilities and/or children neglected, Lord knows what else—they latch on tight enough to squeeze blood from the pores, to choke the life out of anything. All the while they refuse to accept the simple truth that athletes are born not made, no matter how much zeal, talk and cash you throw at the project. Not enough playing time and the coach is mean, unfair, a jerk, ought to be fired. The kid isn't lighting up the scoreboard and the coach is negligent, incompetent, ought to be fired. And that the enterprise of so much pith and moment is a game, children running around kicking a ball. But, hey, my kid's gonna shine.* Just you watch.

As they will, the pressures sometimes erupt: heart attacks, hissy fits, collapses into heaps, foul-mouthed-crimson-faced-

---

* At my nine-year-old's soccer game just the other day, a locked-in dad stood himself foursquare behind the goal, arms folded commandingly across his chest, toes just about touching the netting, and imposed on his goalie son ceaseless micromanagement as the play unfolded before them. Neither vicarious proxy nor surrogate self, the child was his drone, operated by means of verbal command. Stormy of expression, the boy did what he could to comply. Finally the opposing coach complained to the ref. The father was duly admonished—so, with a look of you-can't-tell-me-what-to-do defiance, he stood himself at a little more distance, maybe ten feet, and spoke louder.

vein-popping-spit-flying-nose-to-nose screaming matches, punches thrown, and carping, berating, name-calling, ugly and endless full-throated razzing of other parents, of refs, of opponents, of, I'm not kidding, their own children. With coaches—for purposes of making the team or seeing more playing time—they'll wheedle, cloy, whine, cozy up, pucker up, plead, threaten, and, one hears, stuff envelopes fat enough to make an alderman blush. (At a dinner party not long ago, a dad bragged to me with three twitches and a wink about how much he'd slipped across to get his son a spot in an elite baseball club.) With many parents it's all they'll talk about. Ever. Soccer, soccer, soccer. Lacrosse, lacrosse, lacrosse. Hockey, hockey, hockey. Bright enough, educated enough, grown-up enough parents flanneling, gossiping, exclusively and without relent, about the sport, the team, that day's game, yesterday's practice, the coach's decisions, the coach's comportment, the coach's private life. On and on they go about the nuances of rumors about certain hypothetical scenarios affecting the potential implications of theoretical factors influencing who's eleventh and who's twelfth in the national rankings, the regional standings, the tournament seeding. Intently they discuss which college coaches were in attendance and at whom they seemed to be looking, when, where and why the ref did or did not blow his or her whistle, the muffed corner kick just before the end of the first half, the obnoxiousness of the opposition parents, both individually and in the aggregate. They discuss the wind direction and strength, the temperature, the humidity, the height and athleticism of the opposition's keeper, the suspect gender of the opposition's striker, that kid from the national team who scored three against CFC in that tourney down in Virginia Beach two years ago, you know the one. The game could be happening across the street from a buffalo stampede or the crash of the Hindenburg and they would not turn around for a glimpse.

While the maniacs and the pyrotechnics they inspire are the exception, you see them everywhere, they happen all the time. Invariably their children appear to regard these people with disdain. Cause, I think, for hope.

Overwhelmingly, though, sports parents are good people, loving of their children, trying only to do right by them. That their sons or daughters are dedicated to and adept at something is a good thing and worth encouraging. The benefits are many. That things have blown so wildly out of proportion is—or certainly feels—beyond their control. And you're on the train or you're off.

GET PAST THE CHECK WRITING and the chauffeuring, the critiquing and provisioning and counseling . . . go to a game . . . and there's this—and to me closest to the point from the parent perspective: what one feels in watching his child play. Nowhere else I know of can a parent stand quietly—which is how I prefer it—and for a few hours watch his or her child in action. We can't study you in school, or goofing around with your friends, or in any of your assorted endeavors at home, not for two hours, which would be weird and possibly actionable. But at your soccer game, your baseball game, there you are, unaware of us. We're invisible, Emerson's transparent eyeballs.

And out on the field, you are ever yourself, absent by necessity of any self-consciousness, throwing yourself at a purpose that is entirely absorbing and for that moment only. We see you endeavor and strain and test limits. We see you operate within the framework of team stratagems, the laws of physics and physiognomy, and the rules of the game. We see you interact with your coaches and teammates and opponents and the officials. We see you handle success and failure. We see you sweat and laugh and get pissed off and knocked to the ground. And get up. We see your speed and strength and agility and skill and grace and daring and toughness. We see you think on the fly. We learn all about you as you charge around out there on the field, come to know you in ways we otherwise would not. We also see you take your place in a cultural tradition as many of us did in our day. We've given you to the world, after all, and at a game we can study for a time what in a certain controlled setting that looks like. We also know how important all of it is to you, how hard you've worked, how much you've given up, to be where you are.

And you are not, as many would have it, our surrogate—or at least you're not mine. You are you, freely, you only. And the demands of the game show us something of who that is.

That, ideally, is the parent part, for which I'm happy to pay.

Which, alas, is central to the problem, maybe *the* problem: in their overlapping joy and love and appraisals and hope, parents, sometimes stuntingly, are studying their kids' every move. The poor kids can hardly step right or left, or blink an eye, or breathe, without supervisory scrutiny and inevitable comment. This, I'll point out, is not just sports parents; try music parents. Try chess parents. We know everything our kids are doing and why and with whom and in response to what. Transparent eyeballs? The children know we're there. Of course they know. We're always there. We cheer to let them know they're being supported, that Mommy and Daddy love them, believe in them, root for their success. We'll advise and instruct, too, and sometimes hector. All of which burdens their play—which should be theirs entirely—with Significance. Mom and/or Dad leave work, leave projects around the house, write many checks, get on planes and talk and talk and talk about it . . . and what does that tell the children about the importance of their play? About family priorities?

When we were kids, though, out the door we went. On our own. Dogs went leashless in those days, too. "Be home by dinner" was about all the supervision we had to endure. In packs we hit the streets or the local fields or woods and scared up a little action. We got on our bikes. We built forts and threw dirt clods at one another. We made up games— most, if memory serves, involving potentially harmful projectiles, clods of dirt only the beginning. If we fell in the creek, we got wet. If we skinned an elbow, we dealt with it. A week later to some amusement we would twist the arm around and pick at the scab. I remember climbing a tree for no particular reason at age ten or so and jumping from a branch and when I landed hitting my chin on my knee so hard I chipped a tooth and saw multicolored stars. I signed no disclaimer, wore no helmet, knee or elbow pads, no mouthguard, no safety harness. No one instructed or told me to be careful as I climbed, no one gave me clearance to jump, no one explained jumping technique, no one gasped when I did, no one assessed my landing, nor scolded or consoled me in my duress, nor swept me off to the emergency room to have me looked over just in case. I dared it, did it, processed what happened, moved on. We saw kids behaving badly, doing asinine things, or mean things, or cowardly things, going awry in one way or another, and decided on our own what we thought about it. In this way we developed our own means of navigation. Or didn't and paid for it.

And if we liked a sport we played it, if we didn't we didn't. Parents had nothing to do with any of it. Sports were ours. They were games first, kids' games, played for the exhilaration of playing, but also a means by which to draw out something we sensed in ourselves, or aspired to. We played our version of football in somebody's backyard, tackle football and basketball over at the schoolyard. Sometimes we figured out a way to get into the gym . . . okay, break into the gym. Stickball was big. So too kickball. So too Ghost in the Graveyard. So too loosely organized footballish mayhem called Kill the Guy with the Ball. I invented a variant of Whiffle ball I dubbed Big League and coerced whomever I could to play with me. (Inexplicably, beyond Music Street it never caught on—although today with quiet pleasure I watch my children and pals play a loose derivative.) In all games we kept our own score. We had a pair of sneakers, one pair, that sufficed for everything. Some people called them tennis shoes but no kid I knew ever played tennis. Summers we went barefoot mostly. When we ripped or wore a hole in our jeans our mothers patched them. Patched jeans were emblems of a knockabout life. So too were nosebleeds, split lips, black eyes, head lumps . . . these were interesting to study and borne with a certain pride. Safe or out, fair or foul, we adjudicated and resolved our own disputes. If emotions ran high, so be it. Kind of more fun that way. Sometimes kids got slugged and were often thought to have had it coming. Hard-nosed kids were respected. Wusses—a term from the day—were not.

In high school, when you got there, if you felt like playing a sport you showed up for tryouts. If you made the team your parents appeared for maybe a game or two a season. Maybe. About which you did not feel spurned. If you got cut from the team you got cut. You felt spurned. You went home and watched *The Three Stooges*. Or read a book, a Travis McGee if you were me. Or you grabbed a stick, threw your skates over your shoulder, and played hockey on the Whitings' pond until it was too dark to see or the moon came up. Or you practiced and worked hard and tried again the next year. Your parents might have been aware these things were happening but said only, Dinner'll be ready in ten minutes. Wash up and set the table, please.

Those days are gone.

Gone with them, too, is the age-old notion of athletics as a lesser component of a liberal education. Dog and tail have had it out and the tail has clearly won. Leah's high school soccer alone, the "light" soccer, the "lesser" soccer, requires of her a three-day summer camp and weeklong tryout and preseason practice, then upward of eighteen hours a week once school gets rolling, the club team almost as much, and certainly no other commitment is sending her and a parent to Dallas or Raleigh or Las Vegas or San Diego. None of this is true of an academic endeavor. More and more, we're raising trained and highly focused specialists for whom narrow excellence is the dictum and other responsibilities or pleasures interferences.* Gone, too, long gone, is the notion of sports and competition as simple joyful play. Sure, they're fun and everything, but with parents watching and all too often yapping, and professional coaches wielding carrot and stick and dissecting everything, coaches whose livelihoods depend on the performance of their players, with playing time or even a spot on the roster at stake, which frequently casts teammates as direct threats, with sports influencing if not dictating where one goes to college and, often, how much it will cost, with concussed noggins, ripped ACLs, torn labrums, herniated discs, ruptured spleens, detached retinas, you name it, a daily possibility, with thousands and thousands of dollars on the barrelhead, sports for the athletic child have become serious business.

(And how well and fondly I remember the pickup pond hockey of my youth. A few of us were decent, some okay, most more or less stunk. We didn't care. None of us had cool stuff; we used whatever we could scrape up. For shin pads,

---

* In this, though, young athletes are by no means alone. Among the graduates subject to my recent speech, for example, was a boy who every Saturday would ride a bus the two hundred miles from Boston to Manhattan and back for a ninety-minute piano lesson. During the week he would practice, he told me, three or four hours a day. I've had other musicians, and dancers, artists, equestrians, actors, models—if they count—astronomers, chess players, go-cart racers demonstrate similar commitment . . . commendable from certain angles, to be sure, but one does scratch one's head a bit.

for example, I used *Time* magazines and electric tape, which kind of worked. None of this mattered, either. We showed up and played. It was great fun, especially in the moonlight. The cold stillness of the night. The spectral light and shadow. The scrape of skate blades on hard, uneven ice, the sound carrying as if amplified. The steaming sweat. The thrill of flying along. The crashes. The whoops and laughs.)

Today, paradoxically, in organized little-kid sports, where it all begins, parents, who are the coaches, who are really everything short of putting on a uniform themselves, are often doing whatever they can to emphasize fun and minimize the possibility of pressure or bruises of any kind. For the little ones, no score is kept in any game lest someone suffer the discomforts of losing. Every player gets equal playing time. Every player is praised, every move cheered no matter the execution or outcome. At the end of the season everyone gets a trophy. This goes on weekend after weekend, season after season. In my youngest son's elementary school competitive sports and games and activities have been eliminated from phys ed class for fear, I'm told, of wounded spirits. In Leah's high school, phys ed class is now called "Wellness" in which they sit and discuss healthy choices. In class last week they napped.

Much of the impetus behind travel sports, then, is to find good ol' tooth-and-nail competition—with such achievements as making the team and seeing playing time determined by the participant's abilities and dedication. Since some of the democratizing No Child Left Behind ethos has found its way into sports—not by itself a bad thing—the more traditional venues for spirited organized play (gym class, town sports, high school teams) have had to widen the welcome, pad the corners and gentle things down to accommodate the not necessarily supremely gifted or fully invested. The alternative, club sports, which the ardent and those who excel are almost forced to seek, has escalated into no-limits mania, with parents calling, or seeking to call, many of the shots.

But through it all still I see poetry. I do.

For all the contemporary madness, still I see in sports, any of them, a dramatic aesthetic rite, no two performances alike, beautiful to look at. Beautiful, too, in their impracticality. Sports mean something only when they mean nothing, when they serve no pragmatic function, when we engage in them purely for the exhilaration of the activity. The games, then, are beautiful for the sake of their beauty—as, that is, an aesthetic construct. Work is done; necessities have been addressed. Now we choose for pleasure's sake. Does it matter if Lincoln-Sudbury beats Acton-Boxboro in soccer or baseball? No, it does not. Harvard-Yale? Amherst-Williams? Michigan–Ohio State? Auburn-Alabama? No, no, no and no. Red Sox–Yankees? No. Celtics-Lakers? No. Nor is it about fun, a concept far too cotton candy. Ask a kid—my Ethan, for example—if he had fun in a football game, or if he enjoyed the teamwork or the physical exertion out in the cool autumn air, and he'll shrug and think yeah, he probably did, he might even allow as much, but the look he'll give you will say you're missing the point. To justify sports as endeavors useful in some utilitarian way is in my view to cheapen them. Moreover, to reduce sports to exercises in jolly fun or hearty teamwork or, well, exercise, is to understand music as something to tap your foot to. Which athletes, even small ones, get.

In sports, as in any art, there is also a timelessness; the world stands still in honor of youthful energy and grace and strength and resourcefulness and nerve—of, even, a kind of immortality—with all the existential realities in abeyance. Each game is an ordered universe unto itself, a vivid, brightly colored, microcosmic, improvisational and symbolic celebration of the human condition, of the human spirit—striving, failing, persevering, and, often enough, succeeding. At an athletic event—a soccer game, say—one sees within an ordered frame of time and space the great drama of life played out in metaphor with a pointed clarity life itself lacks. In every moment is possibility; the athlete responds and initiates the next moment . . . until the clock runs out. Sports bring us together. They are our great democratic, communal performance art, our tradition-bound connection to one another across continents, across generations, profoundly beautiful for the participant and spectator alike. Ted's last at bat, Flutie's pass to Phelan, Vinatieri's kick, Fisk's home run, Orr's airborne goal, Havlicek's theft, Roberts's theft—you see in which region my loyalties abide—as well as anything my own, or anyone's, children might achieve are moments here and then gone, a pas de deux, Navajo sand painting, poetic skywriting. Pond hockey in the moonlight. The world sees no material improvement. But in the imagination, where the universe and conscious- ness converge, they are eternal and beautiful.

It's very nice our children have this.

THE ATHLETE, THEN, is alive in a way the rest of us are not. It's in the physicality, the firing-on-all-cylinders immediacy of the moment, body and mind working as one and fully charged. The giving of everything she or he has, right there, right then.

And while every death diminishes us, the death of a young person, any young person, is throat-catchingly tragic, achingly sad. A bleak and brutal cruelty. Agony. There is, though, something uniquely poignant in an athlete dying young. Consequently we've seen deified Princeton's dashing Hobey Baker and Iowa's Nile Kinnick. At Deerfield Acad- emy, where I spent my junior and senior years, there was the hallowed Tom Ashley, the handsome, good-hearted local farm boy everyone admired, who excelled quietly, who car- ried himself with modesty and dignity and who was killed in Château-Thierry in 1918. Lou Gehrig, Harry Agganis, Steve Prefontaine, Hank Gathers, the 1961 Olympic skaters, the 1970 Marshall University football team, the 1977 University of Evansville basketball team. And on and on. Every community seems to have its golden ones gone. Ours does. So perhaps does yours. Taken before the cheering stopped, before the speed and strength and grace had a chance to diminish, before the joy of their play could fade. One grows maudlin with such thoughts, not inappropriately. We name stadiums and arenas for them, give awards in their name. And writers, as they will, have taken note.

Published in 1896, this—inevitably—is the Edwardian classicist and poet A. E. Housman's *To an Athlete Dying Young*:

> The time you won your town the race
> We chaired you through the market-place;
> Man and boy stood cheering by,
> And home we brought you shoulder-high.
>
> Today, the road all runners come,
> Shoulder-high we bring you home,
> And set you at your threshold down,
> Townsmen of a stiller town.
>
> Smart lad, to slip betimes away
> From fields where glory does not stay

And early though the laurel grows
It withers quicker than the rose.

Eyes the shady night has shut
Cannot see the record cut,
And silence sounds no worse than cheers
After earth has stopped the ears.

Now you will not swell the rout
Of lads that wore their honors out,
Runners whom renown outran
And the name died before the man.

So set, before its echoes fade,
The fleet foot on the sill of shade,
And hold to the low lintel up
The still-defended challenge-cup.

And round that early-laureled head
Will flock to gaze the strengthless dead,
And find unwithered on its curls
The garland briefer than a girl's.

As I said, one grows maudlin. No more convinced than
you or I, Housman's speaker believes hardly a word he says,
but seeks solace in saying it. He seeks order, too, and reason,
and thereby comfort, in the traditional quatrains, rhyme
scheme and meter. And he must know, as you and I do, the

fleet of foot takes the road not for any laurel waiting at the end, nor to delight the roadside cheerers, but for the pleasures of the race, of flying along, of testing, then pushing beyond, limits. It's a celebration of being alive, a spiritual rite nearly, if one's thinking tends in that direction. The point is victory . . . victory over one's own doubts and disinclinations, to achieve the sublimity of possibility fulfilled. A victory over gravity, even. To know without equivocation this is the very best you can do. To achieve a oneness of body and will. Yes, the laurel will wither soon enough, but that's okay. Look what I did. And wasn't it fun?

Last December, after a ten-month fight, a dear friend and club soccer teammate of Leah's succumbed to brain cancer. She was a tall and lovely girl, a bit gangly but naturally graceful, and eminently kind, a sweet-spirited, wonderfully regular kid, too. A sophomore in high school, she loved soccer and life and her parents and sister and her friends and tried hard in everything she did. Her initial and instinctive reaction to anything was a wide and genuine smile. She was gentle and trusting and with her family bore through the diagnosis and dying and the outrageous unfairness of it all with exemplary grace and courage. Taking inspiration from her example, so too did the team, the entire club. Funds were raised, benefits held. Opposing teams contributed and shared their sympathies, as did local college and professional teams. Everyone came together. Everyone bore up.

Leah was with Sam just a few hours before she died. I stood in the kitchen with Sam's father—marveling at his strength and enormous heart—and tried with mixed success to hold it together. At the wake a few days later was much embracing and sad laughter and many tears. At the funeral the girls from the team wore their colors and sat together. Their coach and Sam's father gave gracious and loving eulogies.

Six months later, on Sam Prescott's sixteenth birthday, at a big and intense showcase tournament in central New Jersey, the coach stern once more and growly, with college scouts everywhere, with summer heat building, Leah and her Stars teammates whom Sam had left behind gathered before kickoff, arm in arm in a tight circle, at midfield. Sentiments were shared, bonds reaffirmed, their friend remembered. Then to the sky they released sixteen pink balloons that rose from the circle of girls higher and higher until the breeze took them, rising still, off into distant clouds and out of sight.

Sam's mother had come down for the tournament, too. After the game, in the shade of a tree, she made sure the girls got their lunch.

A few months later I tried to tell a friend about the

beauty of all this and could not get the sentences to come out of my chest.

This too is club sports.

USUALLY ATHLETES DO NOT DIE young. Despite what Professor Housman seems at first to suggest, this is a good thing: joy is multifoliate. Usually athletes outlive the gifts that were their youthful delight and distinction. Sooner than anyone would prefer, they join the workaday world and shamble along just like the rest of us, although perhaps achier of knee, intent, usually, on earnest utility, receptive, one hopes, to life's other pleasures. That through injury or the insuperable forces of nature jocks become ex-jocks at an early age is part of the tragedy and therefore the beauty of what they do while they can. And just as everyone else is finding her or his stride in life and gaining a little momentum, athletes are losing theirs. This is the price of their fleeting excellence. They'd committed everything, and now it's gone.

Under ideal circumstances, though, an athlete's experiences will cultivate strengths and qualities of character that translate fluidly to other endeavors at some remove from the green fields of their youth. *On the playing fields of Eton* and so on. More locally, think, say, Bill Bradley or Tenley Albright (although not lost on me is the fact that neither achieved much of anything noteworthy, at least that I know about, on actual green fields). Dwight Eisenhower. Paul Robeson. Benjamin Spock. Alan Page. Byron White. Gerald Ford. George H. W. Bush. Billie Jean King. This, after all, is why schools have athletic departments to begin with. So there's no mistake about it, in both end zones of their magnificent newish zillion-dollar football stadium, and beyond the goal lines of their handsome new soccer stadium, the nice people at Senator Bradley's Princeton have hung identical banners: "Education Through Athletics."

All too familiarly, though, the washed-up jock, underprepared for just about anything not savoring of muscle, sweat and scoreboards, finds himself a child suddenly at the big people's table, his low-grade obtuseness, self-involvement and has-been's inclination to reminisce tending ever more toward buffoonery. He is, alas, among our ripest clichés, somewhat less than relevant and barely tolerated. On those occasions he shows up in literature, he's seen most often from a distance and the subject of scorn. For all his millions and testosteronic swagger, for example, *The Great Gatsby*'s Tom Buchanan is a meathead in riding breeches, and poor Biff Loman is hopelessly adrift, left to find his kicks in kleptomania and discussions with his brother about whom they could beat up, while Tennessee Williams's Brick Pollitt just drinks and mopes. Different is Irwin Shaw's ex-football hero: in his frank but sympathetic 1941 short story "The Eighty-Yard Run," Shaw explores from the inside a bit of the pathos of the faded athlete's lot.

The story is told in a series of flashbacks when our ex-college jock Christian Darling (how's that for a name?) is trying in approaching middle age to reassemble his life after his marriage, career and self-respect have fallen apart. "The pass was high and wide," the story begins, "and he jumped for it, feeling it slap flatly against his hands, as he shook his hips to throw off the halfback who was diving at him." (All right, so the title should really be "The Eighty-Yard Pass Play," but why quibble?) There follows a long, detailed and loving description of Darling's broken-field sprint for the end zone. This is at an afternoon practice, our protagonist a second-string running back at an unnamed midwestern university. The year is 1925. The run for Darling is sublime. He will never again enjoy such unalloyed happiness, and it transpires over the space of a few seconds.

Success builds on success: he graduates, marries his college sweetheart, starts a career. Life is good. Then, perhaps inevitably, it isn't. He stagnates. His wife outgrows him, finds interests that do not include her lumbering husband. The marriage ends. At last in quiet humiliation, having failed at other things, Darling winds up a traveling salesman, which in the last paragraphs of the story brings him back to his old college town. With evening coming on, nostalgia lures him out to the practice field. Helpless to impulse, he re-creates the run, a middle-aged man, all by himself, fleshier now, in street clothes, dashing and dodging his way down the wide and empty field, racing "exultantly for the goal line." Only he's not by himself: a couple of college kids see him. His embarrassment excruciating and complete, he fumbles together an explanation and scurries for his hotel. There the story ends.

Darling's tragedy is not in his yearning for penumbral glories past; rather, it's in his incomprehension of reality. He gets what amounts to just deserts, a childish sentimentalist's defeat. He had failed to evolve, about which C. Darwin shared his warnings. Once social cachet feels like entitlement . . . really, once *anything* feels like entitlement . . . you're headed for problems. Football for Darling should have been another of several important formative experiences, and not merely a perceived ascension to Olympus and all the rights and privileges thereof. The sport, any sport, should aid, not hinder, navigation through life.

And, with apologies, I can't help but think of my own gridiron experiences, my far (by miles) more modest eighty-yard runs, my education through athletics, and I hear perfectly across almost four decades the strong voices of my high school coaches, Jerry Gerolamo at Martha's Vineyard Regional and Jim Smith at Deerfield. Principled, tough, loyal, funny and wise, they were teachers both, and superb at that. Although the textbook was football, the lessons were bigger than any game. One can't expect the kid in helmet and shoulder pads to realize this in the moment. In adulthood, though, he should.

ONE OF ETHAN's coaches this season is the father of a teammate. He, with the handful of other dad coaches, and in the classic manner of football generals going back through Messrs. Smith and Gerolamo to old Glenn Warner himself, offers advice and instruction and chastisement and encouragement, delivered invariably with what we'd have to call old-school vigor. Exuberance, even, when the spirit's on him. He seems to enjoy it. Ethan likes and respects him. And certainly one would guess he knows whereof he speaks. Fred Smerlas is his name, and he's a local legend of my vintage who starred at Waltham High and Boston College and for fourteen years in the NFL, a fearsome, bruising, many-time All-Pro nose tackle with the Bills, Niners and Patriots, and now a Harley-riding opinionizer on local sports radio and television programs. He's also a huge man, who in repose stands in a kind of ursine, counterbalanced lean, who cannot straighten his right arm, who walks slowly, bowleggedly, as if everything hurts and likely does. He has been through twenty-something surgeries. He's riddled with nerve damage. Bone grinds, from the look of things, against bone. In the stands at a Little League game a few years ago he got going on the subject of all the physical wreckage, and

I asked if it was worth it. He turned (stiffly) and looked at me like I was a moron, a word forced of late from circulation but in our day useful.

Now Fred watches his thirteen-year-old son and mine and twenty or so other boys toting the ol' pigskin and smashing into one another, sometimes ferociously, a few slow to get up, a few getting helped to the sideline and, once in a while, someone dashing off in the afternoon sunlight on an eighty-yard run. And I wonder what he thinks.

I do not have to wonder what Ethan thinks. I see it in his face.

Chapter 7

★

Do We Not Bleed?

Our glorious Land to-day,
'Neath Education's sway,
Soars upward still.
Its hills of learning fair,
Whose boundaries all may share,
Behold them everywhere
On vale and hill!
—"America" by Samuel F. Smith

THE SUBJECT NOW IS RACE. WHILE MUCH PROGRESS HAS been made, inequities still abound. Evidence of which you've seen, too, no doubt, even in school, maybe even felt. Haves and have-nots. Gifted and non-. Successful and un-. And, too often, Asian or white and non-. This offends not just essential precepts of education but foundational American ideals, even, finally, the nobility of the human spirit. No one is left unaffected. At the crux is learning.

Consider Phillis Wheatley.

In about 1753 a child was born in West Africa. A few years later she was enslaved, and at the age of seven wound up "for a trifle" the property of a Boston couple, John and Susannah Wheatley. They renamed her Phillis and treated her as one of their own. Recognizing in the child iridescent intelligence, they taught her to read and write—this in an era in which even few white girls received formal education of any kind. By the time she was a teenager, Phillis had blossomed into a scholar and poet . . . and to many a would-be reformer a vital example of what, given the chance, the unjustly disparaged African mind was capable. Skeptics, though, were rife: a board, including John Hancock and the governor of the colony, convened to verify that Phillis had indeed written the work she claimed was hers. In sitting her down and quizzing her they became convinced; and in one child, and a female at that, was any rationale for slavery annihilated. Incontestably, this was a fully dimensional, entirely capable, highly intelligent, *human* being—which opponents of the peculiar, vile institution recognized. Phillis Wheatley became a kind of test-case celebrity, a shining example. Published first in England, her poetry was widely read, widely admired. Soon no less than George Washington and Benjamin Franklin were eager to meet her.

And young Phillis was a clever social critic, advocating justice to the limits of what even a liberal-minded white readership would then tolerate. While her experience differed wildly from that of just about any other slave, she plainly understood the significance of the voice happenstance—and a few sympathetic souls who prized education—had given her. With subtle subversion, she spoke strongly and well; still, cultural might, headstrong self-interest and willful stupidity can make for formidable adversaries, which Wheatley plainly recognized: one hears in much of her poetry certain gentle, chiding efforts to edify. She's trying to help her arrogant, obtuse white readers, to educate them, not just in what she says and how she says it, but in the example she sets in her willingness to be of help. Which is, after all, the Christian thing to do. That she does all this in the cerebral and traditional medium of poetry is significant, too. Quite courageously, she stands herself before them as case in point—to which we should well pay attention today.

Theirs, Wheatley suggests—deftly, kindly—is an ignorant point of view. In her "To the University of Cambridge, in New England," for example, she tells the well-fed young scions at Harvard to get off their privileged duffs, to apply themselves, think beyond their own narrow advantage and do some good. Take it from me, she says, enflamed by an "intrinsic ardor" but denied by the double whammy of sexism and racism what you take for granted and squander, that education can put you among the stars eternal. "Students," she says, "to you 'tis given to scan the heights/Above, to traverse the ethereal space/and mark the systems of revolving worlds." Then, to make them feel guiltier, she reminds them of Christ's suffering on their behalf.

Meanwhile, instead of taking advantage of all they've been handed, the young gentlemen of Harvard are content trusting their entitlement, lazing around and engaging for amusement's sake in low-grade vice and indolence. Here's the last stanza—sensible, mildly rebuking:

> Improve your privileges while they stay,
> Ye pupils, and each hour redeem, that bears
> Or good or bad report of you to Heav'n.
> Let sin, that baneful evil to the soul,
> By you be shunned, nor once remit your guard;
> Suppress the deadly serpent in its egg.
> Ye blooming plants of human race divine,
> An Ethiop tells you 'tis your greatest foe;
> Its transient sweetness turns to endless pain,
> And in immense perdition sinks the soul.

Look, she's saying, identifying herself and her point of view as black, I know what I'm talking about: fritter away your time there in idle pursuits, however sweet they might seem in the moment, and you'll regret it. An education is that important and well worth the work and sacrifice necessary to attain it. Your greatest foe, then, is your own susceptibility to the baser impulses. And for you perdition will be wondering at some later date what might have been. An opportunity to be educated is a great privilege, and privilege is a responsibility . . . to yourself and to others. If you don't like it, too bad. Look at what Jesus went through on your behalf. Ergo, get cracking.

This message is timeless, of course.

Phillis was given her freedom as a young woman. After John and Susannah Wheatley died, she married a freed black man named John Peters, who, evidence suggests, had his faults. Their poverty was severe, opportunities negligible. She bore him three children, two of whom died very young. The third, also very young, died shortly after Phillis and in the same bed with her.

When, nearly two and a half centuries later, talk turns to aptitude, attitude, underperformance and achievement gaps, I think of Phillis Wheatley. When a friend says, "What white suburban kids don't realize is they were born on third base," I think of Phillis Wheatley. When I see race conflated with socioeconomic conditions, I think of Phillis Wheatley. When I see assumptions made about certain earnest and deserving kids who want only what everyone else wants, I think of Phillis Wheatley.

SOON AFTER I arrived in Hawaii—this was in 1986, at a teacher get-together a day or two before summer school began—a new colleague took me aside and explained in professorial tones and without conversational provocation that the islands were a petri dish, a laboratorial commingling of three macrocultures: the Polynesian, the Western and the Asian. He was English, the new colleague, with a bit of a bulldog demeanor. He was also white of hair, bespectacled and billed as widely respected: his words carried a natural heft. "We're in advance of the rest of the planet here," he said. "The fences are down. A new race is emerging, the *human* race."

Nodding politely, I squelched a flutter of bemusement at the old don's cast-iron, self-righteous certitude. In another time and place one would have heard this same accent and floridity blustering about the Raj and bloody wogs and the unlikelihood of a decent cup of tea. Now, though, this. I liked it.

A quick look around my classroom a few days later and I got what he meant: a third of the faces, give or take, were Asian, a third white, a third a coalescence, known locally as *hapa*, "half," although fractional delineations were understood to be loose. Throw in a black kid,* a Polynesian or three, and there you have it. There were, too, blue-eyed, corn-silk blonds with Japanese last names, and kids with Chinese faces and Jewish last names, and Hawaiian kids with last names from the craggy hills of Scotland. There was no racial norm, no standard-setting majority. While I saw almost no sign of what one could call prejudice among them, sensed no wariness or tension, I'd hear now and then jokes and terms tossed about—*haole, flip, mang*—and second- or thirdhand learn of incidents, usually at some remove. I also came to understand in certain neighborhoods to be white was to invite animus, a reality exacerbated, to little surprise, by poverty, which both far and near on Oahu could be extreme.

Nonetheless, what I saw, day after day and overwhelmingly, was the new world order to which the Englishman had referred. In Hawaii people were people, ethnic individuations blending smoothly and enrichingly, with a beautiful hybrid ascendant greater than the sum of its parts. This, I realized, was an emergent postracism world. Everyone appreciated everyone, or pretty near, with much contentment and aloha the result.

---

* One, a *hapa* black kid, known in those days as Barry Obama, had graduated from Punahou a few years before I arrived.

What struck, too, was how natural it all seemed, how effortless and apolitical and enlightened—and such a heartening contrast to the hostility and hand-wringing of the still largely separated, if not outright segregated, Boston I'd left behind, where the attendant ugliness of court-ordered busing still felt quite raw. And primitive. They'd let go of the tiller in Hawaii, it seemed to me, and allowed the breezes of nature, human and otherwise, to blow them where they would. Which was, it appeared, toward one another. To make note of it, even to applaud, was to kind of miss the point—all of it just *was*.

One could see it in student learning and performance as well: even there one simply could not generalize based on race. Such at last had gone the way of phrenology and a flat earth.

Plainly, though, mine was a mainland *haole* point of view, East Coast at that, newly arrived. Even then I knew this. Still, in the Honolulu of those days, Hawaiian, Portuguese, Chinese, English, Tongan, West African, East African, North African, Fijian, Danish, Japanese, Irish, Thai, Italian, Filipino, Indonesian, German, Okinawan, Indian, Vietnamese, Russian, Tahitian, Mexican, Polish, Korean, Samoan . . . everything was everywhere and blended together and no big deal, an unintentional, unselfconscious celebration of humanity united. An *ohana*. Granted, that sunshine and rainbows and balmy ocean breezes and mountain mists and swaying palms and the gentle spirit of *aloha*—which is real—were all features of regular life might have had something to do with it; so too—and here you can subtract the "might"—the generally affluent, educated and insular and, in pockets, elitist nature of the Punahou community in which I spent nearly all my time. The school had been founded, after all, by New England missionaries and spawned the white oligarchy that would soon take control of the islands, and more than a little of that legacy lived on a century and a half later: as another newly arrived white New Englander of a do-gooder bent I might have suffered a certain myopia. And of course admissions people were stopping at the gate those children of any race or ethnicity deemed not up to snuff. Part of it also, a big part of it, was simple proximity: behind its lava-rock wall, Punahou was an island on an island. And on Oahu we were all on the same patch of real estate, everyone a minority, with not a lot of elbow room, pinned tight as we were between mountains and ocean. There was no getting around one another.

And Janice, my girlfriend, then wife, then mother of our *hapa* quartet, was Armenian . . . on both sides of her family, all the way back. Richard, my new and great friend and brother-in-arms at Punahou, fresh from Cleveland by way of Choate and Yale, was black and Native American—not then a term in wide circulation. In the apartment above were Dan and Linda and their kids, he Greek and Irish, she

Hawaiian and *haole* and Korean, and downstairs were Tim and Rita, he German and Irish, she Chinese and Hawaiian. And in my classes and throughout the dazzling campus, the full global variety and every combination thereof, a microcosm within a microcosm within a microcosm.

What twenty-six years ago felt like a kind of revelatory Shangri-la and a great advance in the human condition was, just maybe, something of a precursor after all. One looks around today—even in the Boston late of Louise Day Hicks and Arthur Garrity—and dares, at least a little, cautiously, to take heart. Tolerance, which once seemed so much to ask, has become ever more acceptance, even, frequently, respect, appreciation, and, yes, sometimes, embrace. Minorities are making inroads into worlds de facto segregation denied them even recently. Racial diversity is now a point of pride.

None of which is to say we're there yet. No, no. Inequities and exclusions persist—some pretty close to intentionally. While to some of the holdouts it might feel like a kind of gritty tribal loyalty, bigotry is nonetheless about the most idiotic and toxic form of backwardness afflicting the species. So much is lost. Certainly you've seen it, too. Racism, anti-Semitism, homophobia . . . these are a weakling's manifestations of fear and concomitants of stupidity. Hatred, prejudice, provincialism, ignorance . . . these too often still deliver kicks to the shin or worse. Even the well-meaning can come across as condescending, which is at the very least irritating. And benign-seeming indifference, attitudes of "too bad but not my problem," will exclude and wound as well. Evidence of these will appear in the classroom absolutely. Perhaps you've seen it there, too.

For all the progress, ours is as yet an underevolved culture with too many left out, not just from a voice in the proceedings, but from an opportunity for an opportunity for one. And being somewhat less backward than others is no real cause for celebration. The statistics are all too familiar: by just about every objective measure, African Americans still have it the worst in this country. This is plain five decades after the civil rights movement, more than a century and a half after emancipation, even with a *hapa* man in the White House. Wave after wave of penniless immigrants have arrived, often illiterate in their own language, and within a generation or two stepped right past African Americans. The situation is known to all of us, yet it persists. That in itself is shameful. And our schools bear no small share of the responsibility.

Of which kids across the demographics are aware.

Which makes Mr. Lincoln's redefining of the Civil War at Gettysburg and of the nation as pertinent today as it was in November of 1863. The great task remaining then remains today. A nation conceived in liberty and dedicated to the proposition that *all* people are created equal is humankind's noblest experiment . . . but to succeed requires vigilance, initiative, fair-mindedness, ingenuity, empathy, often courage, often toughness, often sacrifice. And schools doing what they should—for everyone. From this all stand to gain.

To disregard, however innocently, the ideals for which those thousands and thousands who gave the last full measure of devotion at Gettysburg, or Saratoga, or Pusan, or Omaha Beach, or Verdun, or Khe Sanh, or some mountain village in Afghanistan, is worse than ignorant and shameful, it's dangerous.

BY JUNE OF 2002 the time had come: Janice and I and three children and another soon to arrive left Hawaii for Massachusetts, where both she and I are from. I had accepted over the telephone a job teaching English at the public high school in Wellesley, with which I was acquainted by reputation only and loosely at that. I knew, for example, it was a nice town, amply moneyed, that there was a fine women's college there and on marathon day the students lined the route and cheered the runners as they charged by. I knew, too, that Dee Brown, a twenty-one-year-old African American guard for the Boston Celtics and a new resident of the town, coming out of the Wellesley post office one day with his fiancée, minding his own business, had been forced at gunpoint to the pavement by police officers because someone thought he looked like a bank robber.

On the late August morning Wellesley's teachers reported for duty to start the school year—and I to start my new job. We assembled in the middle school auditorium, a few hundred strong. A member of the school committee gave a speech. The superintendent gave a speech. New teachers were introduced. With the others I stood, made a friendly wave and sat back down. At the close of the meeting we were directed to classrooms throughout the building for group discussions—on the topic of race and inequity. First meeting, first subject.

My group was led by a middle school teacher, an African American man, who implored in a pained voice through our hour together that we make accommodations for our black students, that we modify standards, adjust expectations. That we go easy on them and give whatever extra we could. He looked us each in the eye to be sure we got it.

Wondering where I'd landed, I sat there with, among twenty-three other things, issues of fairness banging around the gourd. "Because they're black?" I asked. Okay, blurted.

"Yes," he answered, "because they're black." Then, gratuitously—and, I thought, accusingly—he added this: "You look in the mirror and see a face. I look in the mirror I see a black face."

Had I sixteen eyebrows I'm sure I would have raised all sixteen. Oh come on, I was thinking. This is about you? And: are things here really that bad? And: are we meant to understand being black is a disability? And: since when in a classroom does a social agenda, however laudable, supersede academic concerns? And: doesn't equality mean equal treatment? And: since when does lowering standards help a student? And: doesn't he understand preferential treatment breeds resentment and alienation? And: if we aspire to ideals, shouldn't we try living by them?

But I said nothing. His answer was so immediate, so insistent—and, further, so shot with pain and defensiveness and exasperation with whatever I represented to him—I just sat there trying to look less white and ignorant and privileged. I was hours-new to the school system, to the town, to public school, late of Far-Off Rainbow Land, no less. I didn't know the man nor did he know me. To question him further in a room full of teachers, none but him black, would be construed, I was reasonably certain, as disrespectful to the point of obnoxious, maybe even racist. Make that probably racist. So I nodded, donned a warm benevolence to do any A-list saint proud, and pacified my inner grumblings with an unspoken reminder: the session would soon be over, in a few days I'd be with my students, and across the board I'd treat each of them as fairly, empathetically and respectfully as I was able—that is, everyone the same.

Which was naïve.

I soon learned nearly all the black kids in the Wellesley school system were there as participants in what's called METCO, a voluntary busing program of almost fifty years' standing that brings students of color from Boston to Wellesley and a number of other suburban towns. The kids have to get up and out the door in the dark and quiet of the early, early morning to catch the bus and return home late in the afternoon, in the evening if they participate in sports or another extracurricular. Many are on the bus more than two hours a day. Many see home only in the dark. Many come from rough neighborhoods and modest means. At school they're the city kids, conspicuous in race and, often, dress and demeanor—the student body, like the town, is overwhelmingly white—and the economic and cultural disparity can be gaping. At home the METCO kids are the expatriates, accused, sometimes, of thinking themselves too good for the city schools, too "all that." In both places, then, they're isolated, alienated—by no means an easy row, but for the advantages the students and their families seem willing enough. The program is viewed by most as important and successful. There are, though, too, a few African American kids who live in Wellesley; and a few girls, New Yorkers, who room together in a house not far from the high school, participants in the A Better Chance program. Still, they represent a very small percentage of the student body. Most achieve at levels below the median.

A number of these kids have been my students. And while I take issue in both fact and principle with generalizations about, say, the superior intelligence and automatic grind-it-out studiousness of Asian kids, or the snooty entitlement of wealthy Anglo-Saxon kids, I take greater issue with generalizations about the weakness of African American students. This is not to say, though, I have not had under-performing black students and driven, high-achieving Asian students. I have, and in far greater number than the other way around. But too often are the lazy- or empty-headed, or the flat-out racist, ready to interpret certain responses to personal experience and cultural encouragements or the socioeconomic circumstances under which an individual lives as functions of race. Too often they're ready, even eager, to suggest dispositions of personality and/or intellectual aptitude are somehow genetically encoded along with the pigmentation of one's skin or the shape of one's nose.

Every Asian kid, though, somewhere along the line, has to deal with the stereotype that he or she is a math wiz with no detectable personality, a well-oiled homework machine with a semipsychotic Tiger Mom clawing at his or her backside. Every black kid has to deal with the stereotype that he or she is a recalcitrant student or worse. And it's tempting for anyone in any endeavor to perform to expectations. For a teenager still trying to figure out who he or she might be, this is triply so. The universe seems to ordain it. And those who would defy a stereotype suffer the condemnations of those who cannot. You feel like you're betraying your own. Then there's no one to go home to. Even if their heart isn't in it, Asian kids then feel compelled to knuckle down, while black kids, goes the thinking, need not. Or cannot. An A–, then, is (somewhat) jokingly called an Asian F, a C+ a black A, a B+ a white birthright. And in the name of diversity, college admission practices would seem to bear this out: Asian applicants have to get As because their real competition is understood to be other Asian applicants. Black kids are competing against black kids. And so on.

To me all this stinks.

Stinks.

Spend five minutes in a classroom and you don't see race. At least the teacher doesn't. At least this teacher doesn't. You don't even see students, really. Or for that matter kids. Each before you is a *person*, an individual, different from any other, complete unto himself or herself, important, vital, eager to grow, and each could use your help wherever he or she might sit. Black, white, Asian, male, female, gay, straight, tall, short, thin, plump, these are adjectives, not nouns. To see kids—people—as representatives of categories or specimens in evidence of genetic or social or cultural trends is for a teacher difficult if not repugnant. And, further, contrary to the avowed spirit of our republic. Yet trends exist, so too categories, and concerns are more than just valid, they're pressing.

To many a young person, irrespective of race, going to school is being asked, as Langston Hughes would have it, to subsist on tomorrow's bread: work hard in October and you might get a good grade in June. Work hard and do well through four years of high school and you might get into college. Work hard and do well through four years of college, if you can figure out a way to pay for it, and you might get a good job. Work hard and do well there and we might show you some respect and welcome you among us on something like equal footing. Meanwhile, for any student to struggle amid those who soar is, or certainly can be, discouraging, even humiliating—and encourages the stereotype and condescenders. To be forever thwarted by circumstances is debilitating. To be the object of assumptions is irritating. Easier by far is to convince yourself it doesn't matter, that you don't need anyone else's approval, that you don't have to play someone else's game. That you can do just fine on your own. Easier, if things get really bleak, to just say screw this, and screw them, too. And to find then like-minded company. Add to the mix the long, ugly legacy of racism and poverty and exclusion and disrespect and their many consequences, and pretty soon a kid sees himself up against immutable social forces. And what's one person against all that? Resignation becomes that much easier. Soon enough underachievement becomes part of his identity: school, he winds up thinking, that's their thing, not mine. So screw school, too. And where does this leave him?

Still, for all the complexities and imperfections schools

remain where disparity is best addressed. Among many other essential functions, schools can be, should be, the great elevators, the great *E Pluribus Unum* machines. How and from where children come in should not matter. What happens to them while they're there, as well as how and in what state they emerge and in what direction they go, does. Education is the equalizer.

And fair doesn't always look the same.

Experience in the classroom at Punahou and in Wellesley has told me again and again what common sense has asserted all along: every student needs to be valued for herself or himself, irrespective of the circumstances of upbringing and features of genetics. Or, for that matter, aptitude. Every student needs to take responsibility for her or his own education. Cultural differences, economic disparity, achievement gaps . . . these are real; to pretend otherwise is silly and counterproductive. To allow them to get in the way, though, is in ways large and small a betrayal. I keep hearing Zora Neale Hurston: "At certain times," she wrote, "I have no race, I am *me*." Every kid is always and forever her or his own "me" and should be appreciated for it. Anything else is a betrayal. And to be a "me" is to need a place to belong.

Today high school students are careful on the subject of race. They find, most of them, even a whiff of racism abhorrent but also feel forever preached at about it. On this subject—like so many others—they think they get it and probably do. They see, too, what everyone else sees. Talking about issues helps—at the right time and in the right context—and here courtesy and respect matter entirely. So too candor. But to countenance differences is to acknowledge them, which they fear grants assumptions, stereotypes and prejudice some legitimacy. Treading lightly, they'd rather let be, think racism a problem of yesteryear and move on. This comes at least in part, I think, from faith in our capacity to do the right thing, about which I choose to be optimistic. But of course optimism isn't enough.

EVERY FALL I'M ASKED to write recommendations for students applying to college. I've never stopped to count for how many I've done them, but yearly averages say it has to be on the far side of five hundred. Along with a narrative component, a letter, usually there's a form with some questions to answer and boxes to check. (For teachers there are no boxes to check concerning race. For applicants, though, there are.) Among these boxes are a few that ask for assessments of, in the broadest terms, the applicant's capacities as a student: *Poor, Fair, Good, Excellent, Top 10%, Top 5%, One of the Best of My Career*. These boxes have the look and vibe of the final judgment.

They always give me pause.

One wants to help the kid, of course, one wants to preserve one's integrity, one wants to be helpful to the admissions people . . . and one finds objectionable being asked to make subjective-posing-as-objective qualitative judgments of a student one has been entrusted to educate and of whom, invariably, one has grown quite fond. Some teachers I know and admire skip these forms altogether. Others will check no boxes. I do, however reluctantly, for fear it might somehow handicap the applicant if I don't. Usually I know how much getting into this college or that means to her or him.

In a few weeks I'll be sending off another batch, including some for an African American girl . . . or, rather, for an enthusiastic, personable, principled, accomplished, eminently sensible, hugely intelligent, ferociously hardworking, wholly superlative student, one of the best of my career, who happens to be female and African American. I cannot, though, nor would I if I could, think of her as an exemplar of anything but the human race. She is herself, complete and magnificent, and kind, and funny, and lovely, and does the planet, the greatest of all petri dishes, proud.

I hope someday, someday soon, I'll find this not worth mentioning.

Chapter 8

Getting and Spending

"It has always seemed strange to me," said Doc. "The things we admire in men, kindness and generosity, openness, honesty, understanding and feeling are the concomitants of failure in our system. And those traits we detest, sharpness, greed, acquisitiveness, meanness, egotism and self-interest are the traits of success. And while men admire the quality of the first they love the produce of the second."

—*Cannery Row* by John Steinbeck

ADMITTEDLY, A TEACHER ON THE SUBJECT OF MONEY IS a little like an Eskimo on the subject of flip-flops. I do recognize, though, it comes in handy, money does, and not enough of it can be vexing, even terminal.

I also know Paul of road-to-Damascus fame is quoted out of context: money is not the root of all evil, according to the epistle writer, the *love* of money is—and therein lies a significant difference. But however you parse it, across the long centuries since Paul's pronouncement I'll suggest we've seen little to no improvement on the money-love score. So much, I suppose, for epistle writing. Venality, greed, materialism . . . these remain among the more common and debasing of human flaws. Against the backdrop of the desperate poverty that afflicts so many around the world, all the examples of wild excess can be shriekingly obnoxious if not downright criminal. Still, with due respect to Paul, I cannot call money-love the root of *all* evil. A little too narrow, that, in the face of so much readily apparent wickedness and willful ignorance, which I'll call a far sight worse. In the face of, say, cruelty, it seems almost innocent, does money-love, childish even. But, then, what's a little hyperbole among friends?

And, further, why stop digging? The love of money has its roots, too. Clear away more soil and there's vanity, for example; go deeper still and you'll find narcissism, then insecurity, which has its roots, I'll submit, in our dread of death. Beneath the dread of death you'll find just dirt. Mostly, it all comes back to this: I'm here only a minute, a fleeting minute at that, with eternal oblivion on the other side, so I'd like my moment to be, if you don't mind, and the heck with you if you do, the way I'd like it to be. How can this be unreasonable? And, assorted nutcases and a hairball poet or two notwithstanding, why walk when you can drive? And who's happy rattling along in a cranky little rust bucket when a sleek and shiny Porsche Panamera GTS goes gliding by with that gorgeous muscular hum? If you prefer red, why try to content yourself with gray? This, I think, is only human.

So we scheme, we grab.

And shame on us.

Concerned about this, too, was Thomas Jefferson and not without an informed perspective: across a lifetime of privilege, fairly addicted was he to the finer things, although few talked a better game. And in a pinch, he seemed to feel, why not borrow? Books, art, wine, human labor on his behalf . . . he had from time to time little trouble not paying for any of these—which, even he would have to admit, strains the definition of "borrow." And in borrowing from John Locke for purposes of inventing a nation, the brainy redhead made an important adjustment: "life, liberty and the pursuit of property" became "life, liberty and the pursuit of happiness." Less vulgar, that. Recasts, really, the whole spirit of the enterprise.

Look around today, though, and sometimes one wonders why he bothered.

Turn left or right and there's another example of Wordsworth's sordid boon. Whether it's with the innocent-enough conspicuous consumer's designer this or deluxe that or the sleight-of-hand tax dodge, or the stately, dogwood-shaded, eight-thousand-square-foot pseudo-manor with a commercial-grade kitchen and, while we're at it, a bluestone-decked lap pool out back . . . too often we're in it for the material reward. Money—it's how the big people keep score. Raw sexy net worth. Less is *so* not more, and the journey is definitely *not* the destination. Of course on some abstract level we endorse such holy notions as working for the greater good, or for passion's sake, or for belief in the intrinsic value of an endeavor, or paying our fair share, or the nobility of selfless dedication, or concern for a healthy planet . . . but, well, none of that puts the free-range sage hen and Provençal shallots in the Viking convection oven, now does it? And if prosperity is good, why isn't more prosperity better?

So we make our choices.

And not always easy to achieve is this version of success. Brains, toil, dexterity, luck . . . these would seem necessities. Not easy either in the teenage arena is the showy report card, the science fair citation, the MVP award, admission to Stanford. To achieve any of these also requires sacrifice and pluck and guile and much hard work. There is, too, for many the adrenal rush of competition. The high-end everything, far-ranging leisure, significant net worth, these, then, are the rewards, are they not, for ingenuity, resourcefulness, dedication? The major haul is free enterprise's trophy, the spoils of Darwinian victory, cosmic homage for kicking ass.

Which brings us back to Paul and his roots.

Nonetheless, as the squire of Monticello's cut-and-paste

suggests, Americans have long been ambivalent about wealth. Sure, we'd love a pile of our own. Yes, we'll deify the Astors, the Carnegies, the Jobses, the Gateses, the empire builders, the potentates. Energy, ambition, innovation, dedication, smarts . . . holy words each and not wrongly. We dream of wealth, work hard for it, enjoy it as just deserts when at last we achieve it; all the same, we're careful to maintain every appearance of the common touch, of being at heart just regular folks; and we reserve the right to quietly envy, and perhaps secretly resent, those who have more. And always there are those who have more. In fact, generally, perhaps to ease the conscience, the rich will not consider themselves particularly rich.* Ours, after all, is a culture that prizes modesty, too, and the competence, the tenacity, that comes from struggle and the clean efficiencies of frugality. "Rich," moreover, is a relative term: there are important gradations and tonalities. It's hierarchical, too. (The disapproving, or those prone to resentment, might say these run from "filthy" to "stinking" to "obscenely.") To the ordinary rich—the nicest-house-on-the-block rich—genuine rich is vast and exotic portfolio rich,

---

* Not long ago a friend, a rich friend, explained, in all earnestness, that a million dollars isn't that much anymore, pocket change, really, when you get right down to it. Tax exposure, he said, market instability, commissions and fees, asset vulnerability. You're lucky if you wind up looking at half. Okay, two-thirds. Buy yourself a car. Pay down the mortgage. Put a couple kids through college. Take a vacation. Not exactly a game changer, a million bucks.

Aston Martin rich, slope-side place in Deer Valley rich. To the slope-side guy in Deer Valley, truly rich is the guy with a Gulfstream over at the airport. To the guy with a Gulfstream, as the novelist Tom Wolfe suggests, authentic rich is the guy with a Gulfstream and a Modigliani hanging in it. And so on. Because the moneyed tend to live among and interact with one another, privilege is their norm and the gradations and tonalities mean everything.

But there are catches: live too large and you risk separating yourself not just from others, but from the earth itself, violating certain essential qualities of character associated with apple pie authenticity. One must be careful to retain, then, a grassroots connectedness from which one has ascended in everything but spirit. Look at what happened to Richard Cory. Then there's the old/new conundrum: old money smacking as it does of unmerited privilege, of effete aristocracy, of inbred lassitude and self-protective snobbery, while new money is garish, trashy, coarse . . . belly-scratching peasants playing dress-up. Either way excess looks bad, smells bad. Hence the ambivalence. Hence the disavowals.

With perhaps a sentimental catch in the throat, we prefer instead, or purport to, the sensibilities of the working stiff from whence we'd like to think we come, the sons and daughters of the soil, of the small town, of amber waves of grain, of the heartland as probably Madison Avenue has us calling it. We admire pious, able, good-hearted, hardworking, unassuming just folks who put on no airs, do for others, care for their own, expect no more than their due, bear the label "average American" with quiet pride. Such as these—or so goes the perception—have an authentic humanity the wealthy lack and in quiet moments envy. It seems about the one thing their money can't buy. Often, then, the wealthy try to mask their wealth, no matter its heft, with a kind of proletarian veneer. They indulge in and at the same time try to minimize their privileges, or deny them altogether. Not so easy, that.

Which for the teenager in the house trying to chart his or her life's course can be highly confusing. Like the rest of us, young people don't do ambivalence particularly well. Absolutely they'd like to make a bundle—high tech or Wall Street, probably, cool clothes, rooftop nightclubs— but fear it might cost them their soul. They'd like to help humanity—care for orphans in Soweto, perhaps, sleep on a straw mat, get a meaningful tattoo—but fear it might cost them, well, nice stuff and fun. They know they should follow their passions—easier if these passions lead in at least the general direction of a six-figure income. Interestingly, most will imply—or outright state—the last thing they want is a life like the one in which they grew up. What, and be like their parents? No, they'll say, they want to get out, go somewhere, *do* something; not so much a conscious rejection of their upbringing, but consequent to a vague sense that they're missing something and have been for quite some time. This appears as much a function of their phase of life as weariness with responsibility. But any escape to freedom is still so far into the future, many will defer to others in their dream-building. Five years from now is to them just mists and whispers. Most can't think past that great monolithic abstraction on the horizon, college. And college, they think, college'll take care of all that stuff anyway. Few recognize this indecision, this ambivalence, is a luxury.

And few parents, however considerable their means, are lighting cigars with flaming hundred-dollar bills, are drowning their children in abundance, are redirecting their vanity through them. Rather, most have for reasons of love sacrificed and worked hard across the years on behalf of their children and will stay within reason in doing what they can for them. More than just natural, this is honorable. This is entirely human. Their driving hope, their steadfast aim, is to provide their children the best start in life available to them. To see them fulfill their promise and lead productive and happy lives. While they may not glide to perfect success every time, most think carefully about how best to dispense their resources in the raising of their children. They understand automatic indulgence can be toxic. That preparing and positioning for college have become the whirling center of such an expensive arms race feels to them, and probably is, beyond their control. Most understand that to participate in an inflated economy is to inflate it further. But opportunities for kids today are enriching and abundant, from club sports to travel programs to interest-focused summer camps to extra-help tutorials, and on and on. For this alone pressures to spend are great. Parents love their children so they do what they can—which is sometimes quite a lot. And the highly competitive among them will rev their engines.

The larger consequences of wealth, both personal and cultural, and however unintended, are many. Conspicuous among the cultural one sees a sociogeographical phenomenon that seems to be gaining momentum everywhere: affluence gravitates toward affluence, toward pricey houses in pricey towns. Which will mean robust tax revenue. Which will mean, generally, well-financed and high-performing public schools. Which will attract to the community more well-heeled families with options. This demand tends to increase property values and therefore tax revenue. The schools improve. With these resources able, dedicated, well-supported kids will achieve and conspicuously. More affluent people with children will want in. Prices will climb. Around it goes, and upward.* Those with children but lesser means are priced

---

* It's probably no coincidence—and probably you can remove the probably—that the towns in my own Massachusetts with the highest per capita income are also the towns with the most expensive real estate and top-ranked schools. In struggling communities we see this same phenomenon happening in reverse.

out of the market. Those with the means but no stake in high-performing schools move away, creating space for others. Those already invested are swept along. The swankier zip codes offer, then, ever more fertile soil for the raising of children bound for the finest colleges, the choicest jobs, and, soon enough, their own spot in the golden vortex.

Thus the perpetuation of privilege. It's a powerful force. And foundational notions of equal opportunity and upward mobility based on demonstrated merit can get tossed about in its wake. Most kids raised in such an environment recognize they're perceived to be privileged and anything short of excellence from them would be hugely disappointing.

WHILE HE HAS no children in the game, money and real estate and golden vortices bring us inevitably to Jay Gatsby . . . who, for all the acclaimed "heightened sensitivity," the "romantic readiness," the "extraordinary gift for hope," is in my view an unregenerate putz and a cheat. He misconstrues ostentation for wealth and wealth for class and class for some vague but highly seductive notion of worthiness. It's a fool's delusion. In his romantic readiness, his indefatigable hope, he somehow mistakes the American Dream for the American Guarantee and the purpose of human enterprise the amassing of wealth—with the devoted princess, dewy and chaste, who just happens to take the form for him of Daisy Fay, as his prize. He's at best naïve.

And for us an interesting, even important, case study.

Yes, *The Great Gatsby* is a superb novel. Its insight. Its tightness and subtlety. Its balance and complex simplicity. Its lyricism. And at its center the raw, crazy-logical mutant extreme of the great American materialist. In Gatsby—naïf, putz and cheat notwithstanding—Fitzgerald tapped the universal vein: Gatsby is Fitzgerald, Gatsby is you, he's me. In all of us churns at least a little of young Jimmy Gatz's soaring, starry-eyed idealism untouched by cold reality, his unanswered longing and the simple hope that tomorrow will bring us what today did not. This is the great human quest, is it not, to see not merely our own experience, but that of the human species, as an exercise in progress, as we pull ourselves ever upward? To see confirmed that virtue, at least virtue in spirit, does matter after all? How can he know he'll be killed for daring?

While there's something commendable in Gatsby's doggedness, there is more a tragic imbecility. In his pursuit of happiness Jimmy Gatz took the dimwit's shortcut to property, and he was done before he began. The Great Jay Gatsby, then, is a carnival sideshow, a sequined trapeze artist up there without a net, swinging for all he's worth, reaching for something that isn't there.

And kids recognize . . . all right, some kids recognize . . . something of themselves in Gatsby, the stealthy, tragicomic scrambler, in the "service of a vast, vulgar and meretricious beauty." They too believe in the green light and all too often see conspicuous achievement as the method by which to make it theirs. I hope this isn't you. Every day, then, brings another conscious reinvention of the self, a contrivance to suit someone else's imagined standards, someone to impress whom they believe could be useful to their advancement. To slow down for just a minute to consider the merits of their ambitions or the means by which they hope to see them fulfilled is to give others the advantage in getting there first. And so they beat on.

As perhaps you've noted, on the title page of the novel Fitzgerald shares an epigraph, four lines by Thomas Parke D'Invilliers—early to mid-nineteenth century, one guesses, certainly British. One imagines Fitzgerald, his manuscript nearly finished, coming upon a thin volume, the gold leaf of the title flaking from its spine, the calfskin smooth and dry, tucked on a forgotten shelf in a silent private library, wan shafts of sunlight from a high window catching tiny dust motes in the air. At the wide mahogany table the writer sits, adjusts the green-shaded lamp, then with gentle fingertips opens the book, turns the crisp pages, scans them and in a minute or two, with a muted cry, discovers the perfect little poem. Eureka!

Only . . . and here's the fun part . . . it's a phony. A scam.

Fitzgerald wrote the verse himself. The poet's name he made up, Thomas Parke D'Invilliers, as euphonious and aristocratic-sounding and fraudulent as "Jay Gatsby," the sturdy Anglo-Saxon Thomas, the worldly française of D'Invilliers, even the inspired gentrifying *e* at the end of Parke. The satire redolent in the lines, the pathos, the materialism and acquisitiveness, the debasement, the inanity of the whole exercise, make for the novel that follows a lovely beginning; one tidy quatrain in which the speaker encourages an aspirant for a woman's love to "wear the gold hat, if that will move her," and bounce, too, if bouncing might impress—no extreme is too silly—until, at last, in a delirious outburst, she cries, "I must have you!"

Kids, I'm thinking, should attach it to their college applications.

SOME MONTHS AGO headquarters asked me to swing by the supermarket on my way home from school. At the checkout counter I came upon a recent student of mine, a junior—let's call him Max—who, in collared white shirt, maroon apron, and name tag, was bagging groceries. At the sight of me he reddened to high scarlet . . . as if he'd been caught at something shameful. I said hello. He nodded a furtive greeting, asked if I preferred paper or plastic, then hid in his busyness. At this establishment the last stage of a bagger's duties includes helping customers to their cars, packing up and getting them on their way. Although I was reasonably sure I could handle my gallon of 2%, half dozen bagels and bag of romaine hearts on my own, I accepted Max's rote and mumbled offer of assistance. We needed to talk.

Max, you should know, is an admirably regular kid—albeit more self-conscious than most—who tends to operate within a persona of mild eccentricity. He sports tufty sideburns, a confusion of hair, and a demeanor of droll befuddlement. He's tall and gangly, with a poet's sunken chest and a lively brain. He talks meanderingly and often. Everyone seems to like him. In my sophomore honors class he did just fine and appeared to enjoy and benefit from the experience. Gradewise, he was middle of the pack.

Hunching, Max pushed the cart before him as if from the depths of a salt mine. "I kind of need the job," he explained in a rush of candor as we cleared the doors, his tone hushed and apologetic.

"It's good you have it, then," I said.

"Me and my family . . . we're . . . I mean, we're nothing special . . . not, you know, like, well off or anything."

"Ah," I said.

We started across the parking lot and he chuckled. "I've been thinking about calling it an internship . . . at a, like, major retailer of perishable consumer goods."

I chuckled, too. "Why?"

"Sounds less schmucky."

I stopped. We stopped. The car coming at us stopped.

"Max," I said, "nothing about having a job is schmucky. Schmucky is not giving it your best."

"Yeah, yeah, yeah," he exhaled, rolling his eyes like we both knew I was supposed to say that. "Yeah, yeah," he said again to be sure I got it. "I should be out curing cancer or something, right?" He didn't give me a chance to answer. "Thing is, my parents . . . they make too much for us to qualify for financial aid, but not enough to pay full freight at a, you know, a good college. It's doable, but we're gonna have to take, like, a ton of loans. I'm not kidding." He gestured then at the shopping cart as if to say, "So here I am."

Driving home I found the encounter lingered. Too much to qualify, not enough to pay for. Middle of the pack. Eroded self-esteem. Smothering debt. However earnest, however engaged, however receptive, by objective measure according to the local standards Max was an average student, in the current economy a B student, somewhere in the wide middle. I.e., of the norm. I.e., normal. Neither was he an exceptional athlete, as far as I knew, nor a gifted musician nor artist nor actor. He was simply a well-liked and respectful boy who went to school, did fine, went to his job, put on his apron and bagged groceries, went home and did his homework. A good kid. He tried, as far as I could tell, what felt to him like the best he could. He had his friends, too, I presume, and his enthusiasms. Glowing distinction, though, had as yet eluded him, although this seemed not a particular issue. Nor for him, I gather, the physics retreat at MIT, the hockey tourney in Quebec, the youth concert at Symphony Hall, the Outward Bound program in the Tetons, the entrepreneur camp in New York City. Or the cancer-curing internship wherever. The recompense for all this was a vague feeling of failure and an impulse to apologize.

So often in school those who soar and those who struggle attract the attention, be it applause and citations or extra help and encouragement—a consequence, at least in part, of the emphasis on achievement. Those in the wide middle, kids like Max, the "age-appropriate achievers," the "rank and file," tend to march along "under the radar" and sometimes "fall through the cracks." The forgotten middle class, a sociologist might have it, at once too good and not good enough. While some might take this purgatory as motivation to excel, more just shrug and plod on. Still others surrender to entropy and settle to the bottom—where, one hopes, they'll find buoying help. What happens to a guiding sense of self in all of this, or excitement about learning, one is left to wonder.

In a different wide middle are those for whom the expense of a "good" college is "doable" but crippling, those too wealthy but not wealthy enough. College debt totals in this country are approaching a trillion dollars. Two-thirds of college students graduate owing money. This staggering reality will, of course, recast not just attitudes about what college is for, but the experience itself. How can it be about exploring, about enriching the mind, about the exhilarations of learning, of tapping into wisdom, or even fun, with ten-ton debts to repay and interest eating you alive? How can you even fantasize about the excitements of a career fulfilling for reasons beyond just the remunerative with brutal obligation stretching years and years into the future? No job is schmucky if you believe in it, but with today's economic realities it seems ever fewer have the freedom to enjoy this state of mind. And what college graduate has the prospect of a big income right away? Of course, then, he'll follow the money. He has to.

"They are different from you and me," Fitzgerald once wrote—famously—of the wealthy, blending fascination with envy and, perhaps, a certain disdain. In the classroom, though, an egalitarian preserve, at least ideally, any difference, real or perceived, seldom shows and does not matter. Don't ask me which of my students comes from significant money. I couldn't say nor do I want to know. For all I knew of him, I could have just as easily found Max in a corner suite at the St. Regis with room service caviar on his chin. Students—again, ideally—bring their minds to class and nothing else, and—rich, poor, or somewhere in between—none matters to the teacher more nor less than any of the others.

Just the same, too many young people today seem to

confuse net worth with self-worth, and in their own local economy, in which grades are understood to be remuneration, the GPA too often defines the student. The honor roll is the aristocracy, the 3.9s, the 4.0s *la noblesse*. Below them we find Max and the other middlings. Any excitement about intellectual growth is coincidental. They do their time. They plug away. Grades are the dividends. "The more you learn, the more you earn," one will hear a kid say sagely, only because, it would seem, the poet he's quoting couldn't find a way to make "GPA" rhyme with "earn." It's about grades because, real or imagined, admissions officers are thought to see it that way. Very quickly, then, biology class becomes much less about exploring the mysteries and miracles of life than scoring the A at the end of the semester. Is it so small a leap from there to seeing the practice of medicine more about kite surfing in the Bahamas than the health of one's patients? (Or paying off student loans and keeping up with rent, payroll and malpractice insurance?) And bagging groceries at age sixteen is embarrassing because it's menial and peanuts-paying and so obviously not the path to anyone's idea of the top.

That there's satisfaction in work done well—any work, but the unglamorous in particular—is to too many kids today an alien notion. Rather than confronting reality and advancing the greater good, rather than knuckling down as a matter of principle, rather than seeing a real-life need and addressing it, work of any kind—bagging groceries or studying trigonometry—is merely what you endure for the payback.

But should we blame them? They're just kids, after all, responding guilelessly, most of them, to fresh encounters with attitudes established long before they arrived. By seeking to minimize the physical and psychological burden of any task, by overcelebrating and rewarding any material achievement that might result, we can undermine the dignity of honest effort, and endeavors yielding modest or abstract recompense become to them the toil of lesser beings. "Mexican work," a student of mine called it, he thought innocently. In addition to a stealthy Machiavellian ethos, an unintended side effect is latent snobbery, or worse, though any outward manifestations of this are quickly whitewashed. Look in the right spots and you'll even see an emergent caste system. At the top, the privileges of the privileged are marshaled to ensure more privilege, with many if not all of the precepts and attitudes one might expect.

Maybe Paul should write another epistle.

Chapter 9

⭐

The Same Boat

A man, to be greatly good, must imagine intensely and comprehensively; he must put himself in the place of another and of many others; the pains and pleasures of his species must become his own.

—*A Defence of Poetry* by Percy Bysshe Shelley

ENCOURAGED, PERHAPS, BY THEIR OWN HARMONIZING thinking, John Steinbeck and his friend the marine biologist Ed Ricketts adopted a theory that organisms in the collective, humankind included, can behave very much like a single organism. A school of fish, a flock of geese, a herd of gazelles, while composed of individual fish, individual geese, individual gazelles, can perform like a unified organic whole, just as the individual fish, the individual goose, the individual gazelle, is composed of individual cells functioning in close harmony within a single entity. Further, Steinbeck and Ricketts contended, in its behavior a human community also exhibits the pertinent operational characteristics of a single organism: for mutual benefit, the individual subordinates his or her own immediate needs and preferences for the good of the group, whether the group is two pals hanging around a Monterey marine biology lab, a family at the dinner table, a basketball team, an orchestra, a fire department, a corporation, an army battalion, a city. Or kids in a high school classroom.

Pretty quickly the individual finds his or her role to play to help the group, with the intuited thinking that what's good for the group is good for the individual. While some individuals are more apparently important to the success of the whole, others contribute in subtler ways, or will if called upon . . . like the guy standing at the back of the orchestra with the wooden clapper that makes the whip-cracking sound in a performance of "Sleigh Ride."

In all of this with your garden-variety teenager you're working against an instinctive, often encoded self-absorption. It's a phase-of-life thing, to be sure, but aiding and abetting these days are all the me-first impulses enflamed by social trends, social media and positioning for college. Who wants to wear somebody's tukus for a hat on the totem pole of life? You gotta be on top, bro. Smile and we'll take your picture. Or, better, take your own and Instagram it. And where does that leave the poor guy with the clapper? Seeking, achieving, and then capitalizing on individual accolades is no longer a fetish of the few, but a full-time job for many. Legions of parents and children are on a mission, and me, me, me is the refrain. That a bit of the diva can slip in along the way is no surprise, then, not so much as an ego indulgence, although that can surely be part of it, but as an expedient. Focused self-centeredness accelerates the process, makes likelier intended outcomes—and everyone knows there's precious little room at the top. Other kids, then, members of the group, are not companions sharing the adventure, not teammates with whom one works together, they're interferences, they're competition, they're threats. If I don't take the shot, somebody else will. If the teacher calls on somebody else that means she's not calling on me.

But certainly our association with the groups to which we belong enlarges us, enriches our experience, expands our sense of being alive. Teenagers know this because they feel it all the time. Yes, their self-absorption can be considerable, but so too is their eagerness to fit in, to be accepted, to feel the affirmations and satisfactions of belonging, to know stalwart comrades "have their back," a phrase they enjoy using for the perilous, jungle-primeval existence it suggests.

Standing out while fitting in is no easy trick . . . and therein lies much of the gut-knotting stress of being an adolescent. (That, and math tests.) Their yearnings collide. Such pride, though, do they take in the groups to which they belong, the swelling of the chest they feel when they put on the track team half-zip, the theater troupe T-shirt, that they tend to muscle through—and somehow fitting in *becomes* a way to stand out. And on a cool April morning, the season opener just a few hours away, to saunter down a high school hallway for the first time in your sleek new baseball team hoodie, your name and uniform number stitched on the sleeve in a jaunty cursive . . . this is pure bliss.

As a result, high schools are tribal territory of such richness and variety you'd need a Margaret Mead to sort it all out. With subsumed purpose, teenagers forever seek and invariably find a sense of belonging in a group. Even the nonconformists and/or pariahs find it with other non-conformists and/or pariahs. To call a group a "clique" is to trivialize, to call its members "friends" is to miss the mark; and to a teenager little is more important than the group in which he or she finds safety, comity, connection. It's clan dynamics writ small. It's human nature.

In their more formal incarnations these groups find common purpose in an activity—playing tennis, say, organizing the winter semiformal, raising money for hurricane relief—although dedication to the group is as important as or more important than dedication to the group's avowed purpose. Each has its rites and protocols, often its own lingo. These groups can also exist with no more formal purpose than the time-killing handful who hang out fourth period on the between-floors landing near Mr. Mahoney's classroom in the social studies wing. Groups have their table in the cafeteria, their warren backstage in the auditorium, their rolled-up wrestling mat in the corner of the old gym, their clearing in the woods near school. Groups can be acolytes of a particular teacher or coach, they might have an affinity for the same intoxicant or video game or cause du jour. Whatever the glue might be doesn't really matter; the being together does. At what cost to one's individuality—or reputation—this comes is deemed by most worth it for the enrichment of shared perspectives, as well as the protections and assurances circled wagons afford.

Based, generally, on a consensus among a hierarchical inner circle, membership in a group of teenagers is not easily earned, generally, nor is perseverance necessarily rewarded. Parents are not allowed, of course, any scrutiny they might bring to bear from the outside an outrage. Here "mind your own business" would be, often is, the handiest pertinent phrase. Within each group vague and slippery notions of popularity tend to determine acceptance and influence. Popularity, then, is power. While the components of popularity are usually easy enough to identify—among them confidence, good looks, glibness, audacity, social agility—never is there a precise formula. Nor can it be faked. You have it or you don't, and lasting judgments are made quickly; therefore, more often than not, popularity is assumed rather than bestowed . . . it's assumed, then acknowledged. Moreover, to be popular is to be cool, although they're not the same thing.*

College aspirants have been led to believe such notions as teamwork and cooperation and leadership, especially leadership, shine in the hearts of admissions people; therefore, many today polish to a high gloss their smiles and their we're-all-in-this-together zeal. Joiners, are they, eager to pitch in and do some good . . . and, like a politician at a soup kitchen, they know a choice photo op when they see one. (Exceptions might be the locked-in grinds who have no time to even think about anything but homework and viola practice. Theirs is often a lonely existence.) Since the prestigious college is perceived to be the emerald gateway to American Dreamland, and the road to it goes through the Students Against Drunk Driving, the Renewable Energy Club, the Safe Disposal of Mercury Club, most aspirants are

---

* From my observation the designation of cool is reserved for a small percentage of the population of any group. Even within marginalized subsets, the by-comparison coolest will emerge and be acknowledged. And while they differ in timbre, the dynamics of cool and popularity operate in much the same way, although in its aloofness cool occupies a higher plane and therefore has less influence on the ground. To wear the sash and tiara of popularity, though, is not the same as being liked. In fact, popular kids can be, often are, disliked for their popularity—which, of course, defies logic, but this, let's remember, is high school.

the very model of earnestness, happy to join in, link arms and sing a swaying "We Are the World." Few suffer reproach for their motivations because it's all standard operating procedure. Of course their contributions to good causes are appreciated, the lessons learned there of genuine value. They matter beyond self-interest, too. That those in the group for reasons other than résumé building are painted with the same cynical brush is an unhappy sign of the times.

On top of which, there's this: many secondary schools today, both public and private, have stepped in and mandated community service. As part of the curriculum, they require of their students a certain number of verifiable hours of dedicated altruism to qualify for graduation and will place students in worthy programs to fulfill their obligation. This is understood now to be an important component of a liberal education, a (perhaps coincidental) corrective to the rising trend of aggressive self-involvement in so many young people. More tangible than such abstractions as teamwork and cooperation—more immediately helpful, too—community service is also thought to be a more important college admission criterion than other extracurriculars.* (Even the adolescent version of private enterprise should have, it seems, a charitable purpose. Where that leaves kids like Max is, of course, tenuous.) But because volunteerism is

---

* Short of, say, a 4.4 forty, 30+ ppg, or a 90+ mph fastball. These would matter more.

no longer voluntary, kids are feeling forced to contort their dignity, even their integrity, to PR their way into approbation for something that's required of them anyway. As a result, nonvoluntary exercises in selflessness are understood to be additional opportunities to promote the self, albeit tricky ones. And tricky conceptually, if not ethically, is selfish selflessness. So too boastful humility. And the kids picking up litter along the streambed, the kids helping out at the animal shelter, the oncology unit, the public library, the art museum, the old folks' home understand seeking cap plumage for their service runs counter to, if not violates altogether, the selfless spirit of service to others. But since they have to do it, what the heck. And Williams doesn't take just anybody.

With nothing like serving my fellow man, woman or child in mind, nor flora, nor fauna of any denomination, I walked into the classroom on my very first morning as a teacher (at Punahou in June of 1986) fully aware I had no idea what I didn't know. I had, then, no real notion where to direct my learning nor how best to proceed. I was aware this could be something of a problem. Of my presumptuousness I was unaware.

Nor did I know the kids, nor what their needs might be, nor what might or might not be on their minds. I didn't know the curriculum, nor the local culture. I knew no pedagogies, no tricks of the trade. Beyond the name of the course, I didn't even know, really, what I was supposed to be teaching, nor, once I figured it out, how best to do it. Reading? Writing? Thinking? Self-awareness? Social responsibility? Grammar? The ins and outs of literature? The joys of discovery? Mostly on instinct I'd hung my hopes on this last, but what did I know?

And what, finally, was teaching? What did it look like? How could I tell I was doing it? How would I know it was working? I had a BA in English sprouting moss, a love of reading, a key to a classroom, a list of eighteen students who would be in my charge for two hours five mornings a week for seven weeks. And that's it. The man who'd hired me was off on vacation. The head of the summer school shook my hand when we met, said good luck and returned to his office. I found all of this at once enervating and exciting. The adventure in learning would be mine as much as my students', although I suspected I should be reluctant to reveal as much. To know next to nothing at the outset felt to me problematic, yes, of course, but also fitting, even auspicious. I hoped on Tuesday I'd be better than I was on Monday. And to prove sometime soon worthy of my hiring—to my employers, to my students, to myself.

Still, it was a portentous time for me. I was twenty-seven, which felt late in the game to be starting afresh—laughable in retrospect. I'd never taught before, never read a book about teaching, never even thought all that much about it as a path I might follow—although I had a few years earlier substitute-taught a sixth grade class one day as a favor for a friend. "Taught," though, stretches the definition: I read the scholars stories and we went outside and played kickball. School to me had always been something best put behind you.

But when Hawaii is yours for the taking and the need is a paycheck, you make adjustments.

The nice people at Punahou, understanding it wise to break in the rookie gently, gave me a summer school class called Novel/Short Story for recent ninth graders eager (or spurred) to get ahead, recent sophomores who needed another crack at the course and an aspirant or two auditioning for admission to the school. I was both grateful and delighted to give it a try. If nothing else it meant a summer in Honolulu.

How I'd come to be there was this: four months earlier I could not shake a nasty case of bronchitis. All day, all night, I coughed hard enough to rattle windows and crack plaster. My chest ached. My throat screamed. I could sense ennui creeping up my legs like gangrene. I had an inadequate job, a pathetic car, no medical insurance, a tiny, underheated dump of an apartment in a grubby neighborhood of Boston. I had no money. Bed was a strip of packing foam on the floor. Dinner was cereal and M&Ms. No one wanted to publish the novel I'd written. The weather stunk. So too, so too especially, did the new story at which I was irregularly flailing, something about a young paleontologist and the discovery of a fossil. Coughing, coughing, coughing, I was starting to entertain, even enjoy, thoughts of a Keatsian demise . . . inevitable, I suppose, for an untalented, insufficiently careerist English major. I read an awful lot—struggling for purchase, as the novelist Thomas McGuane puts it—which sufficed inconsistently.

Then out of the proverbial blue, Duke, my college roommate, called. Okay, gray: the sky was a bleak, leaden gray. Lively, irreverent, charismatic Duke, Butch to my Sundance. The Seabees had him stationed at Pearl Harbor. Come on out for a visit, he said. Get a little sun. Turn the page.

Hawaii.

Well, shoot, I thought, coughing, picture that . . . me in Hawaii. Then a second later: well, why not? Then: really . . . *Why not?* I'd never even seen California.

I perked right up. From nowhere and almost immediately I had the idea of doing a piece about Ensign Duke for the Lafayette alumni magazine. I called, got the editor; he, stunningly, went for it and bought me a plane ticket.

Snow swirled from a woolly sky the morning I left Boston. After a glimpse at a chilly LA, I stepped from the plane into the brilliant Oahu sunshine, the lush summery warmth, the caress of a breeze perfumed with flowers. In one direction sparkly ocean, in the other crenellated emerald mountains. And over there an honest-to-goodness rainbow. No, a double rainbow! Smiling, a beautiful almond-eyed girl in a flowered sarong stepped up, put a lei around my neck and kissed me.

I like this place, I thought.

Duke and I got into his Subaru and made for the Diamond Head lookout. Like a dog, much of the way there I hung my head out the window. The coughing ceased. Across my chest little strictures—which I'd been unaware were there—loosened. The air, I kept thinking. Step off the plane in Hawaii it's what you notice first, what you can't quite get past. The air. We parked, got out of the car, the blue Pacific wide and forever before us, the sun starting to settle above the horizon, reddening, for the last of its descent. Below us fifteen, maybe twenty surfers, above soaring frigate birds. Dropping hands to hips, I breathed again, deeply, and looked out at the ocean. Here the word "dreamily" suits. And where my eye happened to fall, the exact spot, maybe half a mile offshore, as if I had summoned it, at that precise moment, a humpback whale, black, big as a bus, came rocketing out of the water, rolled in midair, and in a colossal explosion of spray slammed back into the water. A sign, plainly.

I'm not leaving this place, I thought.

I would need, then, a job. I almost didn't care what, although a spin of some inner dial suggested a school . . . the ultimate noble nonprofit . . . schools employ people, don't they, provide perfectly authentic paychecks? I'd heard of Punahou, read mention of it, knew once a guy who'd gone there, liked the sound of it. And had the switchboard operator put me through to Buildings & Grounds I would have happily pushed a lawn mower or paintbrush had the opportunity arisen. Fussy about sources of revenue I was not— hence, I suppose, my situation. But, almost maternally, the operator asked if I'd been to college. Yes, I said. And in what did I major? English, I said. She passed me along to the head of the English Department in the upper school, the academy as it's called. He gave me a nice greeting. I explained myself. Please call me Ed, he said, and invited me over to the campus. I went, found him in his little office in Cooke Hall, and we talked. Friendly and enthusiastic, he showed me around. As for my reaction to the school, the expression "bowled over" suits. We went back to Ed's office and talked some more. "I assume you've read *Moby-Dick*," he said. "I have," I answered. "Well, what did you think?" he asked. I told him. A few weeks later he called and offered me a job.

I was, or would be soon enough, an English teacher.

THE CLASSROOM WAS on the second floor of Old School Hall, a modest lava-rock building, built in 1851, the oldest on campus, two classrooms downstairs, two up. Wooden stairs climbed the outside wall to a narrow second-story porch that functioned as a hallway. Waiting for me on this porch when I arrived that first morning was nearly the full complement: there they sat, all these kids, T-shirted, backs against the wall, fourteen, fifteen years old, looking to me undersized, wide-eyed and direly young. A forthright sun slanted through the monkeypod trees, doves cooed busily, nearby sprinklers tsk-tsked brightly, and from a distance floated the morning sounds of the city.

Near term, my ambitions included these: get through the two hours intact, see if I could maybe inspire in my flock a willingness to come back the next day, start figuring out what I should be doing and how best to do it. A solid enough plan, I thought. I'd worry later about loftier notions. And more practical ones.

With a deep breath and "here we go" exhale, I unlocked the door. Into a silent, shadowy room we stepped, a room in which teachers and students had come together with noble purpose for a hundred and thirty-five years. It smelled to me of chalk dust and Pine Sol and something else—dormancy, maybe. Or expectation. Or apprehension. I turned on the lights, the ceiling fans. The kids found desks.

One would have to call the mood foreboding . . . this, after all, was summer and before eight o'clock in the morning. What normal teenager felt like being upright? What sane kid felt like schoolwork? A summer of schoolwork?

Outside another beautiful Hawaiian summer day was limbering up. Waikiki beach sat less than a mile away. Sandy's, Makapuu, Waimanalo, Lanikai, Kailua—gorgeous beaches all—were around the corner. Not two hundred yards from us the school's handsome Olympic-size swimming pool sparkled in the sun. I was up against all of this and knew it. So too, of course, did the scholars. Stopping just short of whistling, then, at the prospect of the intellectual excitement we were about to share, generous with smiles and winning affability, I set about looking busy, organizing—opening windows, adjusting shades, selecting ceiling fan rpms—with the thought that they'd know we seasoned pros preferred things just so. I could feel them watching me. Staring, really.

As the last of the students arrived, I asked on impulse that they put the desks in a circle. Where this came from I do not know. And they did it. This small but immediate compliance for some reason stunned me. Not one balked. Not one said, "Well, we like 'em where they are." Not one said with a wave, "Do it yourself." I was now, I realized, in charge, a commander of people, an authority figure with power to wield—a new role for me. Quiet observation had always been my specialty, if I could be said to have had one.

Declining the option of the teacher desk, which sat gray and imposing before the blackboard, I found instead a student desk, brought it into the circle and sat. We looked at one another, my students and me, their expressions flat now but expectant. Through the open windows the doves cooed, the sprinklers tsk-tsked. I called roll, which seemed to me eminently teacherly. We were five minutes in.

I introduced myself then and started generalizing rosily about the road ahead. They listened politely. This took a minute and a half, maybe, before the well ran dry. It was going to be great, though, all of it, I could feel it. My nerves were just eagerness, anticipatory happiness. Next I had the fine idea of asking them to introduce themselves—name and a descriptive sentence or two, maybe mention of an interest, a hope for our summer together. This began promisingly enough but soon degenerated into such revelatory outpourings as "Jason; I like water polo," and "Lorena; I like to hang out with friends," and "Nani. So, how long you been teaching anyways?" Four minutes.

On to the next.

Loquacious I was . . . am . . . not. My inclinations had . . . have . . . always been to stay within my head, not merely out of contentment with my own company, and a certain instinctive privacy, but also, truth be told, a mild self-consciousness about being inarticulate, about producing inelegant, uninteresting clumps from the raw material of thought—wholly pedestrian thought at that. And why impose that on others? Unformed notions and observations bang around the gourd, and finding a useful one as

it went clunking by, shaping it into a form possibly beneficial and palatable to others, often took me long enough that
its moment passed, or I began fearing for the patience of
the listener. This would distract me and further confound
any successful outcome. As a consequence I tended in uncomfortable moments toward conversational minimalism.
People would call it shyness, which always felt to me not
quite accurate. All this, though, was now out the window
and I knew it. Who I might be outside that room didn't
matter. In there I was meant to be a teacher. *The* teacher.

Into the silence I waded. Benignly, if a bit yammeringly,
I asked for their opinions of novels they'd studied in school,
short stories, plays, poetry, movies, good English classes, bad
English classes. Each comment from them, I found, however
paltry, brought pattery, chattery, sometimes lengthy, usually
affirming, sometimes teasing, often directionless commen-
tary from me. As if my reaction were the understood purpose
of whatever they might say. They didn't seem to mind. In
fact, they looked relieved. This I chose to construe as momentum, and I was the engine, the beating heart, the man in
the middle. Everything was coming and going through me.
It felt almost showbizzy, and kind of fun, like I was Johnny
Carson or something. Which offered me the odd sensation
of stepping outside myself and watching, listening.

Which, I understood quickly, was not, or at least should
not be, preferred.

So I hit the brakes, straightened, and with some (I thought convincing) let's-get-down-to-business teacherly gravitas, asked them to take out a piece of paper and a pen and write a page about their expectations of the course and of me and of themselves. This, I recognized as it pecked through the shell, wherever it might have come from, was my big idea for the morning. I had instincts. Yes, I did. Everything would be fine. An excellent plan.

A tiny girl, feet hardly reaching the floor, asked in a little parakeet voice if a pencil would be all right. "Yes," I said, then added hilariously: "No crayon or mascara brush, though."

No one laughed.

"Is this going to be graded?" she asked, her opinion on the matter difficult to mistake.

"Of course," I said, although until that moment the practicalities of assessing anything they might produce had not occurred to me. Should have, but had not. Distantly I guess I understood at the end of our time together I would have to provide a grade of some kind for each report card; but what of the work I would have them do along the way? I hadn't thought about that. Nor by what standards or on what criteria I would assess it. Where, for example, I wondered, does the grader set his parameters? How does he know good from bad in fifteen-year-old-kid writing? What's the difference between C+ work and B–? Of what value the honest but unsuccessful effort? Does one assess differently the able but unreceptive hotshot and the less able but earnest learner? Why grade at all? Well, I'd deal with it when the time came.

Meanwhile, they got busy. Forty-five minutes ought to be enough, I figured, an hour if they really got into it. I pictured myself strolling sagely among the scribblers as they summoned reason and wit, as they composed, negotiated an impasse or two, edited, polished and rewrote. I imagined pausing now and then at a shoulder to offer quiet advice and warm encouragement.

What to do when they were done? I had forty-five minutes to figure that out.

They were finished in eight minutes, maybe seven. Every one of them.

Blinking, I collected the essays—three or four hasty sentences here, half a page there. At me all now stared. *Okay, smart guy, now what?* Meanwhile, like a madman I was scribbling cranial notes. These included Always have a Plan B. And a Plan C. And before them, of course, a good, a really solid, Plan A. A planned Plan A . . . sensible . . . edifying . . . hour-consuming. And this, too: remember, it ain't the DMcC show. For reasons numerous and valid. This also: they're the crew of this particular ship, not the passengers. I liked this last. Just came to me. I underlined it. Crew, not passengers.

So now what? We were, what, maybe seventeen minutes in? I patted the papers into a neat stack. Put them on the teacher desk. Used a stapler for a paperweight.

Okay, so . . . so . . . so how about a discussion? There. Perfect. A discussion. Let 'em earn a sense of ownership in the proceedings.

This notion, this phrasing even, felt to me quite advanced, jargony even, John Deweyish. Or what I imagined it to be. *A sense of ownership.* This I noted cranially as well. And they're the crew. And the owners. I could do this. So again I sat, posture quite correct now, donned another let's-get-down-to-business smile, rapped the desktop assertively, and asked what they'd written about. No more Here's Johnny patter. I'd wait and listen. Deftly, I'd draw them out. Engage. Prod. Challenge. Let them see, little by little, they're in this, too. Together we could do this. Captain and crew. "So?" I said. "Who's first?"

Stares.

Tsk-tsk, said the sprinklers. I called on a boy.

Sixteen syllables, tops.

Perhaps a stare would draw him out. He stared back. I called on another.

From this one maybe twelve syllables.

"So what," I tried with the next, my voice by now perhaps slightly tinny, "did you write about?"

Five. (Viz., "I don't know . . . not much.")

They looked at me. I looked at them. I pursed mỳ lips. Fought off chagrin. Fought off anger.

Them: shiftings in seats. Glances at one another. An uncomfortable giggle. Another. Then a giggle at the giggling. Then giggling at that.

All right, so our big discussion got us maybe fifty-seven seconds, with ownership, emergent or otherwise, nowhere to be found. No crew scurrying busily, happily, about the deck. No sails billowing. No Socratic dialectics—a term vaguely remembered from college and fractionally understood. No percolating ideas. No illuminated faces. No eager hands shooting up. No insights shared or challenged. No aloha for the struggling *malihini kumu*, either. Just staring. Giggling. A standoff.

Fair enough. No cracks as yet in the ol' McCullough steely calm.

I relaxed the posture, crossed my feet before me in an enough-with-the-formality pose. I waited for quiet. (And scribbled another inner note, this about body language re. stly clm, etc. It speaks, too.) What, I asked, had they read recently and liked—this more in a hale and friendly spirit of getting to know you. I was a teacher, yes . . . or, rather, perhaps . . . but I was a lover of reading and a warm and caring human being, too. Had I been able to sing and dance like Deborah Kerr perhaps I would have.

Again, though, the staring. Ricketts and Steinbeck would

deem it this organism's particular talent. Then more chitters. In unmistakable tones of *What a dolt*, the tiny girl chirped, "Didn't we just talk about this?"

Dang it. "Yes," I said. "You're right. We did."

And all of this was my fault.

We were floundering because I was floundering, and I was floundering because I was unprepared. I was unprepared because I'd overestimated myself. Teaching was not a breeze. Next note, top of the page: know what you're doing. Underline it twice. Presume to do something, have people relying on you, expect to get paid for it, you better know what you're doing. Have at least a clue. Have respect for responsibility, for good work. Make "Be Prepared" the motto of teachers, too.

We had more than an hour and a half to go. Eighteen teenagers and me.

And the relationship, I noted, was fast assuming an oppositional bent, the staring becoming disappointed, in certain regions dismissive, in a pocket or two disgusted. Who could blame them? A hundred and forty-plus years' worth of Old School Hall teachers and students were also staring at me. And John Dewey and Socrates, too. None had much use for me. And outside the tsk-tsking.

So, Dave . . . now what?

Tsk-tsk.

I would be fired and rightly. Or . . . I could just walk out the door right now. Keep walking all the way to the airport.

Tsk-tsk.

Then . . . then this: fate, my guardian angel, the un-prepared, inept, presumptuous, first-hour teacher's patron saint, something, Dewey's ghost, the Old School Hall fairy godmother, an errant *menehune* with a little time on his hands, providence itself, *something*, intervened. Beyond the starers immediate and ethereal, tucked in a bookcase against the wall opposite, sat a row of books. Books! My eye, darting about in its last stage of desperation, happened to fall upon a row of books almost concealed under a stack of bulletin-board detritus not as yet thrown away. Maybe thirty identical paperbacks, each with a look of long ne-glect. As if a switch had been thrown, I could feel gather-ing suddenly the glow of intuited recognition: I knew these books! Somewhere I'd seen them before.

I leaped, crossed the room, the starers following me with their eyes.

Holy moly and whaddaya know! Yes! These were, no fool-ing, the very short story anthologies we'd used in Mr. Herr's class my freshman year at Martha's Vineyard Regional four-teen years earlier and five thousand miles distant. The exact same book.

Hallelujah and hip, hip, hooray.

Counting nineteen, I pulled them from the shelf, gath-ered them into my arms like a thrown life ring, went around the circle, passed them out almost skippingly, as if this, of course, had been my plan all along, as if everything until now had been just clumsy prelude. Which in retrospect it was. The last I kept for myself. "Turn . . . ," I said decisively, intrepidly, commandingly, drawing out the syllable as I flipped for the table of contents, found it, ran a fleet eye down the lineup, saw a title I recognized, although I remembered the story hardly at all, something about some guys bouncing around in a dinghy, " . . . to Stephen Crane's 'The Open Boat.'"

Then we started reading. Then I started teaching. We became a class.

SINCE THAT MORNING, with a little more forethought and slightly more expertise and confidence, the ever-evolving teacherly incarnation of me has discussed "The Open Boat" with a few thousand students across just about all of the twenty-six years. In the story I am forever seeing new things, taking from it new inspiration, which is always great fun to share. And, I'll assert, beneficial to the students. Invariably I'm reminded of my first hour as a teacher. Invention, I realized then and haven't forgotten since, has a sibling: necessity is the mother of learning, too. The father would be curiosity, I think.

The story's antecedents, which I found out in the Punahou library that afternoon, are these: early in the morning of January 2, 1897, a ship sank off the east coast of Florida. Leaving Jacksonville harbor a few days earlier and bound for Cuba, the *Commodore* had twice run aground, damaging the hull both times. The captain decided to press on, but the ship's overtaxed pumps could not keep up. Then they failed altogether. Among the last into a lifeboat was the young writer Stephen Crane, who, after the recent success of his novel *The Red Badge of Courage*, had been on his way to report on an uprising in Cuba for a newspaper syndicate.

For two days Crane and three others—the captain of the ship, a cook, and a man from the engine room—bounced around in a ten-foot dinghy, short on food and water, exposed to the elements, battered by waves, not knowing if they would live or die. Crane and the man from the engine room, physically the ablest, took turns bailing and rowing. When at last they reached shore somewhere near Daytona, the dinghy capsized in the surf and, in a few feet of water, the man from the engine room drowned. From this experience came the story.

While it works quite well as a simple tale of adventure— and, if you're interested in that kind of thing, as an example of the early modernist style—"The Open Boat" is a vivid allegory of the human condition. The dinghy is the planet. The threatening but indifferent ocean is the universe. The unnamed men are you and me. Their only chance comes through vigilance, perseverance, concern for one another and unity. Still, despite the injustice of it, or at least the apparent injustice, one dies.

From the point of view of the correspondent and midway through the men's watery ordeal, we get this:

> *During this dismal night it may be remarked that a man would conclude that it was really the intention of the seven mad gods to drown him, despite the abominable injustice of it. For it was certainly an injustice to drown a man who had worked so hard, so hard. The man felt it would be a crime most unnatural. Other people had drowned at sea since galleys swarmed with painted sails, but still—*
>
> *When it occurs to man that nature does not regard him as important, and that she feels she would not maim the universe by disposing of him, he at first wishes to throw bricks at the temple, and he hates deeply the fact that there are no bricks and no temples.*

To contemporary teenagers raised in privilege, who've been coddled, often, and indulged, "The Open Boat" can be startling. It forces them to confront what they invariably term "harsh reality," a fashionable and unintentionally telling expression revealing the limitations of their comprehension of reality. Reality lacks consciousness, I point out, and therefore can have no intent. Reality simply is. Any perception of its harshness has to come, then, from unreasonable expectations of it.

What, I'll ask, of all the other victims of drowning across the millennia to whom Crane alludes? Did they want or deserve to die? Were they somehow deficient human beings? Did the ocean dislike them for some reason, just or unjust? Were the seven mad gods out to get the men in the boat for some unknown transgression? Shipwrecks happen. Train wrecks, too. Cars and planes crash. People die. You already know this. Do kids with leukemia, or muscular dystrophy, or malaria, or AIDS, or take your pick, deserve it? The victims of earthquakes, tornadoes, forest fires, mud slides, drought, privation, oppression, violence, exploitation, abuse, take your pick . . . are they somehow bad people deserving kicks in the head? Is, even, the happenstance of to whom you were born and the conditions of your upbringing cosmically appropriate?

Hardship or calamity strikes and always the inclination is to ask "Why me?" Well, why *not* you? What's so surpassingly important about you? Other people deserve these trials but somehow you do not? The better question would be, as the German soldier asks in Kurt Vonnegut's *Slaughterhouse-Five*, why anybody? Fairness, justice, these are constructs that work only within a human community. So we better be very sure they do work.

We are all, Crane reminds us, regardless of merit real or perceived, in the same open boat, on the same planet, vulnerable to whatever comes our way. Essential to the men in the story, therefore, as it should be to each of us, is a spirit of selflessness and mutual respect, of brotherhood, of working together, working hard, for the common good— particularly those in a position to bail and row. This is the best kind of gratifying: to be helpful for the sake of others to the limits of one's ability. To a circle of contemporary high school kids sensing unspoken competition with one another—for grades, for a spot on the team, for a part in the play, for admission to USC, for simple affirming attention—the concept is significant. "It would be difficult to describe," Crane writes, "the subtle brotherhood of men that was here established on the seas. No one said that it was so. No one mentioned it. But it dwelt in the boat, and each man felt it warm him."

Because these ideas are revelatory, because they cut to the heart of their culture, and what they sense ails them, kids over the years have responded eagerly and well to Mr. Crane. The realities illuminated by his story liberate them from the burdens of certain me-centered attitudes encouraged by their culture and upbringing. They're in the spotlight always, the subject of unending attention, parental doting and prodding and judgment and expectations at school and beyond, which can be isolating. And stifling. And misleading. This spirit of comradeship appeals not only to their sense of community, of belonging, but, concurrently and maybe a bit ironically, to the rebellious instinct at the ready in most teenagers. You're supposed to be in it for you, they've been led to believe, because you're exceptional. You're special. With accolades to win, with all the expected rights, privileges and dividends yours to enjoy. Crane's idea that we're all in this together becomes to them, then, not just the refrain to a cheery/cheesy number in *High School Musical*, but an earned and therefore exhilarating truth.

And a relief: as one of many, they don't have to perform forever to an exaggerated ideal that might at the moment be beyond them. They're free to be themselves, purely and simply. Which is not just good enough, but great . . . great in ways that have nothing to do with how they stack up against the competition. Being ordinary, they find, is not a curse, not shameful. They're part, they see, of the biggest, most relevant group; humanity. Because they've learned something that matters to them, seen something of a few larger truths about life and themselves, they feel a renewed faith in the possibilities of their education in the abstract and an hour of class in the concrete. And reading, too. And the teacher. They'll come back the next day ready for a little more.

That's what happened, or started to, that long-ago morning in Old School Hall.

A GREAT UNIFIER is the high school classroom. Any kind of kid imaginable can walk through the door and sit with twenty or so other incarnations of any kind of kid imaginable. The potential for variety, then, and exciting interplay, is endless, with the time and place and purpose and experience pulling them together. And the teacher, too. They see what they have in common and why it matters. They also see how they're unique and why that matters. When I think of all the young people, the interesting, worthy individuals, who have come together in a classroom with me, thousands of them, my head swims. There is parity in the classroom, too, absolutely, and equality, at least in the ideal—and in a classroom ideals have a better chance than anywhere else. In concert with the teacher—or even in opposition to him or her—students are, like the crew of Melville's *Pequod* but with better prospects—federated along one keel.

Now that I've been at it a few decades and in settings six time zones apart, I see this unity transcends time and place: those summer school kids in Old School Hall in 1986 are in most ways that matter just like the kids of Wellesley High today . . . all of them, each one, important. Taking up the pickax and heading into the diamond mine day after day with a cheery "Hi ho!" yields diamonds, certainly, or it can—but even more reliably it yields the fabulous wealth of one another's company, the spirit of a shared endeavor, the spark of human connection. It's difficult to describe the subtle brother- and sisterhood established in a classroom. No one says it's so. No one mentions it. But it dwells there, and students and their teacher feel it warm them.

Chapter 10

So Live

Men must endure
Their going hence, even as their coming hither;
Ripeness is all.
—*King Lear* by William Shakespeare

As she'd been with the first two, Janice was gutsy and beautiful and heroic in delivering number three. He arrived, though, with lungs full of gunk, and not four seconds after touchdown, a commando team, hushed and determined, swept into the room, scooped him up and went to work. Janice was so spent she hardly noticed. I noticed. Within moments, though, after a quick this and hurried that, everything was fine: the little guy was squawking in robust displeasure, his color a magnificent crimson. Dispensing to me calm reassurances and congratulations, the squad of doctors and nurses collected their things and moved along.

But those fifteen or twenty seconds were enough. My heart was throwing hand grenades against a hollow rib cage. Minutes passed before I could commence the new father's elation. Then the kisses and the marveling and the hoorays and the holy mackerels and the phone calls . . . all just a little tentative thanks to those first fifteen or twenty seconds.

After allowing us some snuggling time, a nurse came and brought the baby down to the nursery, as they do, so the pediatrician could give him the once-over. I followed along, asking my questions. Calm and kind, she did her best to answer them. Then, patting my arm, she suggested I keep an eye on the proceedings from the window. This was at Kapiolani Medical Center, a big maternity hospital just down the street from Punahou, where dozens of babies arrive every day. It was nearing midnight. The nursery was brightly lit and pretty close to standing room only: in regimented lines and rows of clear plastic bins atop stainless-steel rigs, snug in cotton blankets, tiny knit caps pulled tight, lay eighteen or more peapods with wee tiny faces. I watched the pediatrician across the way unwrap Ethan (we'd named him during the snuggling . . . it means strong, firm and safe) and begin her examination. She was steady and focused and professional. She and the nurse showed no sign of alarm. Or even concern. The nurse said something and the doctor smiled. The doctor said something and the nurse smiled and nodded.

And whatever it was that had tightened around my throat, began, little by little, to loosen. Breathing came easier, deeper. Each exhale fogged the window in little deltas beneath my nose. Here, I was thinking, is the real cathedral. And that's my baby boy. Ethan McCullough. This is his life beginning. All of these . . . sweet new lives beginning.

"Kinda funny, isn't it?" said a voice.

This, I determined with a glimpse, was a man in an aloha shirt at the far end of the nursery window, both of us peering in. Another new dad, no doubt. I hadn't noticed he was there. His tone, though, was pure buddy-buddy, as if the two of us were eating peanuts together at a ball game. I had a funny urge to go over and shake his hand.

"The only thing you can say for sure about each one of them is they're gonna die someday. Every one."

For a second I wondered if I'd heard him right. But of course I had. Die. He'd said "die." And when I felt the heat rise and the canine grin emerge, I'll confess, not proudly, my impulse was to ball a fist and pop him one. Blame the Celt in me. *Die?* What kind of a jerk would say such a thing? Instead, I clenched the molars and contented myself with a look and a semihostile . . . okay, fully hostile "What?"

He made a vaguely apologetic shrug, which he garnished

with a stupid-me grin. "Just saying," he tried with a friendly little laugh.

New fathers are forgiving, full to the brim with the milk of human kindness, so I holstered the fist and offered instead a diplomatic obviousness about long, full lives before the reaper comes calling.

"Definitely," he hurried to agree, "definitely. Absolutely. Goes without saying."

The doctor had her stethoscope at my half-an-hour-old son's chest. The nurse was holding a clipboard and writing on it as the doctor spoke. The doctor said something and the nurse smiled and nodded.

"So," the man said, "boy or girl?"

"Boy," I answered, over my shoulder, already on my way back to Janice.

But, of course, one day Ethan will die. (How difficult it is for me to type those words, to countenance even the thought, no matter its irrefutability.) So will I. (Much easier.) So will the doctor and the nurse, and every baby in that room, and Janice and that guy. And so will you.

This is the real goes-without-saying. We all know it, but we try very hard not to.

Which is the great human predicament.

While everything ends—all creatures great and small, and the great blue and green globe itself, and the moon and the stars as well, and whatever might lie beyond them, and whatever comes after them, too—we are the only ones who know it will end. We get on Walt Whitman's Brooklyn ferry fully aware we will soon enough . . . too soon . . . have to get off. The squirrel dashing around in the tree outside my window just now has no idea death awaits, has no idea there's a lethal microbe or a Goodyear Ultra Grip out there somewhere with his name on it, or a red-tailed hawk riding a proximate updraft and flexing its talons. We human beings, though, get to live and love life, get to jump out of bed and, singing a bit, feel a hot shower on the back of the neck and towel off and enjoy a cold glass of cranapple juice and a warm blueberry muffin and merry thoughts of the sunshiny day ahead . . . and at the same time we're aware this morning, like all mornings, is one of a finite and ever-diminishing number of mornings, that each morning we subtract another from the total, that one day that total will zero out and, as William Cullen Bryant puts it, we the all-beholding sun shall see no more. The preferred method of handling this chilling reality is to not think about it. Goes without saying. Goes, even, without thinking.

Which doesn't matter. Think about it, don't think about it . . . death doesn't care. Your tap on the shoulder, mine, will come either way. And it's patient, death.

"If it be now," the ever-pensive Hamlet explains, "'tis not to come. If it be not to come, it will be now. If it be not now, yet it will come." To hero and coward alike, it will come. To the stoic, the whiner, the ascetic, the wastrel, the kind, the cruel, to the bold, the brilliant, the generous, the courageous, the inventive, the beautiful, the snide, the snobby, the loving, it will come. To everyone. Says Thomas Gray in his sublime weeper "Elegy Written in a Country Churchyard":

> The boast of heraldry, the pomp of power,
> And all that beauty, all that wealth e'er gave,
> Awaits alike the inevitable hour.
> The paths of glory lead but to the grave.

A safe claim, that, as all paths lead to the same place.

Hence the universal lump of dread lodged in the collective throat. And all the meek contingencies. Unconsciously we use language to mitigate reality, to clear the passage for easier breathing, which clouds comprehension. The effect is soporific. A few paragraphs ago, for example, I personified death, which implies intentionality and therefore governing reason, which suggests that while I might not like it, my death seems to fit some larger plan, which makes it at least slightly less difficult to accept. Although not to me, to someone somewhere, some able consciousness, my death evidently seems apt. And, further, "death" is a noun. Ontologically misleading. Death is not, cannot be, a person, place or thing. Death is not a state of being; rather, it is the absence of being, a nonstate. The great negation. It's not, then, even an "it." Shuffle off the mortal coil and there's nothing. Empty space. So we do not, we cannot, experience death. There's nothing there to experience it with, nor to find comfort in the remembered life however happy and full. Death is *nothingness*, last and lasting, the ultimate non-noun. If verbs are your thing, with the arrival of death one goes, irretrievably, from present to past tense with hardly a gulp between. One does not then pass away; one vanishes.

And, sooner than we'd like, it will happen to you and to me and the squirrel in the tree, and the tree, and the lichen on the tree, and the worm under the tree, and the talon-flexing hawk above the tree and, in a different lichen-clad tree, which will also die, all the talon-flexing hawk's hatchlings waiting at present for lunch. That any of this seems to us unfair, even cruel, is immaterial and presupposes life and its perpetuation as something other than the scientific and metaphysical miracles for which we ought to be nothing but amazed and grateful.

Not that they could change things—or maybe because they couldn't—brains far better than mine have been trying to make sense of these realities since long before man was decorating the walls of caves. Inevitably, all religion, all art, all philosophy come back to this: we die.

In his quietly chilling "Aubade," for example, the poet

Philip Larkin confronts the "total emptiness of for ever." His leaden anguish is paralyzing: "Unresting death, a whole day nearer now,/Making all thought impossible but how/ And where and when I shall myself die." In 1985, eight years after writing these lines, Larkin bowed to the cold inevitability. Sixty-two years before that he was born. The time between he spent mostly, it appears, among ideas . . . in libraries, where he worked, and at his poet's desk, where he worked, too, but in other ways. He had his friendships, a few romances. He and his poems were much admired and celebrated, here and in England, where he lived. This attention made him uncomfortable: he liked the quiet life, and his friends, and his thoughts. He dreaded death. Then one day cancer killed him.

Which brings to mind this: let us neither overlook the agonies of getting there, the physical, emotional, psychological, torment of dying. The final infirmity. Often protracted. Often horribly painful. Always terminal. Also the suffering of the loving family and friends we leave behind. There's that, too. All part of it. And there's accidents. Gaspingly sudden. Or disasters. Or villainy.

None of this is cheery.

Nor, certainly, are thoughts of decomposition, of physical disintegration into base elements. Every last trace of you gone. Even tombstones erode. And legacies fade. Ask Ozymandias.

Also, let's not forget all the kicks and giggles of aging. Normal aging consequent to a ticking clock, a beating heart. Early-stage dying, the autumnal decline, the aches, the pains, the indignities, the struggles and capitulations, the slowing-downs, the wearing-downs, the thinning-outs. All the abilities, strengths and elasticities of youth, the fullness, the smoothness, the tautness, the beauty and bounce, the energy, the unwitting confidence, the instinctive optimism, the ease, the grace, the clear eye, the thick lustrous hair, the dewy breath . . . all of it going or gone before you realize they're what you've been taking for granted, and they're temporary. It's inevitable, aging, linear, punctuated and irreversible—despite what Ponce de Leon and purveyors of assorted cosmetic products and surgical procedures would have you believe. Except for what you've witnessed and mostly willfully denied in the old people of your acquaintance, nothing in your experience prepares you for what will come: you've always been young, after all, every change an improvement—taller, stronger, more capable.

Then the plateau, and then, soon enough, by degrees, the inexorable decline. Which can be, often is, ungentle. The only anodyne lies in what's left, but that's diminishing, too. Yes, there are memories, and in sleep dreams, but after a certain point both can, will, taunt as much as comfort. And memory is porous. Dreams evanesce. And always the unrelenting cadence as winter's chill approaches.

And while the universe in even its broadest definitions exists separate from our awareness of it, not so our experience of even the smallest part of it. To each and all the universe exists only because he or she, or they, has a consciousness with which to conceive it. We live, then, within the limits of our comprehension. Eliminate the consciousness and you eliminate the grand entirety. When at last the electricity in your few pounds of gelatinous stuff sputters out for good, that's that. Next stop, dust. So we love life, not just for the pleasures of living, ladling from the universe where and while we can and as we will, but for the affirmation against nothingness that is the endeavor. This is, we realize, our moment. "Only that day dawns to which we are awake," said the sage of Walden. So we arise—at least ideally—and have at it.

For this reason and others, then, reasons impossible to refute, death is a good thing.

Yes, it is.

And here's why: nothing is what it is by itself. Everything is what it is only in relation to what it's not. The antithesis of life—and therefore the human spirit, and the self, the conscious mind, the courageous, loving heart—death is the unwavering opposition against which we define ourselves, against which all living nature defines itself. Against which *being* defines and asserts itself.

The great and simple universal dialectic is this: there is everything and there is nothing. Death, then, makes precious all that is not death. This is the exhilarating, the transcendent, beauty of birth, of babies, of children. Of teenagers. And of school, too. Each is an iteration of love. Of optimism. Of energy. The looming black enormity at the end of the road gives life and love urgency and thereby meaning. That death wins in the end makes any assertion against it not futile but beautiful and heroic—a refusal of self-pity and despair. An avowal that life is glorious. A quiet December snowfall, the kiss of a girl in love, a slab of chocolate cake with fudgy frosting that thick, the smell of a baby's hair, Lanikai beach at sunrise, the New York Philharmonic laying into *Rhapsody in Blue*, a good day's work, kindness, books, big laughs at the dinner table, a Wodehouse turn of phrase, moonlight, a sharp liner to left with a runner on second, leaning on the accelerator with the open road stretching into distant hills . . . the list has no limit. Yet each would be meaningless without a certain awareness of our own ephemerality, our own transitory capacity to experience and enjoy whatever it might be. Because life is temporary, all its pleasures glow.

Here fundamental principles of economics apply, supply and demand, scarcity and value. Were life eternal, day after day ad infinitum, not only would the planet be pretty crowded,* not only would your 93× great-grandfather's un-

---

* And then try Fresh Pond Circle at rush hour.

ending armchair bloviations get just a bit tiresome, but simply through blunt repetition all of life's pleasures would fade to gray. Fade? They'd never be anything but the drabbest, dullest gray. Life would be an exercise in meaninglessness, a metronomic, arithmetical bludgeoning, slow-drip torture, an inert, eternal, unrelenting *Who cares?* And the living the animated dead.

Run with this a minute: in eliminating death are we also then eliminating change? At what stage of life would evolving, growing, improving cease? Would we top out at, say, thirty? Should I assume, then, we're eliminating illness, too, and accidents? War and murder would have to go, of course, but what about suicide? So once you're in there's no way out. And how in perpetual stasis would we handle procreation without the standard processes of maturation and decline? Or, alternatively, would we procreate and age at the expected pace and in the current fashion and just get older and older and older, and more grizzled, and smaller and feebler and more desiccated, and older and older still, and wrinklier, and weaker, and tinier, and drier, and more fragile, more shriveled, more somnolent, more cadaverous, and just not die, just sit there, lie there, a blinking, gasping pile of dandruff, dentures and opinions?

Sounds fun, huh?

Not eleven seconds with it and from every angle the notion becomes pungently absurd. Odysseus had his chance and said, sensibly, thanks but no thanks. Had he not, were he still here, in whatever condition, he'd explain, I think, his mistake.

No, the true tragedy of death is our denial of it, because in our denials, our mollifications, our delusional evasions, we undermine our capacities, or, worse, our inclinations, to make the most of the brief and finite time we have. While it might appear not much—nor, in any case, is it the point, really—the best fist we can shake at death is the well-lived life. The full, happy, loving, fruitful life. For the living every moment can have, should have, beauty and meaning. The truly alive are those who with their full energy savor being alive. This by itself is generative, the opposite of death. Every stage of life is a pleasure, or can be, because it is part of the full arc of experience. This is our triumph. The challenge lies in making it happen, which requires strength and heart and imagination. At the end of Thornton Wilder's wise and timeless *Our Town*, young Emily Webb, who has just died, wonders with a plaintive cry whether anyone ever appreciates life fully and without relent.

Too often the answer is no. This is our tragedy.

The admonishments go back further than the printed word—forgetful learners, we—and continue through today's ubiquitous and emphatic though syntactically problematic YOLO. "Carpe diem," said the poet Horace in the first century BC, and one guesses he was not the first to the party. "Gather ye rosebuds while ye may," said the poet Herrick seventeen hundred years later. "They are not long," said the poet Dowson two and a half centuries after that, "the days of wine and roses." These are chestnuts of long standing, no less potent for their familiarity. Staying along horticultural lines, the poet Wordsworth points out "nothing can bring back the hour of splendor in the grass, of glory in the flower." Stated or implied, the message is the same: get up, get out, get busy. Joy is an active endeavor, life an adventure, youth but a moment, love a blessing. "So live," says the poet Bryant with admirable frugality. "Try," says William Saroyan, "to learn to breathe deeply; really to taste food when you eat, and when you sleep really to sleep. Try as much as possible to be wholly alive with all your might, and when you laugh, laugh like hell." And here with Hibernian magnanimity is Jonathan Swift: "May you live all the days of your life."

Let's leave it there and call it consensus. For all the rivers of ink spread on this subject, there can be no final word, for there is ever a new word. Make yours next. Every life is a poet's license, and death a revocation.

I DID NOT KNOW Miki Bowers well. He and I never came to be what anyone would presume to call friends. I liked and admired him right away, though, which appeared universal at Punahou. A mathematics teacher of national renown, Miki was an institution, a legend, really, at the school and across the islands. He was a kindly man, too, slightly eccentric, tall and strong and indomitably energetic, with an aquiline face, a white buzz cut and the alligator skin of decades scorching in the tropical sun. He wore starched short-sleeve shirts and a bow tie, always a bow tie, and carried himself with correct military bearing—he'd left Stanford in '45 to join up, then commanded an artillery battalion in Vietnam, earning medals for valor. In a barrel-chested baritone he spoke loudly, confidently. You'd hear him in the cafeteria, at faculty meetings, along the paths, and singing—*booming*—in chapel. When Miki Bowers was around you knew it.

And he was happy . . . enormously, infectiously happy. He loved his family. He loved Punahou—he'd been a student and athlete and musician there for thirteen years, an authentic big man on campus, and, by the time he retired, a highly effective teacher and coach for more than four decades. He loved Hawaii and his country. He loved the Punahou Carnival; he was, famously, the "Malasada Man." He loved to sing Hawaiian songs, too, and did so at the least provocation and exuberantly and, in his manner, well— his volcanic rendition of "Hawaiian Cowboy" will resonate through the ages. And rattle teeth. In the early 1960s he even had his own "Sing Along with Miki" radio show— although within, say, a half-mile radius one would have thought a radio unnecessary. Every morning he would be up well before dawn and out the door and down to the beach at Ala Moana for a good long swim, then at his desk ready to go long before the first of his students arrived. Miki loved advanced calculus and introductory algebra and anything in between. At one time or another he taught every math course the school offered. And he loved kids, too, believed in them. Teaching for him was simply sharing uncontainable enthusiasm. For which he was widely revered, although I sometimes wondered if he noticed.

Through my first weeks at Punahou he and I would pass each other on campus and he'd nod a smiling hello. To me that alone felt like something. Then at lunch one day in October I spotted him taking a seat at an empty table. I hightailed it over and asked if I might join him. The hope was to do a little absorbing. Here was the novice, all right, young and earnest, seating himself at the great man's knee. What I wanted was wisdom, a bit of the long view, and maybe a trade secret or two. Something on which to proceed. I had, after all, more than a hundred students relying on me to do them some good, and on that note the jury was still out.

After the expected pleasantries, I asked, not quite tugging a forelock, what advice he might have for a new teacher. Blue eyes igniting, a grin erupting as if he'd been waiting all morning for just such a question, Miki leaned his big face at me and with an open hand gave the table a whack. "Bruddah," he bellowed—through the years he would always call me that—"just *love* it! Love everything!" To be sure I got it he banged the table again. Then, settling back in his seat, he hoisted a new smile, the kind often described as wry. "And have an idea what you're talking about."

That was it. Miki Bowers's wisdom—all, it seemed, I and anyone like me needed to know—and not just about teaching, obviously. No elaboration necessary. The old artillery man had nailed it. Then he proceeded directly to twisting my arm to proctor an upcoming session of the SAT.

Years later, soon to be seventy, Miki made the sad announcement that at last the time had come. His step, he said, had slowed. Even Hawaiian cowboys have to hang 'em up eventually. Through the spring there were celebrations, tributes, parties. Hardly able to see over the leis piled about his neck, he would grab his uke and sing. Punahou does ceremonies beautifully, especially farewells. For Miki's the school pulled all the stops. Through those final days there was much food and music and laughter and some tears and long embraces. Aloha 'oe, Miki. Until we meet again.

And as it would, of course, not three months later school resumed. A new year. I returned to campus and found Miki's desk was no longer Miki's desk. There another teacher sat. A new crowd of students filed into what for so long had been Miki's classroom. No baritone boomed in chapel. Others sat at that table in the faculty lunchroom. All around the campus, by the mailboxes and the copiers and in the lounge and lunchroom and to and from class, teachers chatted about all the usuals, and kids worked and learned and lazed around and dashed off to the library and to water polo practice and chatted about their usuals, too. As it always does, soon enough the school year gathered momentum, and the weeks, the months, rolled by. And through it all, nothing, not a single syllable I ever heard, was said of Miki Bowers. He was gone. The school had moved on. It was as if he'd never been there.

This too was a lesson.

Twelve and a half years later, at the age of eighty-three, Miki died. On New Year's Day.

MY MARCHING ORDERS LITERARY, early in those Punahou days I began sharing with my students Nikos Kazantzakis's philosophy-disguised-as-fiction *Zorba the Greek*, as I have every year since for reasons rich and many. In his winning earthy wisdom, the lusty coal miner gets it in my view just about exactly right: to be a fulfilled human being is to be free . . . from expectation, from inhibition, from envy, from fear. Man needs folly, says Zorba. Do what you do purely for the sake of the delight it brings you, says Zorba. Indulge your passions. Engage your imagination. Commit to the moment. Live. Give it all you have. Let outcomes be what they will. I think Miki Bowers would agree.

As he does on the reader as well, the great voracious Zorba goes to work on the yearning, inhibited, intellectual narrator. At last—this many pages and many lessons in—finding himself in a field of wildflowers on a sunlit mountain slope in Crete, the narrator gets it. He has his epiphany and the novel its climax. "Little by little," he tells us in an elated burst, "everything around me, without changing shape, became a dream. I was happy. Earth and paradise were one. A flower in the fields with a large drop of honey in its center; that was how life appeared to me. And my soul, a wild bee plundering."

Soon thereafter, as eventually every student and teacher must, the narrator and Zorba part. Just before the novel ends, we learn of Zorba's death. He was somewhere in Serbia, married to a spirited and much younger woman. His last words, we're told, were these: "I've done heaps of things in my life, but I still did not do enough. Men like me ought to live a thousand years. Good night!" Then he struggled out of bed and went to the window, laughed, whinnied like a horse and, standing there, holding fast to the window frame, looking off into the mountains, died.

Even in dying Zorba rejects death. Albeit merely symbolic, this is a kind of triumph, the triumph of life.

On the day Ethan was born nearly fourteen years ago he was joined, we were joined, by 350,000 other new arrivals, give or take, worldwide. What a sight that would have made through the nursery window. Not all of them are with us still. Alas. One day too soon, however distant, none will be. Until then, though, I hope all are, or will be soon and ever thereafter and to the last limit, wild bees plundering. So too the next day's batch, and the next.

And so too, reader, you. Love everything.

Afterword

A WEEK BEFORE THE WELLESLEY HIGH SCHOOL COMmencement, having to that point thought about the speech pretty close to not at all, I loaded daughter and laptop into the pickup and drove down to New Jersey for another soccer tournament. Leah did homework much of the way. I mulled.

The next morning I got up early and wrote with what I guess I'd have to call an alacrity of purpose. Mostly what came out were distillations of what I've been saying in the classroom one way or another for a long time. (One unpacks what's in one's duffle.) Over the next few days I left it alone. Two nights before the ceremony, though, when we'd finished the after-dinner cleanup and the house had quieted, Janice offered to sit and let me read it to her so I could hear how it sounded. "What for?" I said. "Nobody listens to these things anyway."

This I'll confess was partly a dodge. I wanted very much to give to the graduates something that would matter to them as they headed out the door, something of value. Finishing high school is no small event—and the responsibility and fondness a teacher feels for her or his students come the end of May are powerful, so too sentiment at the thought of seeing them go. This, I'm finding, intensifies with age. For the kids it's a giddy, almost delirious, time of year and rightly; but for teachers . . . for this teacher anyway . . . not so much. Not at all. Most of them I'll never see again. While I really hadn't any idea how they might react to it, I was pleased with what I'd written and hopeful—the way a cook with guests coming up the front walk must be. I didn't want to hear Janice say at this late stage some version of "Not pot roast!" And she would have had she thought it.

But my darling wife is one of the species' truly gifted practitioners of the raised eyebrow. Up it went and I relented. In the living room we sat and I read it to her. When I finished she nodded. "It's good," she said and sweetly.

I do wish now I'd eased off on the "you're not special" refrain and its variants. Rhetorical device or no, I hit that note too often. Cumulatively it starts to sound redundant, even a little hectoring. More helpful, I think, would have been a moment's scrutiny of the concept of exceptionalism and its consequences of a kind I've tried to offer across some of these pages, or even a chuckle at the meaning-draining triteness, the treacly preciousness, of the word "special" and its covert intimations of superiority and entitlement. I also wish I'd caught my boneheaded slipup in calling "pursuit" a verb. But, well, one carries on.

Forty-something hours later, after other fine speeches, I stepped to the podium. This is what I said:

Dr. Wong, Dr. Keough, Mrs. Novogroski, Ms. Curran, members of the board of education, family and friends of the graduates, ladies and gentlemen of the Wellesley High School class of 2012, for the privilege of speaking to you this afternoon, I am honored and grateful. Thank you.

So here we are . . . commencement . . . life's great forward-looking ceremony. (And don't say, "What about weddings?" Weddings are one-sided and insufficiently effective. Weddings are bride-centric pageantry. Other than conceding to a list of unreasonable demands, the groom just stands there. No stately, hey-everybody-look-at-me procession. No being given away. No identity-changing pronouncement. And can you imagine a television show dedicated to watching guys try on tuxedos? Their fathers sitting there misty-eyed with joy and disbelief, their brothers lurking in the corner muttering with envy. Left to men, weddings would be, after limits-testing procrastination, spontaneous, almost inadvertent . . . during half-time . . . on the way to the refrigerator. And there's the frequency of failure: statistics tell us half of you will get divorced. A winning percentage like that'll get you last place in the American League East. The Baltimore Orioles do better than weddings.)

But this ceremony . . . commencement . . . a commencement works every time. From this day forward . . . truly . . . in sickness and in health, through financial fiascos, through midlife crises and passably attractive sales reps at trade shows in Cincinnati, through diminishing tolerance for annoyingness, through every difference, irreconcilable and otherwise, you will stay forever graduated from high school, you and your diploma one, 'til death do you part.

No, commencement is life's great ceremonial beginning, with its own attendant and highly appropriate symbolism. Fitting, for example, for this auspicious rite of passage, is where we find ourselves this afternoon, the venue. Normally, I avoid clichés like the plague, wouldn't touch them with a ten-foot pole, but here we are on a literal level playing field. That matters. That says something. And your ceremonial costume . . . shapeless, uniform, one-size-fits-all. Whether male or female, tall or short, scholar or slacker, spray-tanned prom queen or intergalactic Xbox assassin, each of you is dressed, you'll notice, exactly the same. And your diploma . . . but for your name, exactly the same.

All this is as it should be, because none of you is special.

You are not special. You are not exceptional.

Contrary to what your U-9 soccer trophy suggests, your glowing seventh grade report card, despite every assurance of a certain corpulent purple dinosaur, that nice Mister Rogers and your batty aunt Sylvia, no matter how often your maternal caped crusader has swooped in to save you . . . you're nothing special.

Yes, you've been pampered, cosseted, doted upon, helmeted, bubble-wrapped. Yes, capable adults with other things to do have held you, kissed you, fed you, wiped your mouth, wiped your bottom, trained you, taught you, tutored you, coached you, listened to you, counseled you, encouraged you, consoled you and encouraged you again. You've been nudged, cajoled, wheedled and implored. You've been feted and fawned over and called sweetie pie. Yes, you have. And, certainly, we've been to your games, your plays, your recitals, your science fairs. Absolutely, smiles ignite when you walk into a room, and hundreds gasp with delight at your every tweet. Why, maybe you've even had your picture in the *Townsman*! And now you've conquered high school . . . and, indisputably, here we all have gathered for you, the pride and joy of this fine community, the first to emerge from that magnificent new building . . .

But do not get the idea you're anything special. Because you're not.

The empirical evidence is everywhere, numbers even an English teacher can't ignore. Newton, Natick, Nee . . . I am allowed to say Needham, yes? . . . that has to be two thousand high school graduates right there, give or take, and that's just the neighborhood Ns. Across the country no fewer than 3.2 million seniors are graduating about now from more than 37,000 high schools. That's 37,000 valedictorians . . . 37,000 class presidents . . . 92,000 harmonizing altos . . . 340,000 swaggering jocks . . . 2,185,967 pairs of Uggs. But why limit ourselves to high school? After all, you're leaving it. So think about this: even if you're one in a million, on a planet of 6.8 billion that means there are nearly 7,000 people just like you. Imagine standing somewhere over there on Washington Street on Marathon Monday and watching sixty-eight hundred yous go running by. And consider for a moment the bigger picture: your planet, I'll remind you, is not the center of its solar system, your solar system is not the center of its galaxy, your galaxy is not the center of the universe. In fact, astrophysicists assure us the universe has no center; therefore, you cannot be it. Neither can Donald Trump . . . which someone should tell him . . . although that hair is quite a phenomenon.

"But, Dave," you cry, "Walt Whitman tells me I'm my own version of perfection! Epictetus tells me I have the spark of Zeus!" And I don't disagree. So that makes 6.8 billion examples of perfection, 6.8 billion sparks of Zeus. You see, if everyone is special, then no one is. If everyone gets a trophy, trophies become meaningless. In our unspoken but not so subtle Darwinian competition with one another—which springs, I think, from our fear of our own insignificance, a subset of our dread of mortality—we have of late, we Americans, to our detriment, come to love accolades more than genuine achievement. We have come to see them as the point—and we're happy to compromise standards, or ignore reality, if we suspect that's the quickest way, or only way, to have something to put on the mantelpiece, something to pose with, crow about, something with which to leverage ourselves into a better spot on the social totem pole. No longer is it how you play the game, no longer is it even whether you win or lose, or learn or grow, or enjoy yourself doing it. Now it's "So what does this get me?" As a consequence, we cheapen worthy endeavors, and building a Guatemalan medical clinic becomes more about the application to Bowdoin than the well-being of Guatemalans. It's an epidemic—and in its way, not even dear old Wellesley High is immune . . . one of the best of the 37,000 nationwide, Wellesley High School . . . where good is no longer good enough, where a B is the new C, and the midlevel curriculum is called Advanced College Placement. And I hope you caught me when I said "one of the best." I said "one of the best" so we can feel better about ourselves, so we can bask in a little easy distinction, however vague and unverifiable, and count ourselves among the elite, whoever they might be, and enjoy a perceived leg up on the perceived competition. But the phrase defies logic. By definition there can be only one best. You're it or you're not.

If you've learned anything in your years here I hope it's that education should be for, rather than material advantage, the exhilaration of learning. You've learned, too, I hope, as Sophocles assured us, that wisdom is the chief element of happiness. (Second is ice cream . . . just an FYI.) I also hope you've learned enough to recognize how little you know . . . how little you know *now* . . . at the moment . . . for today is just the beginning. It's where you go from here that matters.

As you commence, then, and before you scatter to the winds, I urge you to do whatever you do for no reason other than you love it and believe in its importance. Don't bother with work you don't believe in anymore than you would a spouse you're not crazy about, lest you too find yourself on the wrong side of a Baltimore Orioles comparison. Resist the easy comforts of complacency, the specious glitter of materialism, the narcotic paralysis of self-satisfaction. Be worthy of your advantages. And read . . . read all the time . . . read as a matter of principle, as a matter of self-respect. Read as a nourishing staple of life. Develop and protect a moral sensibility and demonstrate the character to apply it. Dream big. Work hard. Think for yourself. Love everything you love, everyone you love, with all your might. And do so, please, with a sense of urgency, for every tick of the clock subtracts from fewer and fewer; and as surely as there are commencements there are cessations, and you'll be in no condition to enjoy the ceremony attendant to that eventuality no matter how delightful the afternoon.

The fulfilling life, the distinctive life, the relevant life, is an achievement, not something that will fall into your lap because you're a nice person or Mommy ordered it from the caterer. You'll note the founding fathers took pains to secure your inalienable right to life, liberty and the *pursuit* of happiness—quite an active verb, "pursuit"—which leaves, I should think, little time for lying around watching parrots roller-skate on YouTube. The first President Roosevelt, the old Rough Rider, advocated the strenuous life. Mr. Thoreau wanted to drive life into a corner, to live deep and suck out all the marrow. The poet Mary Oliver tells us to row, row into the swirl and roil. Locally, someone . . . I forget who . . . from time to time encourages young scholars to carpe the heck out of the diem. The point is the same: get busy, have at it. Don't wait for inspiration or passion to find you. Get up, get out, explore, find it yourself and grab hold with both hands. (Now, before you dash off and get your YOLO tattoo, let me point out the illogic of that trendy little expression—because you can and should live not merely once, but every day of your life. Rather than You Only Live Once, it should be You Live Only Once . . . but because YLOO doesn't have the same ring, we shrug and decide it doesn't matter.)

None of this day seizing, though, this YLOOing, should be interpreted as license for self-indulgence. Like accolades ought to be, the fulfilling life is a consequence, a gratifying byproduct. It's what happens when you're thinking about more important things. Climb the mountain not to plant your flag, but to embrace the challenge, enjoy the air and behold the view. Climb it so you can see the world, not so the world can see you. Go to Paris to be in Paris, not to cross it off your list and congratulate yourself for being worldly. Exercise free will and creative, independent thought not for the satisfactions they will bring you, but for the good they will do others, the rest of the 6.8 billion—and those who will follow them. And then you too will discover the great and curious truth of the human experience is that selflessness is the best thing you can do for yourself. The sweetest joys of life, then, come only with the recognition that you're not special.

Because everyone is.

Congratulations. Good luck. Make for yourselves, please, for your sake and ours, extraordinary lives.

Schools are a manifestation of love—of parents for their children, of teachers for their students, of learning, of humanity, of life. And like Heraclitus's river of old, you can't step into the same school twice. On it flows, child after child after child. All is flux there, too—and, done right, good work, good fun, inspiriting growth. Minds blossom. Wisdom begins. Lives are made. Lives are saved. And we're several months along now, the kids busy, as ever, being—

intently being—kids. The Wellesley High School class of 2012 is gone, most of them members of the class of 2016 somewhere else. They're happy, I hope, and working hard—making a point of it—reading good things, reading all the time, and feeling free, too, I hope, and loving their days and nights and all they're learning, and eager for what's to come.

How often I think of them.

Acknowledgments

In writing this book I have been helped and encouraged by a number of kind and able people to whom I am very grateful. From the beginning, Amy Williams, my agent, has been an essential source of energy, wise counsel, bright spirits and sustaining confidence. At Ecco, Dan Halpern's quiet faith in an untried writer has inspired through all weather. Hilary Redmon, my editor, has brought to the project great intelligence, enthusiasm, consideration and an astute critical eye. I count myself most fortunate to work with them, and to call them friends.

Friends of far longer standing are Doc Berry, Miles Byrne, Bill Hill, Drew Kelton, Steve Lemenager, Jarrid Whitney and Karyn Wilson, who read part or all of the manuscript and offered much valued insight, criticism and support, as did my nephew Tyler McDonald. My brothers, Bill McCullough and Geoffrey McCullough; my sisters, Dorie Lawson and Melissa McDonald; my nephew Jed McDonald; my nieces Caroline McCullough, Louisa McCullough, Nellie McCullough, and Caitlin McDonald;

friends Shelley Arakawa, Winter Chernak, Jamie Chisum, Andy Cohen, Ann Duffy, Connor Farrell, Anne Ferguson, Joe Finigan, Ronna Frick, Patrick Gallagher, Jeanie Goddard, Peter Hasenfuss, Ray Hazard, Ingrid Jackson, Woody Jackson, Brendan Lee, Debra Levine, Paul Mattison, Charlie Miller, Craig Mustard, Duke O'Neil, Peter Shribman, Peter Simons and Rob Wolkon—all offered important insights, ideas and affirmations.

Also helpful in ways large and small were Beth Barmakian, Gail Barmakian, Andrea Holbrook, Doug Johnson, Mark Mayall, Gretchen Pathak and Mike Walsh. I'm grateful, too, to Amy Anderson, Andrew Keough and Salvatore Petralia for so graciously allowing me time away from the classroom to write. Many thanks, also, to Susan Hobson at McCormick & Williams and, at Ecco, to Emma Janaskie and Kim Lewis.

To my parents, Rosalee and David McCullough, whose support and interest in and thoughts about this enterprise have been steady, steadying and enormously helpful, thank you. To my children—David, Leah, Ethan and Jesse—each of whom has offered much inspiration, edification, good humor, clear thinking, unrelenting encouragement and reasons to believe, thank you.

Finally, always, to Janice, my wife and wise counselor and *kuuipo*, who inspires every day, thank you.

ASIAN TAPAS

ASIAN TAPAS

over 60 recipes for tempting
Asian small plates and bites

RYLAND PETERS & SMALL
LONDON • NEW YORK

Senior Designer Toni Kay
Commissioning Editor Alice Sambrook
Production Controller Mai-Ling Collyer
Art Director Leslie Harrington
Editorial Director Julia Charles
Publisher Cindy Richards
Indexer Vanessa Bird

First published in 2018 by
Ryland Peters & Small
20–21 Jockey's Fields, London WC1R 4BW
and
341 E 116th St, New York NY 10029
www.rylandpeters.com

10 9 8 7 6 5 4 3 2 1

Recipe collection compiled by
Alice Sambrook

Text copyright © Valerie Aikman-Smith,
Caroline Artiss, Jordan Bourke, Dunja
Gulin, Tori Haschka, Carol Hilker, Vicky
Jones, Jackie Kearney, Jenny Linford,
Loretta Liu, Uyen Luu, Dan May, Nitisha
Patel, Louise Pickford, Milli Taylor and
Ryland Peters & Small 2018

Design and photographs copyright ©
Ryland Peters & Small 2018

ISBN: 978-1-84975-934-2

Printed in China

A CIP record for this book is available
from the British Library.

US Library of Congress Cataloging-in-
Publication Data has been applied for.

NOTES:
• Both British (Metric) and
American (Imperial plus US cups)
measurements are included in these
recipes for your convenience, however
it is important to work with one set
of measurements and not alternate
between the two within a recipe.
• All spoon measurements are level
unless otherwise specified.
• All eggs are medium (UK) or large
(US), unless specified as large, in
which case US extra-large should be
used. Uncooked or partially cooked
eggs should not be served to the very
old, frail, young children, pregnant
women or those with compromised
immune systems.
• Ovens should be preheated
to the specified temperatures.
We recommend using an oven
thermometer. If using a fan-assisted
oven, adjust temperatures according
to the manufacturer's instructions.
• When a recipe calls for the grated
zest of citrus fruit, buy unwaxed fruit
and wash well before using. If you can
only find treated fruit, scrub well in
warm soapy water before using.

CONTENTS

INTRODUCTION

Most people are familiar with the idea of tapas in Spanish bars. Originally, it was the practice of offering tempting little dishes to customers on the house to accompany their glass of wine or an ice-cold draft beer, but it is now more widely understood to be a style of dining that involves sharing small plates with others. And this idea of sharing food is not exclusive to Europe. In Japan, bars known as 'izakaya' offer an informal place to enjoy an after-work drink with something small to eat. And unlike other Japanese styles of eating, the dishes in these venues are usually shared by everyone at the table, just like tapas. The modern concept of Asian tapas fuses the unbeatable appeal of socializing over small-portion sharing plates with the more exotic and enticing flavours of Asian cuisine. It offers a multitude of delicious possibilities for tasty dishes and another way to entertain your friends at home in style.

In this mouth-watering collection of recipes you will find ideas for bite-size morsels from Asian cuisines as diverse as China, Japan, Korea, Vietnam, Thailand and India. A chapter of recipes for irresistible Parcels, Rolls & Dumplings includes perfect fingerfood ideas from egg rolls and bao buns to dim sum and wontons. Fritters, Frys & Pancakes make a more substantial snack. Choose from filled crispy pancakes, bhajis, dosas and pakoras. Lighter Bites on offer, such as summer rolls, sushi and tempura are ideal served as little teasers in advance of an Asian-style feast. And if you want to lay on a full sharing menu, choose something from Ribs, Grills & Wings such as sticky Korean ribs, Vietnamese BBQ ribs or Indian grilled lamb chops as the star of the show. With meat, fish and vegetarian options included, it's also possible to create an informal dinner or a feast for a crowd that offers something for everyone.

It makes sense to consider what you serve to drink with your nibbles. A good accompaniment to dim sum, fluffy buns or dumplings is a tea that will cut through any oiliness. Try a black tea such as Pu-Erh tea, a so-called 'blue tea' like Oolong, or a green tea like Dragonwell. And if you prefer a herbal infusion, look in your local Asian market for Chrysanthemum tea which is mild and much like camomile. For sushi, a fresh and fruity sake is the best choice. Although traditionally served warm, most premium sake produced these days tastes better slightly chilled, just like wine. Serve it in little ceramic cups for authenticity! Cold bottled beer is a great choice for grilled sticky ribs and wings, and there are plenty of excellent Asian brands to choose from. Look for India's Cobra beer or Singha lager, or for a Japanese theme, choose Asahi or Sapporo or even a Korean Cass.

Choose your dishes, pair them with something good to wash it all down with and enjoy the Asian tapas experience at home!

BASIC DOUGH RECIPES

WHEAT DOUGH

150 g/1 cup plus 2 tablespoons Asian white
   wheat flour
80 ml/scant ⅓ cup water

MAKES 16 DUMPLING SKINS

Place the flour in a mixing bowl and mix
together with the water to form a dough. Turn
the dough out onto a lightly floured surface and
knead for 20–25 minutes or until the dough
is smooth and elastic. Separate and roll into
two equal cylinders about 2.5 cm/1 inch in
diameter. Cover with a damp kitchen cloth to
prevent from drying out and set aside to rest
at room temperature for 30 minutes.

Use a sharp knife to slice the dough cylinders
into 16 equal pieces. On a lightly floured surface,
roll out each piece with a rolling pin until it has
a neat round shape and a diameter of around
7.5 cm/3 inches.

EGG DOUGH

150 g/1 cup plus 2 tablespoons Asian white
   wheat flour
40 ml/3 tablespoons water
1 egg

MAKES 16 DUMPLING SKINS

Place the flour in a mixing bowl and add the
water and egg. Mix together, then turn the
dough out onto a lightly floured surface. Using
lightly floured hands, knead for 20–25 minutes.
The dough will be sticky at first but will become
smooth and silky. Separate in half and roll into
two equal cylinders, each about 2.5 cm/1 inch

in diameter. Cover with a damp kitchen cloth
and set aside to rest at room temperature for
30 minutes.

Use a sharp knife to slice the dough cylinders
into 16 equal pieces. On a lightly floured
surface, roll out each piece with a rolling
pin until it has a neat round shape and
a diameter of around 7.5 cm/3 inches.

PUFF PASTRY DOUGH

WATER DOUGH
100 g/¾ cup Asian white wheat flour
15 g/1 heaped tablespoon caster/superfine sugar
40 ml/3 tablespoons water
30 g/2 tablespoons unsalted butter, melted

BUTTER DOUGH
100 g/¾ cup Asian white wheat flour
50 g/3½ tablespoons unsalted butter, melted

MAKES 12 DUMPLING SKINS

In a mixing bowl, combine all the ingredients
for the water dough. Form the dough into a ball
and knead lightly until smooth and silky. Wrap
the dough in clingfilm/plastic wrap and rest
in the fridge for 15 minutes. Divide into 12 and
roll each piece into a ball. Cover with a damp
kitchen cloth and set aside.

In a second mixing bowl, repeat the same full
process with the butter dough ingredients but
instead of chilling, rest at room temperature
for 15 minutes.

Take a water dough ball and knead gently and
briefly. Very lightly flour the worktop and use
a rolling pin to roll out the ball of water dough
to a diameter of 7.5 cm/3 inches. Place a

butter dough ball in the centre and wrap the water dough around to enclose it completely. Turn the dough ball over so the join is on the underside. Roll the combined dough into a thick square parcel. Fold the parcel into three and flatten with the rolling pin again. Repeat this fold and roll process twice with each ball. Cover and rest in the fridge for 15 minutes before rolling into the desired shape for the recipe.

BREAD DOUGH

2 teaspoons fast-action dried yeast
450 g/3½ cups Asian white wheat flour
100 g/¾ cup plus 1 tablespoon icing/
confectioners' sugar, sifted
15 g/2 tablespoons dried milk powder
¼ teaspoon fine salt
2 teaspoons baking powder
180 ml/¾ cup water, add more if needed
50 ml/scant ¼ cup vegetable oil, plus extra
for oiling the bowl

MAKES 16 BAO BUNS

Place the yeast in a large mixing bowl, then add the flour, sugar, milk powder, salt and baking powder. Make sure the yeast is separated from the salt by the layer of flour. Add the water and oil and bring together with a dough scraper. When no dry flour remains, remove the dough from the bowl and place on a lightly floured surface. Knead firmly for 5–10 minutes, until smooth and elastic.

Lightly oil the mixing bowl. Shape the dough into two cylinders and place back in the oiled bowl, cover with oiled clingfilm/plastic wrap and leave in a warm place to rise for 40–60 minutes or until doubled in size.

Remove the risen dough from the bowl, punch it down and knead it again briefly, but very carefully rather than firmly this time. Roll the dough out into a big rectangle and portion it out into 16 equal balls. Cover the dough balls with oiled clingfilm/plastic wrap and leave to rest again for 30 minutes in a warm place.

Roll out each dough ball so that it has a diameter of around 7.5 cm/3 inches; try to make the centre slightly thicker than the edges so that it can hold the filling. Cover each dough circle with a damp kitchen cloth as you finish to stop it from drying out.

CRYSTAL SKIN DOUGH

100 g/¾ cup wheat starch
50 g/½ cup tapioca starch
pinch of salt
150 ml/⅔ cup boiling (not hot) water

MAKES 16 DUMPLING SKINS

Combine the wheat starch, tapioca starch and salt in a large bowl. Add the boiling water and mix with a wooden spoon to form the dough. Transfer to a lightly floured surface and knead until smooth. Separate the dough in half and roll into two equal cylinders, about 2.5 cm/ 1 inch in diameter. Wrap in clingfilm/plastic wrap and rest at room temperature for 30 minutes.

Divide the dough into 16 equal balls. On a lightly floured surface use a rolling pin to roll the dough balls into thin discs, about 5 cm/ 2 inches in diameter. Cover the finished skins with a damp kitchen cloth as you work so that they don't dry out.

PARCELS, ROLLS & DUMPLINGS

CHINESE EGG ROLLS

There is something so satisfying about an egg roll. Maybe it's the crunch; maybe it's the texture; maybe it's something about how pork and cabbage come together so well when hugged between egg roll wrappers and deep-fried. Whatever it is, they're delicious!

3 tablespoons olive oil
1 teaspoon sea salt
1 teaspoon freshly ground
    black pepper
1 teaspoon ground ginger
1 teaspoon garlic powder
450 g/1 lb. pork shoulder
2 tablespoons plain/
    all-purpose flour
2 tablespoons water
120 g/2 cups cabbage,
    shredded
1 medium carrot, shredded
8 x 18-cm/7-inch square egg
    roll wrappers
1 litre/quart peanut oil,
    for frying
2 tablespoons toasted
    sesame seeds (optional)

**SWEET & SOUR
DIPPING SAUCE**
1 tablespoon soy sauce
1 tablespoon water
3½ tablespoons caster/
    superfine sugar
3½ tablespoons white vinegar
zest of 1 unwaxed orange

meat thermometer

MAKES 8

Preheat the oven to 180°C (350°F) Gas 4.

Rub the oil, salt, ground black pepper, ginger and garlic powder onto the pork shoulder.

Set the meat on a rack set into a roasting pan. Roast for 20 minutes, and then reduce the heat to 160°C (325°F) Gas 3. Continue to cook until a meat thermometer inserted into the shoulder reads 85°C (185°F), about 1–2 hours. Remove the pork from the oven and let stand until cool enough to handle, about 30 minutes. Shred the pork.

Combine the flour and water in a bowl until they form a paste. In a separate bowl combine the cabbage, carrot and shredded pork and mix them together.

Lay out one egg roll wrapper with a corner pointed toward you.

Place about 20 g/⅓ cup of the cabbage, carrot and shredded pork mixture onto the wrapper and fold the corner up over the mixture.

Fold the left and right corners toward the centre and continue to roll. Brush a bit of the flour paste on the final corner to help seal.

In a large frying pan/skillet, heat the peanut oil to about 190°C (375°F). Place the egg rolls into the heated oil and fry, turning occasionally, until golden brown. Remove from oil and drain on paper towels. Put on a serving plate and top with toasted sesame seeds, if desired.

To make the sweet and sour sauce, mix all the ingredients together in a mixing bowl. Transfer to a small saucepan and bring to the boil, then remove from the heat. Pour the sauce into a small bowl ready to dip the egg rolls into.

TAIWANESE-STYLE GARLIC PORK BAO

Pillowy Taiwanese-style buns contrast beautifully with the gutsy, succulent braised pork, making these a memorably tasty treat.

BRAISED PORK
1 tablespoon olive oil
1 onion, finely chopped
2 garlic cloves, chopped
2-cm/3/4-inch fresh ginger, peeled and chopped
400 g/14 oz. pork belly, cut into 2.5-cm/1-inch cubes
1 tablespoon Korean soy bean paste
1 tablespoon Korean chilli paste
1 tablespoon dark soy sauce
1 tablespoon rice wine or medium sherry
1 teaspoon white sugar
300 ml/1¼ cups chicken stock or water

BAO (TAIWANESE BUNS)
250 g/1¾ cups plain/all-purpose flour
2 teaspoons white sugar
½ teaspoon fast-action dried yeast
½ teaspoon baking powder
¼ teaspoon salt
100 ml/⅓ cup hand-hot water
50 ml/3½ tablespoons whole milk
2 teaspoons white wine vinegar
shredded carrot and spring onion/scallion, to garnish

large frying pan/skillet or casserole dish with a lid

bamboo steamer, lined with non-stick baking parchment

MAKES 8

First make the braised pork. Heat the oil in the large, lidded frying pan/skillet or casserole dish. Fry the onion, garlic and ginger for 2 minutes, stirring, until the onion has softened. Add the chopped pork belly and fry, stirring often, until the pork is lightly browned.

Add the soy bean and chilli pastes and mix to coat thoroughly. Add the soy sauce, rice wine and sugar and cook, stirring, for 1 minute. Next, add the stock or water and bring to the boil.

Cover with a lid, reduce the heat and simmer for 1 hour until the pork is tender. Uncover the pan, increase the heat to bring the liquid to the boil and cook uncovered over medium heat, stirring often, until the sauce has considerably reduced. Set aside until needed.

Meanwhile, to make the bao, mix together the flour, sugar, yeast, baking powder and salt in a large bowl. Add in the hand-hot water, milk and vinegar and mix together to form a soft dough. Knead for 10 minutes until the dough is supple and smooth.

Place the dough in an oiled bowl, cover with oiled clingfilm/plastic wrap and set aside in a warm place for an hour to rise.

On a lightly floured surface, knock back the risen dough and roll to form a thick sausage shape. Cut into 8 even-sized pieces and shape each piece into a ball. Roll each ball into an oval, roughly 12-cm/5-inches long. Fold each oval in half over a small rectangular piece of baking parchment. Cover with oiled clingfilm/plastic wrap and set aside to rest for 20 minutes.

Steam the buns in batches in the bamboo steamer, spaced apart, for 10 minutes or until cooked through. Handling the hot buns carefully, remove the baking parchment.

Reheat the braised pork until piping hot, if needed, and fill each bun with braised pork, garnish with shredded carrot and spring onion/scallion and serve at once.

MUSHROOM PUFF PASTRY DUMPLINGS

These delicious dumplings are filled with a mixture of button, shiitake and oyster mushrooms, but you can adapt the combination to suit what is available. If you can find them, shiitake mushrooms add a nice umami-like depth of flavour.

1 batch of Puff Pastry Dough, see page 8
2 shallots, chopped
1 garlic clove, chopped
1 teaspoon grated fresh ginger
4 button mushrooms, sliced
4 shiitake mushrooms, sliced
4 oyster mushrooms, sliced
2 spring onions/scallions, sliced
1 egg, beaten
salt and freshly ground black pepper
black sesame seeds, to garnish

2 large baking sheets, greased

MAKES 12

Prepare the puff pastry dough following the instructions in the basic recipe on page 8 and rest the balls in the fridge until needed.

Preheat the oven to 200°C (400°F) Gas 6.

In a small frying pan/skillet, fry the shallots over a medium heat for a few minutes until fragrant. Add the garlic and ginger and stir-fry together for a couple of minutes. Add the sliced mushrooms and spring onions/scallions and season with salt and pepper. Fry until the mushrooms are cooked and the mixture is dry. Set aside to cool.

Roll each pastry ball into a rectangle 10 x 6 cm/4 x 2½ inches.

Put a small tablespoon of filling on one side of a skin, brush the edges with beaten egg and fold in half to enclose the filling. Use a fork to make indentations and tightly seal the edges. Repeat with the rest of the dough and filling to make 12 dumplings.

Spread the parcels out on the greased baking sheets, brush the tops with beaten egg and sprinkle with black sesame seeds to garnish. Bake in the preheated oven for 20–25 minutes or until golden brown. Serve warm.

GOLDEN PUMPKIN & LEEK DUMPLINGS

Vegetables take centre-stage in these warming, golden-coloured pumpkin and leek parcels. The interior of the dumpling should be soft in texture, and is flavoured beautifully with Chinese chives, ginger and Sichuan pepper. The egg dough provides just a little bite.

1 batch of Egg Dough, see page 8
100 g/3½ oz. firm tofu, drained and sliced into small cubes
pinch of salt
40 g/¼ cup steamed pumpkin
1 leek, finely chopped
2 Chinese chive stalks, white parts removed, finely chopped
2 Chinese cabbage leaves, finely chopped
handful of freshly chopped coriander/cilantro
1 teaspoon grated fresh ginger
1 teaspoon Sichuan pepper
1 teaspoon black pepper
2 tablespoons vegetarian stir-fry sauce
2 tablespoons sesame oil
black vinegar, for dipping

MAKES 16

Prepare the egg dough following the instructions in the basic recipe on page 8.

While the dough is resting, make the filling. Lightly salt the tofu slices and set them aside for 30 minutes. After that, press out as much excess water as possible paper towels.

In a large bowl, mix together the steamed pumpkin with the tofu, chopped vegetables, coriander/cilantro, ginger, Sichuan pepper, black pepper, vegetarian stir-fry sauce and sesame oil. Chill in the fridge for 30 minutes.

Roll out the egg dough, continuing to follow the instructions on page 8. Put a large teaspoon of filling into the centre of each skin. Dab a little water on one edge of the skin, fold in half over the filling and pinch the corners together to seal. Fold small pleats to seal up the middle. Continue with the rest of the batch, leaving the prepared dumplings on a tray lightly dusted with flour and covered with a damp kitchen cloth as you work.

Put a large pan of water on to boil. Lower the dumplings into the boiling water and cover with a lid. As soon as they start to float, they are cooked. Serve hot with black vinegar for dipping.

Alternatively, you can lightly pan-fry the uncooked dumpling and finish off the cooking by poaching the dumplings in a little stock or water.

CHINESE VEGETABLE CLAMSHELL BUNS

The fashionable clamshell shape of these buns shows off the vibrant colours of the vegetables. Take care with preparation as your knife skills will be on show. These buns are also good stuffed with the braised pork on page 15.

1 batch of Bread Dough, see page 9
1 head of Chinese cabbage leaves
3 handfuls Chinese spinach
2 small leeks
1 carrot, peeled and grated
8 oyster mushrooms, sliced
3 Chinese chive stalks, white parts removed, sliced
2 tablespoons sunflower oil, plus extra for oiling the dough
large handful of freshly chopped coriander/cilantro
vegetarian stir-fry sauce, to serve

bamboo steamer, lined with non-stick baking parchment

MAKES 16

Prepare, rise and roll out the bread dough following the instructions in the basic recipe on page 9.

Divide the dough into 16 round balls and flatten each slightly with a rolling pin into an oval shape, around 12 x 6 cm/4 ½ x 2 ⅓ inches. Cut 16 squares of baking parchment, each 12 cm/4 ½ inches. Use your fingers to lightly oil the surface of a piece of dough, place a square of paper on top and fold the dough in half so that the paper is in the centre. Cut another 16 squares of baking parchment just larger than the buns. Lay the paper squares on a tray and lightly dust with flour. Place a bun on top of each square on its side, cover with oiled clingfilm/plastic wrap and leave to rise for 30–40 minutes.

While the buns are rising, slice the cabbage leaves, spinach and leeks lengthwise into ribbons approximately 6 cm/2¼ inches long and 2 cm/¾ inch thick. Set aside.

Brush the top of each risen bun lightly with sunflower oil. Lift the buns on their squares and place in the bamboo steamer about 4 cm/ 1½ inches apart. Steam over boiling water for 15–20 minutes until light and fluffy.

Heat the sunflower oil in a wok and stir-fry all the vegetables and herbs for around 2–3 minutes. Add vegetarian stir-fry sauce to taste and give the vegetables a quick toss.

When the buns are ready, remove the baking parchment from the middle of each one and fill with the hot vegetables. Serve.

SALMON & MUSHROOM DUMPLINGS

Salmon is a popular ingredient in any cuisine. It works well with the light texture of a crystal skin dough and the pink against the white is attractive.

1 batch of Crystal Skin Dough, see page 9
1 oyster mushroom
1 bunch enoki mushrooms
3 shiitaki mushrooms
20 g/¼ cup chanterelle mushrooms
1 tablespoon sunflower oil
1 garlic clove, finely chopped
1 small salmon fillet
1 tablespoon grated fresh ginger
1 bunch of Chinese chive stalks, white parts removed
chilli/chile oil, to serve

small round pastry cutter

bamboo steamer, lined with non-stick baking parchment

MAKES 12

Prepare the crystal skin dough following the basic recipe on page 9, and make the filling while the dough is resting.

Slice the mushrooms into small, even pieces. Heat the sunflower oil in a pan/skillet and fry the mushrooms and garlic over a medium heat until fragrant. Set aside to cool, discarding any excess juice.

Roll out the crystal skin dough and stamp out 24 circles using the small round pastry cutter. Portion the salmon fillet into 12 pieces and cut the Chinese chive stalks into 3-cm/2-inch lengths.

Place a salmon piece in the centre of a skin, add a sprinkle of grated ginger and a chive piece neatly on the top. Lastly, top with a teaspoon of the cooked mushrooms. Cover with another round skin and press around the edge to seal.

Place the dumplings into the lined bamboo steamer and steam over boiling water until transparent and the salmon is cooked through. Serve hot with chilli/chile oil for dipping.

FRIED SHRIMP & SCALLOP BAO

These bread buns are intensely delicious yet classy comfort food. With the surprise of a whole scallop in the centre, they are sure to be a winner. Separate dipping sauces are not usually needed with bread buns such as these as the filling inside should be juicy enough.

1 batch of Bread Dough, see page 9
2 spring onions/scallions, chopped
¼ head of cabbage, chopped
400 g/14 oz. raw prawns/shrimp, peeled and deveined
3 tablespoons oyster sauce
2 tablespoons Korean chilli flakes/hot red pepper flakes
1 tablespoon sesame oil
2 tablespoons Shaoxing rice wine
16 raw, fresh scallops

bamboo steamer, lined with non-stick baking parchment

MAKES 16

Make the bread dough following the instructions from the basic recipe on page 9, and leave to rise while you prepare the filling.

Mix the spring onions/scallions and cabbage together in a large bowl. Mince the prawns/shrimp by chopping them very finely with a sharp knife. Add these to the vegetables along with the oyster sauce, chilli flakes/hot red pepper flakes, sesame oil and Shaoxing rice wine. Mix together well and chill in the fridge.

Continue to follow the instructions from the bread dough recipe on page 9. Once the skins are ready, place 1 tablespoon of the prawn/shrimp filling in the centre of each and add a scallop on top. Pull and pleat the edges of the dough to enclose the filling and pinch to seal the tops of the buns. Cover with oiled clingfilm/plastic wrap and let rise for a final 30 minutes.

Set the buns in the lined bamboo steamer about 5 cm/2 inches apart. You may have to do this in batches depending on the size of your bamboo steamer.

Steam the buns over boiling water for 8–10 minutes until the dough is light and fluffy and the scallop inside is cooked. Let cool slightly and serve warm.

SCALLOP & CRAB DUMPLINGS

The scallop is the opalescent jewel in the crown of these dumplings, which are great for impressing guests at a dinner party. The spicy lime-based dipping sauce is the perfect complement to the luxurious seafood filling.

1 batch of Crystal Skin Dough, see page 9
1 leek, finely chopped
60 g/2¼ oz. fresh mixed white and brown crab meat, flaked
1 teaspoon grated fresh ginger
1 teaspoon crushed garlic
½ teaspoon salt
½ teaspoon ground white pepper
½ teaspoon Shaoxing rice wine
½ teaspoon white sugar
1 teaspoon oil
1 teaspoon cornflour/cornstarch
16 raw, fresh scallops

DIPPING SAUCE
4 tablespoons sugar
2 tablespoons water
2 tablespoons white vinegar
1 garlic clove, crushed
1 tablespoon fish sauce
1 teaspoon Indonesian chilli/chile sauce
freshly squeezed juice of 2 limes
handful of freshly chopped coriander/cilantro

bamboo steamer, lined with non-stick baking parchment

MAKES 16

Begin by making the dipping sauce. Boil the sugar, water and vinegar in a small saucepan until the sugar has dissolved. Turn down the heat to medium, stir in the garlic, fish sauce and chili/chile sauce and simmer for 1 minute. Remove from the heat. Cool and add the lime juice and coriander/cilantro. Set aside ready for later.

Prepare the crystal dough following the instructions in the basic recipe on page 9. While the dough is resting make the filling. In a bowl combine the leek, crab meat, ginger, garlic, seasoning, Shaoxing rice wine, sugar, oil and cornflour/cornstarch; mix well.

Roll out the crystal dough skins, continuing to follow the instructions on page 9. Put a large teaspoon of the crab mixture into the centre of each skin and place a scallop on the top. Fold the skin in half over the filling, and pinch together the sides to create the traditional crescent shaped dumpling. Fold the two ends of the crescent inwards so that they overlap. Press together to seal and form the Chinese ingot shape.

Place the dumplings into the lined bamboo steamer. Steam over boiling water for 15–20 minutes or until the skin is transparent. Serve the dumplings hot with the dipping sauce.

TRADITIONAL SHRIMP DUMPLINGS

Also known as *har gao*, these little dumplings are one of the most iconic dim sum dishes. The crystal skin should be delicate enough to just about see the pink shrimp peeping through.

1 batch of Crystal Skin Dough, see page 9
50 g/1¾ oz. firm tofu, drained and excess water pressed out
150 g/5¼ oz. raw prawns/shrimp, peeled and deveined
1 teaspoon minced fresh ginger
1 teaspoon crushed garlic
½ teaspoon Shaoxing rice wine
½ teaspoon salt
½ teaspoon sugar
½ teaspoon ground white pepper
1 teaspoon olive oil
1 teaspoon cornflour/cornstarch

DIPPING SAUCE
1 small piece fresh ginger, peeled and finely sliced
6 tablespoons black vinegar

bamboo steamer lined with non-stick baking parchment

MAKES 16

Finely mince the drained tofu using a sharp knife.

Chop each prawn/shrimp into 4–5 small pieces and place in a bowl. Add the drained and minced tofu, ginger, garlic, Shaoxing rice wine, salt, sugar, white pepper, oil, and cornflour/cornstarch. Mix well and set aside in the fridge to marinate while you make the dough.

Prepare, rest and then roll out the crystal skin dough following the instructions in the basic recipe on page 9. Place a large teaspoon of filling neatly into the centre of a skin. Fold the skin in half over the filling. Pinch one end together and start to crimp the edge by making small folds to form pleats to create the traditional crescent shape.

Put the dumplings into the lined bamboo steamer. Steam over boiling water for 15–20 minutes or until the skin is transparent and the prawns/shrimp are red.

To make the dipping sauce, stir the sliced ginger into the black vinegar. Serve the dumplings hot alongside the dipping sauce.

LOTUS LEAF RICE DUMPLINGS

The lotus is considered a sacred plant in Chinese culture, the fruit of which is delicious but hard to find. More prevalent are the giant strong-textured leaves, perfect for holding filling but still pleasant to eat.

370 g/2 cups sweet glutinous/sticky rice
4 dried lotus leaves
½ teaspoon salt
1 teaspoon sesame oil
1 chicken breast, finely chopped
1 tablespoon cornflour/cornstarch
2 teaspoons vegetable oil
4 shiitake mushrooms, sliced
1 leek, sliced
1 Chinese sausage (marinated and smoked pork sausage found in Chinese markets), thinly sliced
2 teaspoons oyster sauce
2 teaspoons soy sauce
1 tablespoon Shaoxing rice wine
2 tablespoons caster/superfine sugar

rice cooker

bamboo steamer, lined with non-stick baking parchment

MAKES 8

Rinse and drain the rice, then soak in 600 ml/2½ cups water for 2 hours.

Meanwhile, fold and cut each lotus leaf in half lengthways. Submerge the leaves in hot water and leave to soak for 30 minutes, pressing down if they float up. Trim the leaves with kitchen scissors/shears until they are a similar size and trim off the hard stalk end.

Drain the rice thoroughly. In the bowl of a rice cooker, place the rice, salt, sesame oil and 250 ml/1 cup water. Cook following the packet instructions.

Mix the chopped chicken with the cornflour/cornstarch. Put the vegetable oil in a large frying pan/skillet over a high heat and fry the chicken for 3 minutes. Add the mushrooms, sliced leek and sausage and cook, stirring, for a further few minutes. Lower the heat and add the oyster sauce, soy sauce, Shaoxing rice wine and caster/superfine sugar. Stir-fry until chicken is cooked and the vegetables are tender. Set aside to cool.

Divide the cooked rice into 8 portions. With wet fingertips, divide each portion of rice in half. Shape 8 half-portions into rectangles in the centre of each lotus leaf half. Put 1 tablespoon of chicken mixture on top and spread evenly. Top the meat with the other halves of rice to cover them completely.

Fold the bottom of the leaves up over the rice. Fold in the left and right sides, and then roll each leaf away from you towards the curved edge to make a rectangular packet. Place the dumplings seam-side down on the bamboo steamer. Steam over boiling water for 45 minutes, or until heated through. Serve warm.

RED THAI CURRY & LENTIL BAO

A fragrant taste of Thailand is fused with traditional Chinese bao buns in these beautiful red curry buns.

1 batch of Bread Dough, see page 9
2 tablespoons sunflower oil
2 onions, finely sliced
2 garlic cloves, crushed
1–2 tablespoons Thai red curry paste (to taste)
2 raw chicken breasts, cut into bite-size pieces
500 ml/2 cups hot chicken stock
80 g/scant ½ cup dried red lentils

bamboo steamer, lined with non-stick baking parchment

MAKES 16

Make the bread dough following the instructions in the basic recipe on page 9. While the dough is rising, prepare the filling.

Heat 1 tablespoon of the oil in a large frying pan/skillet and add the onions. Cook for 3 minutes over a gentle heat until soft and fragrant. Stir in the garlic and curry paste and cook for 1–2 minutes more.

Add the chicken pieces and cook for 2–3 minutes. Stir in the stock and lentils, bring to the boil, cover and simmer for 25 minutes, stirring occasionally, until the lentils are tender and the chicken is cooked. Set aside to cool.

Continue to follow the instructions from the bread dough recipe on page 9.

Once the skins are ready, place 1 tablespoon of the filling in the centre of each round. Gather and pleat the edges, pinching to seal the top of the bun. Cover the finished buns with oiled clingfilm/plastic wrap and allow to rise for another 30 minutes.

Set the buns in the lined bamboo steamer about 5 cm/2 inches apart. You may have to do this in batches depending on the size of your steamer.

Once risen, steam the bao over a high heat for 15–20 minutes or until the dough is light and fluffy. Leave to cool slightly and serve.

SPICY CHICKEN & SHRIMP DUMPLINGS

A simple and delicious favourite served with a garlic, ginger and chilli/ chile oil. These are the classic flavours of Asia. The amount of hot pepper powder can be added more or less to taste.

1 batch of Wheat Dough, see page 8
1 chicken breast
60 g/2¼ oz. raw prawns/ shrimp, peeled and deveined
1 leek, chopped
2 Chinese chive stalks, chopped
a large handful of freshly chopped coriander/cilantro
½–1 tablespoon Korean hot pepper powder (to taste)
1 teaspoon freshly ground black pepper
1 tablespoon oyster sauce
½ tablespoon sesame oil

DIPPING SAUCE
1 garlic clove, finely chopped
1 tablespoon grated fresh ginger
6 tablespoons soy sauce
2 tablespoons chilli/chile oil

MAKES 16

Prepare the wheat dough following the instructions in the basic recipe on page 8, and rest wrapped in clingfilm/plastic wrap until needed. Meanwhile, mince the chicken breast and prawns/shrimp using a sharp knife to very finely chop. Transfer to a mixing bowl and combine with the rest of the filling ingredients. Chill in the fridge for 30 minutes.

Roll out the skins, continuing to follow the basic recipe on page 8. Put a large teaspoon of filling into the centre of each skin. Dip your fingertips in a small dish of water and slightly moisten the edge of half the skin. Seal the dumpling up tightly using your fingers to pinch, pull and fold the skin into 4 pleats at the join. Repeat the process until all the mixture and skins have been used.

Bring a large pan of water to the boil. Gently lower in the dumplings and cover with a lid to poach. The dumplings are cooked when they float to the top of the liquid.

To make the dipping sauce, mix together all the ingredients. Drain the dumplings and serve at once accompanied with the dipping sauce.

If you prefer a crispy base, you can lightly pan-fry the uncooked dumplings in a small amount of oil and finish off the cooking by poaching in water or stock.

HOISIN DUCK PUFFS

Here, slow-cooked juicy confit duck is flavoured with five-spice, star anise, cinnamon and cloves, and enclosed in puff pastry to make these delectable treats.

1 batch of Puff Pastry Dough, see page 8
2 duck legs
60 g/¼ cup sea salt flakes, plus extra for serving
1 tablespoon freshly ground black pepper
1 garlic clove, crushed
2 tablespoons Chinese five-spice powder
5 star anise
1 cinnamon stick
2 cloves
500 g/1 lb. duck fat
2 spring onions/scallions, chopped
2 tablespoons hoisin sauce
1 egg, beaten
white sesame seeds, to garnish

small round pastry cutter

2 large baking sheets, greased

MAKES 12

Rub the duck legs with the sea salt flakes, black pepper, crushed garlic clove, five-spice powder, star anise, cinnamon stick and cloves. Pack the duck and these ingredients tightly into a dish, skin-side down. Cover the dish with clingfilm/plastic wrap and leave to marinate in the fridge for 24 hours.

Preheat the oven to 150°C (300°F) Gas 2.

Scrape the marinade off the duck pieces. Heat the duck fat in an ovenproof dish until melted, then add the duck legs, ensuring they are completely submerged.

Bake the duck in the preheated oven for 3½ hours, or until the meat is very tender when pierced with a skewer and the fat in the skin is rendered. Once cooked, remove the duck from the fat and allow to cool uncovered. Shred finely and mix with the chopped spring onions/scallions and hoisin sauce.

Prepare and roll out the puff pastry dough following the instructions from the basic recipe on page 8. Using a small round pastry cutter, stamp out 2 rounds from each dough ball portion. Put a spoonful of filling on one half, brush the edges with beaten egg and position the second piece of pastry on top. Use a fork to make indentations around the edge to tightly seal.

Preheat the oven to 200°C (400°F) Gas 6.

Brush the tops with beaten egg and sprinkle with white sesame seeds. Place on the prepared baking sheets and bake in the preheated oven for 20–25 minutes until golden brown.

BEEF BULGOGI PUFFS

Translating literally as 'fire meat' in Korean, beef bulgogi is a flavoursome dish of marinated grilled beef. The recipe was introduced to China by the migrant population of Korea. Using a good cut of beef here is key; you want the meat to be almost as soft as the flaky pastry on the outside.

1 batch of Puff Pastry Dough, see page 8
4 spring onions/scallions finely chopped
½ onion, finely chopped
¼ pineapple (pear or kiwi will also work), finely chopped
1 tablespoon dark soy sauce
1 tablespoon sugar
1 teaspoon sesame oil
freshly ground black pepper
2 garlic cloves, crushed
1 tablespoon freshly squeezed lemon juice
150 g/5¼ oz. sirloin steak, sliced into bite-size strips
1 egg, beaten
white sesame seeds, to garnish
chilli/chile sauce, for dipping

stove top griddle pan/grill pan, lightly greased

2 large baking sheets, greased

MAKES 12

Stir together the filling ingredients, apart from the meat, in a large bowl to form a marinade paste, adding a little water to loosen if necessary.

Mix the beef strips with the paste, making sure that each strip is well coated. Leave in the fridge to marinate for at least 30 minutes and up to 2 hours; left longer than this the beef may become too salty.

While the meat is marinating, prepare the 12 puff pastry dough balls following the instructions in the basic recipe on page 8. Chill in the fridge until needed.

Heat a griddle/grill pan over a medium-high heat, add the beef strips and juices to the pan and cook until the meat is browned around the edges and cooked to your liking, around 3–7 minutes. Remove from the pan and leave to cool.

Preheat the oven to 200°C (400°F) Gas 6.

Roll each pastry ball into a square about 10 cm/4 inches along each edge. Put a tablespoon of filling in the middle and brush the edges with a little beaten egg. Fold the pastry in half diagonally to create a triangle. Seal the edges then tuck the seams underneath to create a smooth finish on top. Repeat with the remaining dough and filling.

Place the puffs on the greased baking sheets and brush with beaten egg. Sprinkle with sesame seeds and bake in the preheated oven for 20–25 minutes until golden brown. Serve with the chilli/chile dipping sauce on the side.

BARBECUE PORK PUFFS

Light flaky pastry is here the yin to the yang of the dark and rich barbecue pork. The Chinese way of making puff pastry using combined butter dough and water dough originates from Hong Kong, and it's a little healthier than the Western way of packing in as much butter as possible.

1 batch of Puff Pastry Dough, see page 8
1 tablespoon sunflower oil
1 shallot, chopped
2 tablespoons dry sherry
225 g/8 oz. pork loin, diced
1 teaspoon crushed garlic
2 tablespoons honey
2 tablespoons hoisin sauce
1 teaspoon Chinese five-spice powder
1 tablespoon soy sauce
1 egg, beaten
black sesame seeds, to garnish

heat-proof casserole dish

2 large baking sheets, greased

MAKES 12

For the filling, heat the oil in the heat-proof casserole dish and add the chopped shallot. Cook until softened and lightly caramelized, about 5–7 minutes. Pour in the sherry and let the alcohol cook out. Lower the heat to medium and add in the diced pork. Cook, stirring, for an extra 2 minutes or until lightly browned.

Meanwhile, mix the garlic, honey, hoisin sauce, five-spice powder and soy sauce in a bowl with 2 tablespoons of water. Add this to the pork and shallot, stirring well. Cover and cook for 1 hour over a low heat until the sauce has thickened and the pork is soft. Check occasionally during cooking to ensure the sauce does not dry out, adding a little extra water if needed.

While the pork is cooking, prepare the puff pastry dough balls following the instructions from the basic recipe on page 8. Chill in the fridge until ready to cook.

Preheat the oven to 200°C (400°F) Gas 6. Finely chop the pork once it is cool, ready for filling the pastry.

Roll each pastry ball into a rectangle 10 x 6 cm/4 x 2½ inches and then cut each in half widthways. Put a small tablespoon of filling on one half, brush the edges with beaten egg and position the second piece of pastry on top. Use a fork to make indentations and to tightly seal the edges.

Place the parcels on the greased baking sheets, brush the tops with beaten egg and sprinkle with black sesame seeds. Bake in the preheated oven for 20–25 minutes or until golden brown. Serve warm.

PORK & CABBAGE SHUMAI

Pork and cabbage are a popular choice of filling for home cooks in China because they are protein-packed yet inexpensive ingredients. But that doesn't stop these dumplings from being ridiculously tempting. Create the flower shape by lightly squeezing the egg dough cup in the middle.

1 batch Egg Dough, see page 8
100 g/3½ oz. raw prawns/
    shrimp, peeled and
    deveined
100 g/3½ oz. lean minced/
    ground pork
60 g/1¼ cups chopped
    cabbage
1 tablespoon oyster sauce
½ tablespoon sesame oil
1 teaspoon freshly ground
    white pepper
1 tablespoon cornflour/
    cornstarch
1 teaspoon salt
toasted white sesame seeds,
    to garnish

DIPPING SAUCE
125 ml/½ cup soy sauce
2 tablespoons sesame oil
large handful of freshly
    chopped coriander/cilantro
2 spring onions/scallions,
    sliced
1 teaspoon crushed garlic
1 tablespoon grated fresh
    ginger

*bamboo steamer, lined
    with non-stick baking
    parchment*

MAKES 16

Prepare the egg dough following the instructions from the basic recipe on page 8. While the dough is resting, make the filling. Mince the prawns/shrimp using a sharp knife to finely chop into small pieces. Transfer to a large mixing bowl, add the rest of the filling ingredients and mix thoroughly.

Roll out the egg dough, continuing to follow the instructions from the recipe on page 8. To assemble the shumai, place a wrapper on your palm and add a small tablespoon of filling to the centre. Gather the edges of the wrapper and gently pleat so that a basket shape is formed up and around the filling, leaving the middle exposed. Lightly tap the base of the dumpling on a work surface to flatten the bottom and make sure the filling fills the nooks and crannies. Lightly squeeze the middle with your thumb and forefinger to create the classic flower shape. Repeat for the rest of the wrappers and filling.

Arrange the shumai at the bottom of the lined bamboo steamer, leaving plenty of space between each one. Cover and steam the dumplings over boiling water for 7 minutes or until cooked through.

Make the dipping sauce while the dumplings are steaming by stirring the ingredients together in a small bowl.

Remove the dumplings from the steamer using the baking parchment to assist. Serve warm sprinkled with toasted white sesame seeds and alongside the dipping sauce.

PORK & LEEK JIAOZI

Traditional jiaozi are extremely popular at holiday celebrations such as Chinese New Year. Often prepared in an assembly line by various family members, these tasty dumplings are enjoyed by children and adults alike. The folded, plump pleated shape is a nice easy one to make.

1 batch of Wheat Dough, see page 8
100 g/3½ oz. firm tofu, drained and sliced into small cubes
pinch of salt
100 g/3½ oz. minced/ground pork
2 Chinese chive stalks, white parts removed, finely chopped
large handful of freshly chopped coriander/cilantro
1 teaspoon Sichuan pepper
1 teaspoon black pepper
2 tablespons dark soy sauce
2 tablespoons sesame oil
1 leek, finely chopped
2 button mushrooms, finely chopped
1 tablespoon sunflower oil
black vinegar, for dipping

MAKES 16

Prepare the wheat dough following the instructions from the basic recipe on page 8. While the dough is resting, begin the filling. Sprinkle the tofu slices with salt and set aside for 30 minutes before squeezing out any excess water.

In a large bowl mix the minced/ground pork with the tofu and the rest of the ingredients apart from the sunflower oil and black vinegar.

Roll out the skins, continuing to follow the instructions from the recipe on page 8. Place a small tablespoon of filling neatly into the centre of a skin. Dip your fingertips into a small dish of water and slightly moisten the edge of half the skin. Fold the skin in half over the filling. Pinch one end together and make small folds to form pleats. The end result should be a plump sealed pocket.

Tap the dumplings base-down on your work surface to finish. As you are working, set aside the finished dumplings on a floured baking sheet under a damp cloth so they do not dry out.

Heat the sunflower oil over a medium heat in a large frying pan/skillet. Lightly fry the dumplings until golden brown on the bottom. To finish off the cooking process, place the dumplings in a large pan of boiling water. Cover with a lid and poach until they float to the surface.

Serve the dumplings hot with black vinegar for dipping.

CRISPY CHICKEN WONTONS

Deep-frying these dumplings until they are crisp transforms them into an appetizing snack. When served with the dipping sauce, they go perfectly with pre-dinner drinks. Chinese black rice vinegar is available from Asian stores.

1 chicken breast fillet (approx. 140 g/5 oz.), finely minced
4 tablespoons finely chopped fresh Chinese chives
pinch of ground Sichuan pepper
1 teaspoon light soy sauce
½ teaspoon sesame oil
16 wonton wrappers
sunflower or vegetable oil, for deep frying
salt and freshly ground black pepper

DIPPING SAUCE
2 tablespoons Chinese black rice vinegar
1 teaspoon sugar
1 garlic clove, finely chopped
½ red chilli/chile, finely chopped (optional)

MAKES 16

Thoroughly mix together the minced chicken, Chinese chives, Sichuan pepper, soy sauce and sesame oil. Season well with salt and pepper.

Mix together the ingredients for the dipping sauce and set aside.

Take a wonton wrapper and place a teaspoon of the chicken mixture in the centre of the wrapper. Brush the edges with a little cold water and bring the wrapper together over the chicken to form a parcel, pressing together well to seal properly. Set aside. Repeat the process until all 16 wrappers have been filled.

Heat the oil in a large saucepan or deep-fryer until very hot. Add four of the wontons and fry for a few minutes, until golden brown on both sides, turning over halfway through to ensure even browning. Remove with a slotted spoon and drain on paper towels. Repeat the process with the remaining wontons.

Serve at once with the dipping sauce.

SHRIMP & MANGO WONTONS

Deep-fried golden crispy wontons are a moreish pleasure to eat. The tropical mango dipping sauce provides a sweet and sharp tang to cut through the savouriness of the skin. Folding in this rustic way is simple to do but the finish is very effective.

350 g/12½ oz. raw prawns/
  shrimp, peeled and
  deveined
1 teaspoon salt
1 teaspoon freshly ground
  black pepper
small handful of freshly
  chopped coriander/cilantro
50 g/1¾ oz. firm tofu, drained
  and sliced, excess water
  pressed out
16 wonton wrappers
sunflower oil, for deep-frying

DIPPING SAUCE
4 tablepoons mayonnaise
2 teaspoons condensed milk
¼ small mango, diced into
  small cubes

MAKES 16

Use a pestle and mortar to mince the prawns/shrimp to a fine paste. Season with the salt and pepper and mix in the coriander/cilantro. Mash the tofu with a fork and add to the paste, stirring in well.

Hold a wonton skin on the palm of your hand and add a heaped teaspoon of filling to the centre. Dab the edges of the skin with a tiny bit of water and gather and scrunch the sides together in a rustic fashion. Repeat until all the filling and skins are used.

Heat the oil in a deep-fryer or large pan until it reaches 180°C/350°F. Cook the wontons in the hot oil in small batches for around a minute on either side. The wontons are cooked when they float up and the skins have turned golden brown. Drain the excess oil on paper towels.

To make dipping sauce, sweeten the mayonnaise with the condensed milk and stir in the diced mango. Serve the wontons hot with the mango dipping sauce.

FRITTERS, FRYS & PANCAKES

JAPANESE OKONOMIYAKI PANCAKES

These chunky cabbage-based pancakes are a great dinner party dish to make with friends, frying them up one at a time and adding different toppings. Originally from Osaka, the name means 'grill as you like it', so you really can make it your own. Omit the prawns/shrimp for a vegetarian option.

100 g/¾ cup white spelt flour
¼ teaspoon baking powder
½ teaspoon sea salt
150 ml/⅔ cup instant dashi, or fish or vegetable stock
2 eggs
300 g/10 oz. cabbage, thinly sliced
3 spring onions/scallions, finely chopped diagonally, reserve some for garnish
2 tablespoons vegetable oil
100 g/3½ oz. raw prawns/shrimp, peeled and deveined
2 tablespoons kewpie (Japanese mayonnaise, see tip right), or normal mayonnaise
2 tablespoons Okonomiyaki sauce (see tip, right)
2 tablespoons bonito flakes – (dried, smoked tuna flakes, see right)
1 tablespoon pickled sushi ginger

frying pan/skillet with a fitted lid

MAKES 2

In a large bowl combine the flour, baking powder and salt. Whisk in the dashi (or fish or vegetable stock) and eggs. Then add the cabbage and most of the spring onions/scallions and combine together.

In the non-stick frying pan/skillet add a tablespoon of the vegetable oil and heat over a medium-high heat. Add half the batter in a neat round shape about 15 cm/6 inches in diameter; don't flatten it out, as Okonomiyaki should be thick. Place half the prawns/shrimp on top so they sit into the batter, cover the pan with the fitted lid and cook for about 3–4 minutes until the bottom is set and golden. Carefully turn over, place the lid back on and cook for a further 3–4 minutes until the prawns/shrimp are cooked through and the surface is golden. Turn over one last time and cook for a further 2 minutes with the lid off.

Slide the pancake onto a plate, then drizzle over half of the kewpie or mayonnaise and the Okonomiyaki sauce, top with the bonito flakes and remaining spring onions/scallions. Serve immediately with the pickled ginger on the side. Repeat for the second pancake.

TIP: You can buy Okonomiyaki sauce (as well as kewpie mayonnaise, dashi stock and bonito flakes) in an Asian market, or online. You can make your own less sugary version of Okonomiyaki sauce at home by mixing 1 tablespoon of soy sauce with 1 teaspoon of rice vinegar. It will be too thin to drizzle on top, so serve it as a dipping sauce on the side.

VIETNAMESE SHRIMP-STUFFED CRÊPES
with nuoc cham dipping sauce

**Bánh xèo is a street-food favourite of many Vietnamese when the sun sets –
it is a light savoury crêpe served with an abundance of salad leaves and herbs.**

NUOC CHAM DIPPING SAUCE
2 garlic cloves, finely chopped
2 Bird's Eye chillies/chiles,
  very finely chopped
2 tablespoons rice wine
  vinegar
1 tablespoon fresh lime juice
3 tablespoons fish sauce
  (see tip, right)
2 tablespoons maple syrup
110 ml/scant ½ cup water

PANCAKES
220 g/1¾ cups rice flour
1 tablespoon cornflour/
  cornstarch
1 teaspoon ground turmeric
1 teaspoon coconut palm
  sugar
400-ml/14-oz. can coconut
  milk
300 ml/1¼ cups cold water
vegetable oil, for frying
200 g/2 cups beansprouts
250–300 g/8–10 oz. cooked
  prawns/shrimp
sea salt and black pepper

TO SERVE
large lettuce leaves
fresh mint leaves
handful of spring onions/
  scallions, sliced

*22–24-cm/8½–9½-inch
  non-stick frying pan/skillet*

MAKES 8

For the nuoc cham sauce, combine the garlic, chillies/chiles, rice wine vinegar and lime juice in a small bowl and leave for 5 minutes. Add the rest of the ingredients, mix well and leave to one side.

To make the pancake batter, sift both flours and turmeric into a large bowl. Stir in the sugar and a pinch of salt and pepper. Slowly whisk in the coconut milk and water, ensuring there are no lumps.

Place the frying pan/skillet over a high heat. Add a little vegetable oil, and once smoking hot, ladle in a thin layer of the batter, swirling around to evenly cover the base of the pan. Turn the heat down to medium-high and fry for 3 minutes, then add some beansprouts and prawns/shrimp and cook for a further 2 minutes. The bottom of the pancake should be crisp and golden. When it is, fold over the pancake and slide it off onto a plate and serve immediately. They are best when just cooked, so serve them immediately one at a time. Start cooking another one when you are nearly finished eating the first.

To eat, place a good chunk of the pancake, some mint and slices of spring onions/scallions in a lettuce leaf, wrap it up tightly and dunk in the dipping sauce with each bite.

TIP: For the 'nuoc cham', use a good-quality Vietnamese fish sauce. Look out for the word 'nhi' on the label, which means the liquid has come from the first extraction from the fish.

COURGETTE/ZUCCHINI ONION BHAJIS
with sumac yogurt & pomegranate molasses

This stellar Middle Eastern twist on the classic Indian dish is the perfect way to use up those few extra courgettes/zucchini that you might have leftover.

SUMAC YOGURT
250 g/1 cup soy or Greek yogurt
1 tablespoon pure maple syrup
1 teaspoon sumac
sea salt

BHAJIS
450 g/1 lb. courgette/zucchini, coarsely grated
70 g/½ cup chickpea/gram flour
40 g/⅓ cup rice flour
80–100 ml/5–6 tablespoons of water
2.5-cm/1-inch piece of fresh ginger, peeled and finely grated
2 garlic cloves, peeled and crushed
1 teaspoon ground coriander
½ teaspoon cumin seeds
½ teaspoon fennel seeds
½ teaspoon mustard seeds
1 large or 2 small red onion(s), thinly sliced
small handful freshly chopped coriander/cilantro, plus extra to serve
vegetable oil, for frying
2 tablespoons pomegranate molasses, to serve

SERVES 4–6

First, make the sumac yogurt. In a bowl combine together the yogurt, pure maple syrup, sumac and a pinch of salt and set aside.

Place the grated courgette/zucchini in a sieve/strainer and press firmly to remove as much liquid as possible, then wrap in a clean dish towel and press firmly again to dry them off.

Place the flours into a large bowl and whisk in the water to create a thick batter the consistency of double/ heavy cream. Add in the ginger, garlic, spices, onion, set-aside courgette/zucchini, 1 teaspoon sea salt, most of the fresh coriander/cilantro and combine very well.

Pour 2.5 cm/1 inch of vegetable oil into a frying pan/skillet and set over a medium–high heat. If you have a cooking thermometer, it should be 180°C (350°F), if not test that the heat is right by dropping in a tiny amount of batter – if it turns golden and crisp after about 40 seconds it's ready. Carefully place separate heaped tablespoons of the mixture into the hot oil, shaping into circular mounds. Do not overcrowd the pan as it will bring the temperature of the oil down. Fry, turning once or twice until crisp and golden. Remove and drain on paper towels. Keep the cooked bhajis warm in a low oven while you fry the rest.

Serve immediately with the extra coriander/cilantro sprinkled on top. Dollop the sumac yogurt and pomegranate molasses generously over each crispy bite.

CHINESE TURNIP CAKE

In China, turnip cake is made in big batches, brought round on a trolley and fried at the dinner table until caramelized and golden. Omit the sausage for a pescatarian version of the dish.

1 Chinese turnip, peeled and grated (carrot or pumpkin will also work)
4 tablespoons sunflower oil
50 g/2 oz. raw prawns/shrimp, peeled, deveined and coarsely chopped
5 shiitake mushrooms, sliced
1 Chinese sausage, sliced
1 spring onion/scallion, sliced
127g/1 cup rice flour
1 tablespoon cornflour/cornstarch
1 teaspoon salt
1 teaspoon superfine/caster sugar
1 teaspoon ground white pepper

DIPPING SAUCE
2 tablespoons oyster sauce
1 tablespoon sesame oil

450-g/1-lb. loaf pan, lined with non-stick baking parchment
steamer large enough to hold your pan

MAKES 1 LOAF

Simmer the grated turnip in 250 ml/1 cup water for 10 minutes until softened. Keep stirring while simmering and leave the pan uncovered so that the liquid gradually reduces by half. Set aside to cool.

Heat 2 tablespoons of the oil in a large frying pan/skillet over medium heat. Add the chopped prawns/shrimp, mushrooms and sausage and stir-fry for 5 minutes. Stir in the chopped spring onion/scallion and fry for a minute longer. Let cool.

Combine the rice flour, cornflour/cornstarch, salt, sugar, and pepper in a large mixing bowl. Add the cooked turnips with their liquid and mix well. Lastly, stir in the cooked prawns/shrimp, mushrooms and sausage.

Pour the cake batter into the lined loaf pan. Place the pan into a steamer with plenty of water and steam over medium-high heat for 50 minutes. Cool the turnip cake for 10 minutes before removing from the cake pan.

Use a sharp knife dipped in water to slice 3-cm/1-inch thick pieces. Add the remaining oil to a non-stick cast iron pan/skillet over medium-low heat. Fry the cake slices on both sides until golden and crispy.

Mix together the oyster sauce and sesame oil to form a dipping sauce and serve alongside the hot cake slices.

VIETNAMESE PORK-STUFFED CRÊPES

Oriental food is often naturally healthy, yet full of flavour. This Vietnamese pancake is a perfect example, made with rice flour and coconut milk. For a pescetarian version, try the recipe on page 55.

DIPPING SAUCE
2 garlic cloves, finely chopped
2 Bird's Eye chillies/chiles, finely chopped
2 tablespoons cider vinegar
5 tablespoons fish sauce
3 tablespoons sugar

CRÊPES
200 g/1½ cups rice flour
2 teaspoons ground turmeric
400 ml/1½ cups coconut milk
2 spring onions/scallions, thinly sliced
pinch of sea salt
pinch of sugar
cooking oil, for frying
4 shallots, chopped
400 g/14 oz. pork belly, thinly sliced
200 g/7 oz. raw king prawns/ jumbo shrimp, peeled and deveined (optional)
200 g/3½ cups beansprouts
sea salt and black pepper

TO SERVE
lettuce leaves
spring onions/scallions, cut into short lengths
coriander/cilantro
Thai sweet basil garden or hot mint

20-cm/8-inch non-stick frying pan/skillet with a lid

MAKES ABOUT 12

To make the dipping sauce, mix together the garlic, chillies/chiles and vinegar in a bowl. Set aside for 2 minutes. This 'cooks' the garlic. Now add the fish sauce, sugar and 400 ml/1½ cups water.

For the crêpes, mix together the flour, turmeric, coconut milk, 400 ml/1½ cups water, spring onions/scallions, salt and sugar in a bowl, making sure it is smooth and free of lumps.

Heat 1 teaspoon oil in the frying pan/skillet over medium heat and fry 1 teaspoon of the chopped shallots until browned. Season the pork belly and prawns/shrimp (if using) with salt and pepper and add a few pieces to the pan until cooked through. Using a shallow ladle, pour in a thin layer of the crêpe batter, add a handful of beansprouts and cover the pan with the lid. Allow to cook for 2 minutes. Remove the lid and cook for a further minute, making sure the crêpe is crispy and brown. Fold the crêpe in half and set aside. Repeat this whole process with the remaining shallots, batter and other ingredients to make several more crêpes.

To eat, put a piece of crêpe onto a lettuce leaf, add the onions/ scallions and herbs, roll it all up and dip it in the dipping sauce.

KOREAN KIMCHI PANCAKE
with black garlic crème fraîche

This popular Korean dish contrasts the chewy-textured, chilli/chile-hot pancake with the subtle coolness of crème fraîche, enriched with the mellow sweetness of black garlic. Kimchi is a traditional Korean fermented relish, usually made with cabbage.

100 g/¾ cup plain/
  all-purpose flour
½ teaspoon salt
100 ml/⅓ cup water
3 tablespoons kimchi liquid
  (reserved from kimchi)
130 g/1 cup kimchi,
  finely chopped
1 spring onion/scallion,
  finely chopped
150 ml/⅔ cup crème fraîche
  or sour cream
3 black garlic cloves,
  finely chopped
1 tablespoon sunflower
  or vegetable oil
thinly sliced spring onion/
  scallion, to garnish

SERVES 4

Make the batter by whisking together the flour, salt and water into a thick paste. Stir in the kimchi liquid, then mix in the kimchi and spring onion/scallion.

Mix together the crème fraîche and black garlic and set aside.

Heat a large frying pan/skillet until hot. Add the oil and heat well. Pour in the batter, which should sizzle as it hits the pan, spreading it to form an even layer. Fry for 3–5 minutes until set, then turn over and fry the pancake for a further 3–4 minutes until it is well browned on both sides.

Cut the kimchi pancake into bite-size portions and serve topped with the black garlic crème fraîche. Sprinkle with extra spring onions/ scallions to garnish.

OOTHAPAM Indian vegetable pancakes

Oothapam is a thick pancake made with semolina flour. The fermented version looks a bit like a crumpet, with fresh vegetables dropped into the batter as it cooks. The traditional recipe is fermented for hours, but there is also a quick version which doesn't come out as thick but is equally delicious.

vegetable oil, for frying
1–2 green chillies/chiles, to taste, thinly sliced
3 fresh or dried curry leaves, chopped
1 red onion, thinly sliced
2 tomatoes, finely chopped
1 carrot, grated
small handful of chopped kale
coconut chutney or spicy sambar chilli/chile paste, to serve

TRADITIONAL BATTER
300 g/1⅔ cups basmati rice, rinsed until the water runs clear, then drained
100 g/generous ½ cup hulled whole urid dal
½ teaspoon fenugreek seeds
½ teaspoon salt

QUICK BATTER
300 g/2 cups coarse semolina flour
300 g/1⅓ cups plain or soy yogurt
1 teaspoon freshly squeezed lemon juice
1 teaspoon bicarbonate of soda/baking soda
1 teaspoon salt
pinch of asafoetida powder (hing)

MAKES 10-14

For the traditional fermented batter, put the rice in one bowl and the dal and fenugreek seeds in another bowl, and add water to cover both by at least 5 cm/2 inches. Soak for at least 6 hours or overnight.

Drain the rice and dal mixtures, reserving both the drained liquids. Put the rice in a food processor or blender and blitz until smooth, adding about 6–7 tablespoons of the soaking water, or more if needed. Repeat with the dal mixture, adding 5 tablespoons of the soaking water and blending until smooth.

Put both mixtures in a large bowl. Mix together with the salt and cover with clingfilm/plastic wrap. Leave overnight in a warm place to ferment. The batter will keep for up to 1 week in the fridge once it is fermented, or can be frozen for up to six months.

For the quick batter, mix all the ingredients together with enough water to make a thick pouring consistency. Set aside for 10–15 minutes.

If using the fermented batter, add a little more water as necessary to make a thick pouring consistency. Add ½ tablespoon oil to a large non-stick frying pan/skillet over medium heat. Using a ladle, spoon the batter into the centre of the pan and use the back of the ladle to smooth it out to the edges. Add a little oil around the edge to ensure it doesn't stick.

Quickly remove the pan from the heat and scatter the top of the pancake with some of the prepared vegetable topping ingredients. Use the back of the ladle to push the vegetables slightly into the batter. Return the pan to the heat and cook for 3 minutes or until the pancake begins to brown underneath, then turn it over and cook for another 1–2 minutes. Repeat to make the remaining pancakes. Serve immediately with the suggested accompaniments.

INDIAN LENTIL & RICE DOSAS

The preparation for these classic Indian pancakes needs to start 36 hours in advance. A veggie curry is a good filling, but you can customize as you like.

350 g/1¾ cups basmati rice, rinsed and drained
125 g/⅔ cup white urid dal, rinsed and drained
1 teaspoon fenugreek seeds
spring or bottled water
1–2 teaspoons salt
vegetable oil, for frying
potato and pea curry, to serve
fresh coriander/cilantro and mint chutney, to serve

MAKES ABOUT 12

Put the rice and dal in separate bowls, adding the fenugreek seeds to the dal. Cover each with spring or bottled water by 5 cm/2 inches and leave to soak for 8 hours. After soaking, drain the dal, retaining the soaking water, and grind the dal and fenugreek in a food processor to a fine paste. Add 100 ml/⅓ cup of the soaking water to the paste and blend again, to achieve a smooth batter. Pour into a large bowl.

Repeat the process with the rice, grinding to a fine grainy texture, then add 125 ml/½ cup of the soaking water and blend again. Pour the rice batter into the bowl with the dal and mix thoroughly. Mix in another 250 ml/1 cup of water. The batter should coat the back of a spoon when dipped in. Cover the bowl with clingfilm/plastic wrap and set aside in a warm place to ferment for 24 hours.

When ready to make the pancakes, stir the batter, which will be frothy by now, and add the salt. It may be necessary to add more water, but make a trial pancake first. Heat a non-stick frying pan/skillet or pancake pan until medium-hot and brush with oil. Wipe off the excess oil with a paper towel. Pour a ladleful of batter onto the centre of the pan, then quickly spread it as thinly as possible, using the back of the ladle, moving it around in a spiral, starting at the centre of the pan. This has to be done quite quickly, before the batter starts to cook. The pancakes should be at least 20 cm/8 inches in diameter – if the batter doesn't spread that far, add a little more water to the bowl.

When the edges start to look lacy and crisp, lift the edge of the pancake to see if it is golden brown underneath. At this stage a little extra oil can be drizzled round the edge of the pan. Using a spatula, turn over the dosa and cook on the other side for a few minutes. Keep the pancakes warm on a plate covered with kitchen foil as you make them.

Serve each one with a spoonful of potato and pea curry spread across the centre. Spoon some fresh coriander/cilantro and mint chutney on top, and fold the pancake over from either side to seal.

KOREAN MOONG PANCAKES with pork

These savoury pancakes often contain kimchi, the Korean spiced pickled cabbage that is becoming increasingly popular around the world, but this version uses green beans instead. Either way, they make a delicious light bite.

400 g/2 cups dried moong dal (skinned and split mung beans), soaked overnight
400 ml/1⅔ cups of water
2 tablespoons soy sauce, plus extra to serve
4 garlic cloves, crushed
1 tablespoon grated fresh ginger
4 tablespoons vegetable oil
250 g/8 oz. minced/ground lean pork
1 teaspoon salt
1 leek, trimmed and finely chopped
125 g/4 oz. green beans, fresh or frozen, chopped into small pieces
chopped pickled cucumber and sliced red chilli/chile (optional), to serve

MAKES ABOUT 12

Drain the moong dal and put them in the food processor. Blend them finely, then add the water, soy sauce, all but 1 crushed garlic clove and all but ½ teaspoon of the grated ginger. Process the mixture to a smooth purée. Transfer the moong dal purée to a bowl, then leave the batter to sit for at least 30 minutes.

Meanwhile, heat 2 tablespoons of the oil in a frying pan/skillet or wok and fry the remaining garlic for 1 minute before adding the pork, together with the remaining ½ teaspoon of grated ginger and salt. Stir well and continue to cook until the pork is cooked through, then add the chopped leek and green beans and continue to cook gently until the vegetables are al dente. Take off the heat and set aside.

Heat a teaspoon of oil in a non-stick frying pan/skillet over a medium heat, and when it is hot, pour a spoonful of the batter into the pan. Spread out the batter with the back of the ladle until it forms a 8-cm/3-inch circle. Repeat the process with more batter, frying several pancakes at a time.

Cook the pancakes until golden brown on the underside and until tiny holes have begun to appear on the upper surface, then flip them over and cook the other side. This will probably take around 5 minutes on each side. It is important not to overheat the pan and burn the surface before the inside is cooked, but it must be hot enough for the pancakes to brown and crisp.

Keep warm while you make the other pancakes in the same way, brushing the frying pan or wok with oil before cooking each batch. Serve straight away with a bowl of soy sauce for dipping, and pickled cucumber and some sliced red chilli/chile, if desired.

GREEN CHILLI/CHILE BHAJIS

These exotic and tasty bhajis are wonderfully adaptable. Substituting the mild green chillies/chiles for deseeded and shredded green Habaneros makes a bhaji with an intense heat that will live long in anyone's memory!

500 ml/2 cups sunflower oil

4 tablespoons coriander seeds

4 tablespoons nigella (black onion) seeds

4 tablespoons yellow mustard seeds

4 tablespoons fenugreek seeds

1 tablespoon fennel seeds

½ teaspoon whole cloves

1 large onion, diced

3–4 garlic cloves, finely chopped

5-cm/2-inch piece of fresh ginger, peeled and finely chopped

100 g/3½ oz. mild green chillies/chiles, finely chopped

60 g/¼ cup plain yogurt

grated zest and freshly squeezed juice of 2 limes

250 g/2 cups chickpea/gram flour

250 g/2 cups cornflour/cornstarch

250 ml/1 cup water

3 tablespoons hot curry powder (either Madras or Malay-style citrusy)

sea salt and freshly ground black pepper

CARAMELIZED LIME, MINT & YOGURT DIP

1 teaspoon groundnut/peanut oil

1 lime, quartered, plus extra lime zest, to garnish

300 g/1½ cups plain yogurt

few fresh mint leaves

cooking thermometer (optional)

MAKES ABOUT 16

To make the dip, heat the oil in a frying pan/skillet over a medium heat. Add the lime quarters and fry each cut side until the surface begins to develop a strong colour. It can be useful to push the lime onto the hot surface of the pan to speed this process – this will force out a little more of the juice, aiding the caramelization. Mix the yogurt and a pinch of black pepper in a small bowl. Squeeze the juice from the caramelized limes into the bowl. Take half the mint leaves and roughly tear them, then add to the bowl, too. Stir, then garnish with the rest of the mint leaves and a little lime zest. Set aside.

Put the sunflower oil in a large saucepan. Heat until it reaches 190°C (375°F) on a cooking thermometer. If you don't have a cooking thermometer, the oil is ready when a 2.5-cm/1-inch cube of white bread dropped into it browns in less than 60 seconds.

Meanwhile, toast all the seeds and the cloves in a dry frying pan/skillet over a medium heat until the seeds start to pop. Grind them using a pestle and mortar. Put the ground spices along with all the remaining dry ingredients in a bowl and mix. Gradually add the water until the mixture is firm but will drop from a spoon.

Place about 3 separate tablespoonfuls of the bhaji mix in the hot oil and fry for about 8 minutes, or until golden brown. Remove the bhajis from the pan using a slotted spoon and let drain on paper towels before serving. Continue to cook the remaining bhajis in batches and keep the already cooked bhajis warm until needed.

Serve with the caramelized lime, mint and yogurt dip.

CHINESE DUCK BREAST PANCAKES
with ginger jammy plums

You could roast and serve a whole duck if you want it crispy, but it will take a couple of hours. This recipe uses just duck breast to save time on roasting and shredding – it's juicy and easy to portion. The ginger jammy plums add flavour and look gorgeous too.

175 g/6 oz. duck breast
2 teaspoons Chinese five spice mixed with ½ teaspoon salt
10 ready-made Chinese pancakes (about 14 cm/ 5½ inches in diameter)
10 teaspoons hoisin sauce
½ cucumber, cut into matchsticks
5 spring onions/scallions, cut into matchsticks

GINGER JAMMY PLUMS
2 fresh plums, cut into 20 wedges
freshly squeezed juice of 1 orange
1 teaspoon grated fresh ginger
1 teaspoon caster/granulated sugar

MAKES 20

To make the jammy plums, simmer the plums in the orange juice, ginger and sugar for 3 minutes in a shallow frying pan/skillet until they take on a jam-like texture.

Take the duck out of the fridge 20 minutes before cooking. Score the skin of the duck and trim off any excess fat around the sides.

Rub the five spice and salt mix all over the duck. Put it in a frying pan/skillet skin-side down and turn on the heat.

When the pan is hot and you can hear the duck start to sizzle, let it cook for 5 minutes.

Sear the duck on the sides and the bottom, cooking for a further 5–8 minutes, or until cooked to your liking.

Take the pan off the heat and leave the duck to rest.

Lay the pancakes flat on a chopping board and cut in half.

Spoon ½ teaspoon hoisin sauce on a half-pancake and arrange a piece of duck, a wedge of jammy plum and a few matchsticks of cucumber and spring onions/scallions on top. Tightly roll into a flat cone. Repeat with the remaining ingredients and serve.

MUSHROOM PAKORAS

There is something irresistible about deep-fried food! These Indian pakoras – made with nutty-tasting chickpea/gram flour and flavoured with fragrant spices – are ideal for a drinks party served alongside other Indian small plates. Serve with a herbed yogurt dipping sauce or simply with lemon wedges.

115 g/¾ cup chickpea/
   gram flour
1 teaspoon ground cumin
1 teaspoon cumin seeds
½ teaspoon ground turmeric
½ teaspoon salt
½ teaspoon baking powder
120 ml/½ cup water
½ onion, chopped
200 g/6½ oz. mushrooms,
   chopped
2–3 sprigs freshly chopped
   coriander/cilantro
vegetable oil, for deep-frying
lemon wedges, to serve
   (optional)

YOGURT DIP
4 tablespoons freshly
   chopped coriander/cilantro
   or mint leaves
200 ml/1 scant cup plain
   yogurt

MAKES ABOUT 12–14

First, make the yogurt dip. Stir the chopped coriander/cilantro or mint into the yogurt and set aside.

Place the chickpea/gram flour, cumin powder and seeds, turmeric, salt and baking powder in a mixing bowl.

Whisk in the water to form a smooth batter. Fold in the onion, mushrooms and coriander/cilantro.

Heat the oil in a wok or large pan until very hot. Cook the pakoras in batches, dropping in a tablespoon of the mixture for each pakora. Fry for about 3–5 minutes, until golden brown, turning over each pakora as it cooks to ensure even browning. Remove the pakoras with a slotted spoon and drain on paper towels.

Serve at once with the yogurt dip or lemon wedges for squeezing.

AMRITSARI FISH PAKORAS

It does not get more 'Indian street food' than Amritsari fish pakoras! Deep-fried, diced cod is coated in an aromatic spiced batter, making the perfect crispy morsel. These tasty treats are traditionally found at the street-food stalls of Amritsar in Punjab, northern India, however, they are so hugely popular that they are now eaten all over the country.

500 g/1lb. 2 oz. cod loin, diced into 2.5-cm/1-inch cubes
plain/all-purpose flour, sifted, for dusting
vegetable oil, for deep-frying

MARINADE
½ green chilli/chile (or more to taste)
2 garlic cloves
1 teaspoon grated fresh ginger
2 tablespoons vegetable oil
freshly squeezed juice of ½ lemon
½ teaspoon ground turmeric
½ teaspoon salt
½ teaspoon chilli/chili powder

BATTER
4 tablespoons rice flour
8 tablespoons gram/chickpea flour, sifted

1 teaspoon ajwain seeds
1 teaspoon chilli flakes/hot red pepper flakes
1 teaspoon ground turmeric
½ teaspoon baking powder
1 tablespoon freshly chopped coriander/cilantro
180 ml/¾ cup ice-cold water
1 teaspoon salt

TO SERVE
mango powder, for sprinkling
black salt, for sprinkling
sliced chilli/chile
freshly chopped coriander/cilantro
lemon wedges

deep-fat fryer (optional)

SERVES 4–6

Rinse the diced fish under cold running water and gently pat dry.

Blitz the chilli/chile, garlic and ginger in a food processor to make a coarse paste. Combine with the rest of the ingredients for the marinade and mix with the diced fish. Let the fish pieces marinate for a minimum of 30 minutes at room temperature and a maximum of 24 hours in the refrigerator.

Combine all of the ingredients for the batter together, then set aside for 30 minutes to allow the ingredients and flavours to all come together. It should be the consistency of double/heavy cream.

Pat the marinated fish pieces in sifted flour and shake off any excess. Dip the floured fish pieces into the batter, ensuring that the fish is fully coated in the batter, with the spices distributed evenly.

Heat the oil for deep-frying in a deep-fat fryer or large, heavy-bottomed pan to 180°C (350°F). Deep-fry the fish pieces in batches of 6–8 pieces until golden-brown and the fish is cooked through; this should take no longer than 3–4 minutes per batch. Sprinkle over a pinch of mango powder and black salt, to taste, then serve with sliced chilli/chile, coriander/cilantro and lemon wedges.

SALT & PEPPER SQUID with Sansho spicy dip

This recipe, using spicy, citrusy Sansho pepper, is a spin on the ever-popular salt and pepper prawns/shrimp served in Chinese restaurants around the world. Dip the freshly fried squid into the spiced mayo and enjoy.

½ teaspoon ground
   Sansho pepper
2 teaspoons sea salt
65 g/½ cup rice flour
450 g/1 lb. squid, cleaned
   and sliced
freshly squeezed juice
   of 1 lemon
vegetable oil, for frying

SANSHO SPICY DIP
115 g/½ cup good-quality
   mayonnaise
5 g/¼ cup Vietnamese or
   regular basil leaves
½ teaspoon Sansho pepper
½ teaspoon sea salt
grated zest of 1 lemon

SERVES 4

To make the dip, whisk all the ingredients together in a small bowl until well combined. Set aside.

In a large shallow bowl mix together the Sansho pepper, salt and rice flour. Put the squid in another bowl and pour over the lemon juice.

Pour enough oil to come halfway up a large saucepan, then place over a medium–high heat until the oil starts to simmer.

Take a few pieces of squid at a time and toss in the flour mixture to coat.

Working in batches, deep fry for 2–3 minutes until golden and cooked through. Transfer to a wire rack to drain.

Pile the cooked squid in a shallow bowl and serve with the dip.

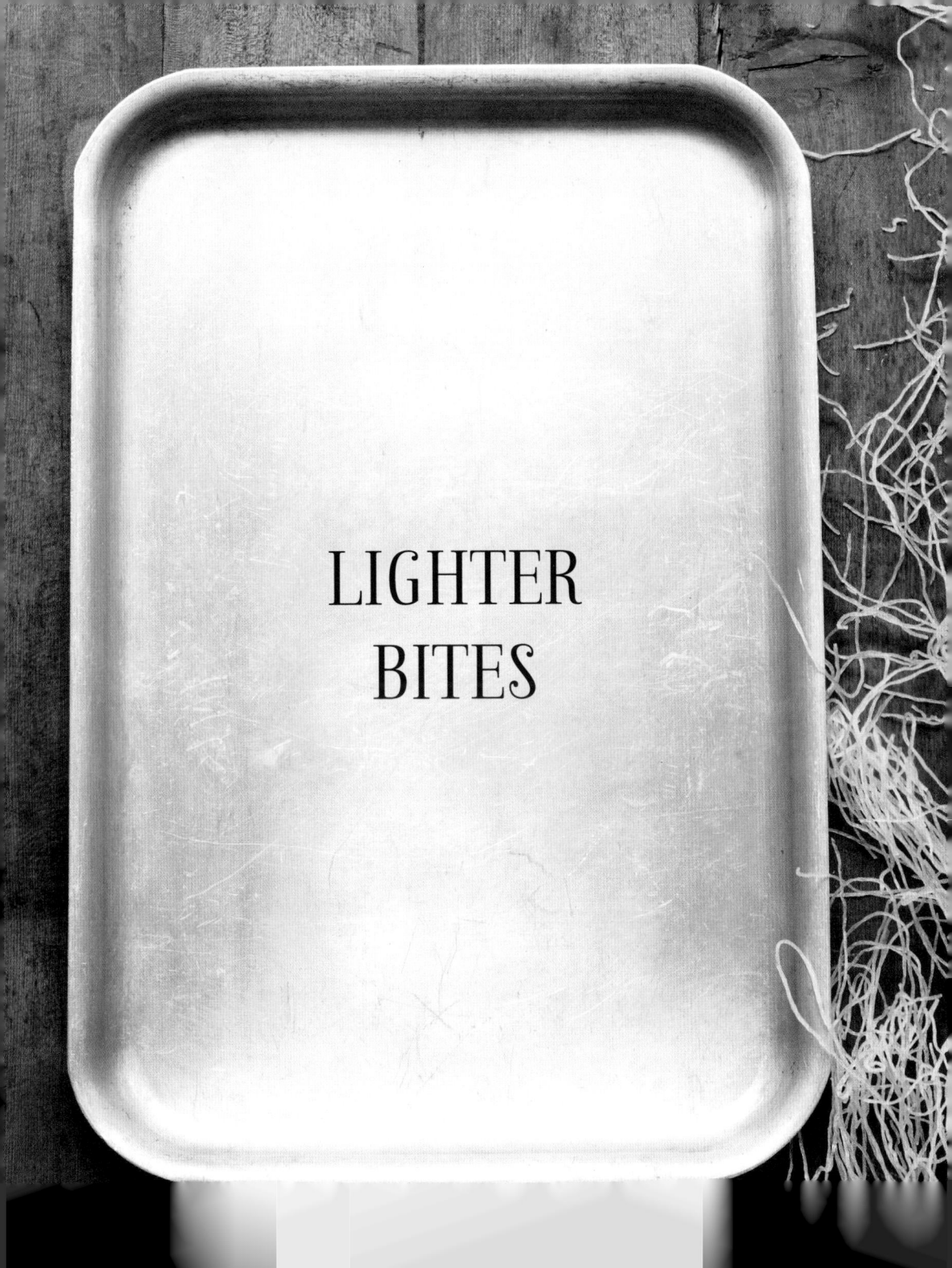

LIGHTER
BITES

VIETNAMESE SUMMER ROLLS

There are so many names for the ever-popular Vietnamese summer roll, including salad roll and crystal roll. Whatever the name, they are a fresh yet flavourful, delicious option if you are looking for an Asian bite that is not deep-fried. Here, they are stuffed with fragrant herbs and served with punchy dipping sauces which pep up the mild-tasting rice wrappers.

55 g/2 oz. rice vermicelli noodles
8 rice wrappers (21.5 cm/ 8½ inches in diameter)
4–6 shiitake mushrooms, cut into matchstick pieces
115 g/½ cup medium to firm tofu, sliced into matchstick pieces
30 g/½ cup cabbage, shredded or finely chopped
1⅓ tablespoons freshly chopped Thai basil
3 tablespoons freshly chopped mint leaves
3 tablespoons freshly chopped coriander/cilantro
2 lettuce leaves of choice, chopped
4 teaspoons fish sauce
60 ml/¼ cup water
2 tablespoons freshly squeezed lime juice
1 clove garlic, crushed
2 tablespoons caster/ granulated sugar
½ teaspoon garlic chilli/ chile sauce
3 tablespoons hoisin sauce
1 teaspoon peanuts, finely chopped

MAKES 8.

Bring a medium saucepan of water to boil. Boil the rice vermicelli for 3–5 minutes, or until al dente, and drain.

Fill a large bowl with warm water. Dip one rice wrapper into the warm water for 1 second to soften. Lay the wrapper flat. In a row across the centre of the wrapper, place 1 tablespoon of shiitake, 1 tablespoon tofu, a handful of cabbage, basil, mint, coriander/cilantro and lettuce, leaving about 5 cm/2 in. uncovered on each side. Fold the uncovered sides inward, then tightly roll the wrapper, beginning at the end with the lettuce. Repeat to make another 7 spring rolls.

In a small bowl, mix the fish sauce, water, lime juice, garlic, sugar and garlic chilli/chile sauce. In another small bowl, mix the hoisin sauce and peanuts.

Serve the spring rolls at room temperature and dip them into both sauces at will!

STEAMED ASIAN BLACK GARLIC SCALLOPS

A simple yet luxurious seafood dish, in which the natural sweetness of the scallops contrasts nicely with the savoury, smoky saltiness of the garlic dressing.

3 tablespoons dark soy sauce
2 black garlic cloves, finely chopped
2-cm/¾-inch piece fresh ginger, peeled and finely chopped
1 spring onion/scallion, finely chopped
12 king scallops
4 tablespoons groundnut/ peanut or sunflower oil
2 black garlic cloves, finely chopped

steamer

SERVES 4

Mix together the soy sauce, black garlic, ginger and spring onion/scallion in a bowl and set aside.

Steam the scallops until they turn opaque and are cooked through.

Heat the oil in a small frying pan/skillet, add the garlic and fry, stirring often, until fragrant. Pour the hot garlic oil into the soy sauce mixture, mixing well to form the dressing. Spoon the garlic dressing over the freshly steamed scallops and serve at once.

VIETNAMESE CHICKEN & QUINOA BITES

The quinoa and chicken in these tasty little meatballs are both packed full of protein, making these light bites the perfect high-protein dish to serve to health-conscious dinner guests, especially after they've hit the gym.

85 g/½ cup quinoa
450 g/1 lb. minced/ground chicken
½ teaspoon sea salt
1 tablespoon sweet chilli/chile sauce, plus extra to serve
1 tablespoon cornflour/cornstarch
2 teaspoons sesame oil
2 tablespoons vegetable or coconut oil
lettuce leaves and fresh coriander/cilantro, to serve

SPICE PASTE
50 g/½ cup sliced shallots
20 g/½ cup fresh mint
20 g/½ cup fresh coriander/cilantro
2 lemongrass stalks, outer leaves discarded and roughly chopped
2.5-cm/1-inch piece fresh ginger
3 garlic cloves
½ tablespoon fish sauce
2 Bird's eye chillies/chiles
1 tablespoon vegetable or coconut oil

high-speed blender

baking sheet, lined with non-stick baking parchment

MAKES 20

Start by cooking the quinoa. Put it in a small saucepan and pour over 250 ml/1 cup of water. Set over a medium heat and bring to the boil, then reduce the heat to low. Simmer with a lid on for 10 minutes, until the quinoa is soft and fluffy and all the water has been soaked up. Leave to one side to cool down.

Preheat the oven to 200°C (400°F) Gas 6.

Add all the ingredients for the spice paste to a blender and whizz until smooth. Transfer to a large mixing bowl.

Add the ground chicken to the spice paste, then the cooled quinoa, the salt, sweet chilli/chile sauce and cornflour/cornstarch, and mix everything together.

Dampen your hands with water and roll the mixture into balls about 1 tablespoon in size. Lay the balls on the prepared baking sheet and drizzle with both the sesame and vegetable oils.

Bake in the preheated oven for 10–15 minutes, depending on the size of your balls. Once cooked, they will be white all the way through – no pink bits inside – and slightly browned on the base. Cut one open to check it is cooked all the way through.

You can eat these straight away – they are good wrapped in lettuce leaves with some fresh coriander/cilantro and sweet chilli/chile sauce on the side to dip into. You can keep them in the fridge for up to 2 days.

SMOKED DUCK SUMMER ROLLS

Called 'summer rolls' and typically served in summer months due to their refreshing nature, these can have many different fillings. This recipe uses thin slices of smoked duck breast (available from specialist food stores), but if you can't find smoked duck you could use smoked salmon or smoked trout instead.

100 g/3½ oz. rice vermicelli
   noodles
2 teaspoons fish sauce
2 teaspoons freshly squeezed
   lime juice
2 teaspoons caster/
   granulated sugar
8 x 20-cm/8-inch dried rice
   paper wrappers
100 g/3½ oz. smoked
   duck breast
100 g/3 cups thinly sliced
   lettuce
1 carrot, peeled and cut into
   thin batons
½ cucumber, deseeded and
   cut into matchsticks
20 fresh Thai basil leaves

**HOISIN & PEANUT
DIPPING SAUCE**
2 tablespoons hoisin sauce
1 tablespoon smooth peanut
   butter
1 tablespoon warm water
2 teaspoons freshly squeezed
   lime juice
1 teaspoon dark soy sauce
¼ teaspoon caster/
   granulated sugar

SERVES 4

Put the noodles in a bowl, cover with boiling water and soak for 30 minutes until softened. Drain the noodles, pat dry and transfer to a large mixing bowl. Whisk the fish sauce, lime juice and sugar together until the sugar is dissolved and pour over the noodles. Toss well and set aside.

Next make the dipping sauce. Put all the ingredients in a small saucepan set over a low heat. Heat gently, stirring until the peanut butter is softened and the sauce smooth. Remove from the heat and set aside to cool.

Working one at a time, dip the rice paper wrappers into a bowl of warm water for about a minute until softened and then pat dry on paper towels. Lay each wrapper out flat and top with a few noodles, the smoked duck slices, shredded lettuce, carrot, cucumber and basil leaves. Fold the ends of the rice paper over the filling and then roll up tightly to form parcels.

Serve with the dipping sauce.

RICE ROLLS WITH PORK & SHRIMP

Bánh cuôn are noodle sheets similar to lasagne, traditionally made from rice flour, tapioca starch and water and then steamed. They are folded or rolled, with or without a filling, and dipped into a spicy dipping sauce. They are light yet full of gorgeous flavours and textures.

FILLING
80 g/1 cup dried shredded wood ear mushrooms
dash of cooking oil
2 Asian shallots, finely chopped
300 g/10½ oz. minced/ground chicken or pork
½ teaspoon sea salt
½ teaspoon coarsely ground black pepper
2 teaspoons sugar
170 g/6 oz. king prawns/jumbo shrimp, peeled, deveined and finely chopped

NOODLE SHEETS
300 g/2¼ cups tapioca starch
300 g/2¼ cups rice flour
1 teaspoon cooking oil, plus extra for frying
2 spring onions/ scallions, finely chopped
½ teaspoon salt
900 ml/scant 4 cups water

DRESSING
2 garlic cloves, finely chopped
2 Bird's Eye chillies/ chiles, finely chopped
2 tablespoons cider vinegar
5 tablespoons fish sauce
3 tablespoons sugar
400 ml/1½ cups water

GARNISHES
deep-fried shallots
Thai sweet basil, finely chopped
coriander/cilantro, finely chopped

20-cm/8-inch non-stick frying pan/skillet with a lid

SERVES 6

To make the filling, put the mushrooms in a bowl, cover with warm water and soak for at least 30 minutes. Drain and pat dry.

Heat the oil in a frying pan and fry the shallots briefly. Add the meat and mushrooms and stir-fry for a couple of minutes. Add the salt, pepper, sugar and prawns/ shrimp. Cook for 3 minutes, then allow to rest.

To make the noodle sheets, mix the ingredients and the water in a bowl, making sure the batter is smooth and free of lumps. Heat a dash of oil in the 20-cm/8-inch frying pan. Using a shallow ladle, pour in 1 ladleful of the batter and tilt the pan to spread the batter. Cover with the lid and cook for 2 minutes, then slide the cooked noodle sheet onto a plate. Repeat with the remaining batter.

Divide the filling between the noodle sheets. Fold the sides over the filling, then roll up tightly from the bottom. Place, seam side down, on a serving dish.

For the dressing, mix together the garlic, chillies/chiles and vinegar in a bowl. Set aside for 2 minutes. This 'cooks' the garlic. Now add the fish sauce, sugar and the water.

Serve the rolls warm or at room temperature with the garnishes and dressing sprinkled on top.

VEGAN TEMAKI ROLLS WITH SEED PÂTÉ

This hand-rolled sushi is really easy to make. Temakis are a great choice for parties since they are best rolled directly at the table, just before eating, and everybody can join in, which leaves you with less work. Prepare and serve all ingredients in the middle of the table and let the fun begin!

FERMENTED SEED PÂTÉ
240 g/2 cups pumpkin seeds
840 ml/3½ cups water, for soaking
50 ml/scant ¼ cup olive oil
60 ml/¼ cup water
1 garlic clove
¼ teaspoon turmeric powder
1 tablespoon nutritional yeast (optional)
3 teaspoons vegan rice or barley miso
2 teaspoons lemon juice
¼ teaspoon salt
freshly crushed black pepper

MAKES 250 G/2½ CUPS

TEMAKI ROLLS
2 medium carrots (around 100 g/3½ oz. total weight)
1 ripe avocado (around 190 g/6½ oz. in weight)
2 handfuls rocket/arugula or 50 g/1 cup alfalfa sprouts, plus extra to serve
3 spring onions/scallions
6 sheets of nori seaweed
2 cups Sauerkraut or other fermented vegetables, plus extra to serve
soy sauce, to serve

MAKES 12

First make the pâté. Soak the pumpkin seeds in the water for soaking for 2–3 days, until slightly fermented, without changing the soaking water. Discard the soaking water and rinse them thoroughly under running water. Drain well. Place in a high-speed blender jug/pitcher, together with the remaining ingredients. Blend until smooth, using a tamper tool to push down the ingredients. If you don't own a high-speed blender, the pâté will probably turn out chunkier in a less powerful blender, and more water will need to be added, resulting in a somewhat runnier consistency. Let sit in the fridge for another day; the flavours really develop in this final stage of setting. There will be some leftovers, but you can store these in the fridge and use within a week.

Wash and julienne the carrots. Peel the avocado, slice in half, discard the stone and cut both halves in strips. Wash the rocket/arugula or sprouts and pat dry. Take only the green parts of the spring onions/scallions, wash them well and cut into 10-cm/4-inch pieces. Cut each nori sheet in half with scissors.

Make sure your hands are dry before starting. Place a piece of nori (shiny side down) in the palm of your hand and add 1½ tablespoons of pumpkin seed pâté. Spread it gently on the left third of the nori sheet. Place your chosen fillings diagonally over the pate. Do not overfill; a couple of carrot matchsticks, 1 slice of avocado, 1 tablespoon of sauerkraut and some greens are more than enough. Fold the bottom left corner of the nori over and begin rolling into a cone shape. Wet the edge with little water and seal. Continue until all nori is used. Serve the temaki rolls with more fermented vegetables, condiments, some soy sauce and leftover greens.

SMOKED MACKEREL SUSHI ROLLS

This is a recipe for inside-out 'uramaki' rolls, which look far more difficult than they actually are! They will impress your guests.

255 g/1¼ cups brown
   or white sushi rice
550 ml/2⅓ cups water
50 ml/3 tablespoons mirin
   (sweetened rice wine)
5 sheets of nori seaweed
black sesame seeds
350 g/12 oz. smoked
   mackerel, cut into
   thin strips
2 spring onions/scallions,
   cut into thin strips
½ red (bell) pepper,
   cut into thick strips

TO SERVE
wasabi
picked Japanese sushi ginger
light soy sauce

bamboo sushi mat

SERVES 4

Wash the sushi rice under cold water and drain. Place in a saucepan with a lid and add the water. Bring to the boil (uncovered), then reduce to the lowest heat and simmer until nearly all the water has been absorbed (about 20–25 minutes). Remove from the heat, place the lid on top and allow it to stand for 15 minutes.

Spread the rice out over a clean baking sheet. Drizzle the mirin all over the rice, turning it with a spatula to help it cool down.

While it is cooling, wrap the bamboo sushi mat in clingfilm/plastic wrap, squeezing out any trapped air. This helps prevent the rice from sticking. Lay the mat lengthways in front of you. Take one nori sheet and lay it out, shiny side down, on the mat. Wet your hands and take a small handful of rice. Starting at the far end, pat the rice across the nori sheet leaving a bare ¼-cm/½-inch gap running along the edge of the sheet closest to you. Add more rice if needed, but it should be no more than 1 cm/½ inch thick.

If it starts sticking to your hands simply wet them again. You can also use the back of a spoon dipped in water.

Sprinkle black sesame seeds over the rice, then flip the nori sheet over so that the rice is facing downward with the edge free of rice closest to you and in line with the edge of the bamboo mat. Across the middle of the nori lay 3 lines of mackerel, spring onion/scallion and red pepper.

Then, using the bamboo mat, roll the edge of the nori sheet closest to you over the filling in the middle, tucking it over firmly so the filling is enclosed. When it looks like you are about to roll the mat into the sushi roll, pull the mat back and continue to roll applying even pressure and tightening as you roll, using the mat to shape it. Once the roll has come together, carefully take it off the mat, lay the mat over it and press and smooth the roll. The roll will actually be more of a rectangular shape. With a sharp and wet knife, cut the roll in half and then each half into 3.

Repeat this process with the remaining ingredients. Serve with wasabi, pickled ginger and soy sauce in a dish on the side.

SASHIMI & CUCUMBER BITES

Seasoned raw fish with flavours of ginger, soy, sesame and spring onions/ scallions, topped with avocado make a perfect Japanese-inspired light bite. A little bit of extra chilli/chile keeps things sprightly. You can serve this sashimi mix in lettuce cups or on cucumber slices.

600 g/1 lb. 5 oz. fresh or sashimi-grade fish (tuna is classic, but you can substitute any other sashimi-grade fish)
½ teaspoon white sugar
3 tablespoons soy sauce
1 tablespoon sesame oil
1 tablespoon grated fresh ginger
1 tablespoon finely chopped red chilli/chile
35 g/½ cup (about 5) chopped spring onions/scallions
1 tablespoon black sesame seeds, plus extra to garnish
1 tablespoon white sesame seeds, plus extra to garnish
1 large avocado, peeled, pitted and diced into 1-cm/½-inch dice
1 head iceberg lettuce, or thick cucumber slices, slightly hollowed out, to serve

SERVES 6-8

Trim any sinew or bloodlines off the fish. Cut the flesh into 1-cm/¾-inch dice.

Stir the sugar into the soy sauce until it dissolves.

Mix with the sesame oil, ginger and chilli/chile. Combine the soy dressing with the fish. Gently fold through the spring onions/scallions, sesame seeds and avocado.

Serve with lettuce leaves to wrap around or pile onto thick slices of cucumber. Garnish with extra sesame seeds if you like.

MUSHROOM-FILLED LETTUCE CUPS

Light and elegant, with pleasantly contrasting textures, these filled lettuce leaves make an appealing light bite. Fresh oyster or shiitake mushrooms would work well in this Chinese-inspired dish. Similarly, radicchio or chicory leaves, with their distinctive bitter note, could be used instead of lettuce leaves.

1 tablespoon vegetable oil
1-cm/½-inch piece fresh
  ginger, finely chopped
1 garlic clove, finely chopped
2 spring onions/scallions,
  finely chopped, separated
  into white and green parts
300 g/10 oz. white/cup
  mushrooms, cut into
  1-cm/½-inch dice
1 tablespoon rice wine
  or Amontillado sherry
2 teaspoons light soy sauce
1 tablespoon oyster sauce
8 even-sized Little Gem
  lettuce leaves
coriander/cilantro sprigs,
  to garnish
finely chopped red chilli/
  chile, to garnish

MAKES 8

Heat the oil in a wok or large frying pan/skillet. Add the ginger, garlic and white spring onion/scallion pieces and stir-fry over a medium heat for 1 minute.

Add the diced mushrooms and stir-fry for 2 minutes. Add the rice wine or sherry and stir-fry for 1 minute, until cooked off. Add the soy sauce and oyster sauce. Stir-fry for 2 minutes. Toss through the green spring onion/scallion pieces.

While the mushroom mixture is hot or at room temperature, spoon it into the lettuce leaves, filling each one with the mixture.

Garnish with coriander/cilantro leaves and finely chopped red chilli/chile and serve at once.

TEMPURA VEGETABLES & SHRIMP
with wasabi mayonnaise

Tempura vegetables and shrimp are always a hit. This lighter, wheat-free version is made using rice and cornflour/cornstarch to give a thin crispy coating of batter to the fresh ingredients.

selection of vegetables,
  eg. carrot, sweet potato,
  aubergine/eggplant,
  squash, broccoli, (bell)
  pepper, spring onion/
  scallion, beet(root)
600 ml/2½ cups vegetable,
  sunflower or rapeseed oil
4 king prawns/jumbo shrimp,
  peeled and deveined,
  but tails on
100 g/¾ cup rice flour,
  plus extra for coating
100 g/¾ cup cornflour/
  cornstarch
1 teaspoon baking powder
small bottle of ice-cold
  sparkling water
2 egg whites
few cubes of ice
sea salt and freshly ground
  black pepper
5 tablespoons mayonnaise
  mixed with wasabi powder
  or paste to taste for dipping

SERVES 4

Cut the hard vegetables into thin slices about ½ cm/¼ inch thick. Cut softer vegetables like aubergine/eggplant, spring onion/scallion or (bell) pepper a little thicker.

If you have a deep fat fryer, heat the oil to 190°C/375°F, otherwise heat it in a deep saucepan. If you don't have a cooking thermometer, check the temperature by dropping a small cube of bread into the oil. It should turn golden in about 25–30 seconds. Any faster than this and the tempura will burn before the vegetable inside is cooked through.

While the oil is heating, mix together the flours, baking powder, ½ teaspoon salt and a good pinch of pepper in a bowl. Slowly stir in just enough cold sparkling water until you have a yogurt-like consistency, but don't over-whisk. It doesn't matter if the batter is lumpy; traditionally Japanese tempura batter is not mixed too thoroughly, as the lumps in the batter help to form a more crunchy tempura. Using an electric whisk, beat the egg whites in a separate bowl until they form hard peaks. Fold the eggs into the batter, stir the ice cubes through to keep it as cold as possible.

Lightly coat the vegetables and prawns/shrimp in rice flour. Shake off any excess, then dip into the batter. Carefully place them into the hot oil. Don't overcrowd the fryer or pan, as it will bring down the temperature of the oil. The prawns/shrimp will take about 3 minutes and the vegetables about 2 minutes. Remove all the tempura with a slotted spoon and drain on paper towels. Serve with the wasabi mayonnaise on the side for dipping.

SWEET-&-SOUR POPCORN TOFU

This is a Chinese-inspired fusion-style dish with healthy tofu at its core and fresh plums used to make a dipping sauce. There are quite a lot of processes involved to give the tofu perfect texture and flavour, but you can save time by using a ready-made plum sauce, if you like. For an impressive and fun way of serving, put a little sauce in a Chinese soup spoon and top with a piece of crispy tofu.

6 tablespoons light soy sauce
2 teaspoons Chinese five-spice powder
400 g/14 oz. firm tofu, drained, excess water pressed out and sliced into small cubes
150 g/1 cups cornflour/ cornstarch
100 ml/⅓ cup soya/ soy cream
150 g/2¾ cups panko breadcrumbs
1 teaspoon hot smoked paprika
600 ml/2½ cups vegetable oil, for deep-frying

PLUM SAUCE
12 plums, stoned/ pitted and roughly chopped
2 tablespoons water
4–6 tablespoons soft brown sugar, if using fresh plums
8 tablespoons rice vinegar, or to taste
1 tablespoon tomato purée/paste, or to taste
½ teaspoon salt

SERVES 4–6

To make the sauce, put the plums in a pan over medium heat and add the water and sugar. Bring to the boil, then simmer for 15 minutes or until the fruit is completely softened. Add the remaining sauce ingredients and bring to a simmer again, adding a little water if necessary so that the sauce is not too thick. Using a food processor or blender, blend the sauce until smooth. Check the seasoning and adjust the sugar, salt or vinegar to taste. The balance of sweet-and-sour flavours means one should not overpower the other.

Mix the soy sauce and five-spice powder in a bowl, then drizzle this marinade over the tofu pieces. Put the cornflour/cornstarch in one bowl, the soya/soy cream in another bowl and the panko breadcrumbs in a third bowl. Add the paprika to the breadcrumbs and mix well.

Heat the vegetable oil in a wok over a medium–high heat. Put a sheet of non-stick baking parchment on the work surface. Dip each piece of tofu in the cornflour/cornstarch, then in the soya/soy cream and then in the breadcrumbs, shaping it a little to form a ball. Lay each coated ball on the baking parchment as you go.

Fry the tofu in batches, until golden brown and crispy. Lift out using a slotted spoon and drain on paper towels. You can keep the tofu balls warm in a low oven, if you like, or reheat them later at 170°C (350°F) Gas 4 for 10–15 minutes. Serve with the plum sauce.

KIMCHI NOODLE DUMPLINGS
with dipping sauce

The super-healthy, super-flavoursome wonder-ingredient kimchi is the star of the show in these delicious crispy-bottomed dumplings. Traditionally kimchi is quite fiery so just one tablespoon of chilli/hot red pepper flakes is added here, which is far less than you will find in most Korean recipes. Add more if you dare!

150 g/⅔ cup minced/
  ground pork
150 g/scant 1 cup cooked
  prawns/shrimp, peeled
  and very finely chopped
100 g/4 oz. kimchi
2 teaspoons dark soy sauce
½ beaten egg
20 gyoza wrappers
4 tablespoons vegetable oil
125 ml/½ cup water to the pan

DIPPING SAUCE
2 tablespoons dark soy sauce
1 tablespoon brown rice
  vinegar
pinch of toasted sesame
  seeds
spring onions/scallions,
  thinly sliced, to serve

*baking sheet, lined with
  non-stick baking parchment*

SERVES 4

Put the pork, prawns/shrimp, kimchi, soy sauce and beaten egg in a large mixing bowl and mix together until evenly combined.

Working one at a time, lay the gyoza wrappers out flat and place a teaspoon of the mixture on one half of each wrapper. Dampen the edges with a little cold water, fold the wrapper over the filling and carefully press the edges together to seal.

Preheat the oven to 110°C (225°F) Gas ¼ (or the lowest heat setting).

Heat the oil in a wok or large non-stick frying pan/skillet set over a high heat. Add half the dumplings and fry for about 1 minute until the bottoms are golden. Add the water to the pan, cover and simmer for 5 minutes until the filling is heated through. Remove the lid and cook for a further 1–2 minutes until the bottoms are crispy. Transfer the dumplings to the prepared baking sheet, turn off the oven and set in the still-warm oven while you cook the remaining dumplings in the same way.

Mix together the ingredients for the dipping sauce in a small bowl. Arrange the dumplings on warmed plates and serve with the sauce, scattered with spring onions/scallions.

VEGAN MAKI & CALIFORNIA ROLLS

These two types of sushi are so easy to make at home. Maki is where the nori is on the outside of the roll, and California rolls are where the nori is on the inside.

SPREAD
65 g/½ cup dry-roasted
  sunflower seeds (or use
  4 tablespoons tahini)
3 teaspoons umeboshi paste
1 tablespoon dark sesame oil

SUSHI
475 g/2⅔ cups cooked
  brown rice
2 medium pickled gherkins,
  cut lengthways into strips,
  or other pickled vegetables
  (sauerkraut, daikon, etc.)
1 long carrot, cut lengthways
  into thin sticks
4 long spring onion/scallion
  leaves, washed and drained
4 toasted nori sheets

DIPPING SAUCE
2 tablespoons fresh ginger
  juice
2 teaspoons tamari
2 tablespoons dry-roasted
  sesame seeds
4 tablespoons water
extra pickles and wasabi
  paste, to serve

sushi mat

MAKES 32

Prepare the spread by blending the sunflower seeds in a blender into a powder/butter, and then adding the umeboshi and oil.

Prepare a bowl full of lukewarm water to wet your hands with while making the sushi. Place each nori sheet in turn on a sushi mat, shiny-side down. Wet your hands and spread 120 g/¾ cup of the cooked rice evenly over the nori, except the top side, where you'll want to leave a 1-cm/⅓-in. margin to make it easier to roll and seal.

To make the maki, spread a tablespoon of the spread across the middle of the roll. Place a quarter of the gherkin strips, carrot sticks and spring onion/scallion leaves over the spread, making sure the layer is not thick, as this will make for an overly thick sushi.

Starting from the bottom, roll up the nori and tuck in the vegetables. Continue rolling and press tightly so that the rolled sushi stays sealed. Before serving, slice each sushi into 8 pieces. Repeat the process for the a second nori sheet, so you end up with 16 pieces of sushi.

To make California rolls, cover the sushi mat with a sheet of clingfilm/plastic wrap and place one nori sheet on top. Wet your hands and spread 120–150 g/¾–1 cup of the rice over the nori, distributing it evenly up to the edges. Carefully flip the nori so that the rice side goes on top of the clingfilm/plastic wrap on the mat. Spoon a tablespoon of the spread in a strip across the middle of the roll. Place half the remaining gherkin, carrot and spring onion/scallion leaves over the spread. Starting at the edge while pressing it firmly, roll up the sushi mat and continue until you reach the end of the mat. Be careful not to wrap the clingfilm/plastic wrap inside! Squeeze the sushi inside the mat with your hands. Unwrap before serving, and slice into 8 pieces. Roll each of these pieces in toasted sesame seeds. Repeat with last nori sheet and remaining vegetables.

To make the sauce, mix the ginger juice, tamari and water. Dip a piece of sushi in it. Before eating, coat in some sesame seeds (but not for the California rolls, as they won't need it!) Serve the sushi with extra pickles and, if you wish, a little wasabi paste, to spice things up!

CAULIFLOWER & KALE PAKORAS

Pakoras are easy to adapt to whichever seasonal vegetables you have available. Cauliflower and kale are a great combination because the kale adds extra crispness. You can make a big batch at home, as they keep well in the fridge and can easily be reheated in the oven. Gram flour is made from chickpeas, which is a good source of protein, it is also a naturally gluten-free recipe (although it's a good idea to check the asafoetida powder if you are serving to coeliacs/celiacs).

1 small cauliflower, cut into 2-cm/¾-inch florets
1 tablespoon sunflower oil, plus extra for deep-frying
2 onions, thinly sliced
a bunch of kale or dark leaf cabbage, thinly sliced
2–4 small green chillies/chiles, to taste, finely chopped
2 large red chillies/chiles, finely chopped
1 tablespoon chilli/chili powder
½ teaspoon asafoetida powder (hing)
250 g/2 cups chickpea/gram flour
2 teaspoons black cumin seeds
2 tablespoons fennel seeds
2 tablespoons dried pomegranate seeds (anardana)
bunch of fresh coriander/cilantro, roughly chopped
¼ teaspoon bicarbonate of soda/baking soda
1 teaspoon salt
daniya or raita, to serve

MAKES ABOUT 24

Parboil the cauliflower for 2–3 minutes, then drain in a colander/strainer and leave for 5 minutes.

Heat the oil in a small pan over medium heat and fry the onions for 5 minutes or until softened. Add the kale, green and red chillies/chiles, chilli/chili powder and asafoetida, and cook for 3 minutes. Set aside.

Sift the chickpea/gram flour into a large bowl. Toast the cumin and fennel seeds in a dry pan over medium heat for 30 seconds, stirring occasionally, to release the aroma, then add to the gram flour followed by the onion and kale mixture. Add 120 ml/scant ½ cup water to make a thick paste, then add all the other ingredients and mix well. The batter should have a thick porridge-like consistency, so add a little more gram flour or water if necessary.

Heat the oil for deep-frying in a deep pan or deep-fat fryer. Using a tablespoon, gently drop spoonfuls of the mixture into the hot oil, frying in batches of three or four. Cook until golden brown, turning halfway through to cook both sides. Remove with a slotted spoon and drain on paper towels. Serve hot, with some daniya or raita for dipping.

BEEF BULGOGI & RICE NOODLE WRAPS

The word bulgogi means 'fire meat' and refers to marinated and grilled meats, usually beef. Here it is stir-fried and combined with shiitake mushrooms and Korean sweet potato noodles, wrapped in lettuce leaves and topped with kimchi and ssamjang.

500 g/1 lb. beef rib-eye steak
2 tablespoons light or dark soy sauce
2 tablespoons soft brown sugar
1 Asian shallot, finely chopped
1 garlic clove, crushed
2 teaspoons sesame oil, plus extra for dressing
½ teaspoon Chinese five-spice powder
125 g/4 oz. spiralized sweet potato noodles
2 tablespoons peanut oil
125 g/4 oz. shiitake mushrooms, trimmed and cut into quarters
4 tablespoons kimchi
Ssamjang (Korean spicy sauce), to serve

SERVES 4

Begin by preparing the beef. Thinly slice the steak and arrange in a single layer in a wide, shallow dish. Combine the soy sauce, sugar, shallot, garlic, sesame oil and Chinese five-spice powder, and pour over the beef. Set aside to marinate for at least 1 hour.

Plunge the sweet potato noodles into a pan of boiling water and cook for 4–5 minutes until al dente. Drain, refresh under cold water and drain again. Shake the noodles dry and dress with a little sesame oil to prevent them from sticking together. Set aside.

Heat the oil in a wok or large frying pan/skillet set over a medium heat until it starts to shimmer. Add the beef in batches and stir-fry for 2–3 minutes until golden. Remove with a slotted spoon. Add the mushrooms and any remaining marinade and stir-fry for 1 minute. Return the beef to the pan along with the noodles and stir-fry for 1 minute, until everything is heated through.

Serve with lettuce leaves, kimchi and the ssamjang Korean spicy sauce. Wrap, roll and eat.

RIBS, GRILLS
& WINGS

KOREAN STICKY RIBS

Gochujang is a red pepper paste used in Korean cooking. It comes in varying degrees of heat, so make sure to check the label and choose something to suit your tastebuds. These ribs are great for the barbecue; serve them with an Asian coleslaw or kimchi.

8 Korean-style beef ribs,
 1 cm/½ inch thick
3 spring onions/scallions,
 finely sliced
2 tablespoons black
 sesame seeds

MARINADE
60 ml/¼ cup soy sauce
60 ml/¼ cup toasted
 sesame oil
140 g/½ cup orange-blossom
 honey
2 heaped tablespoons
 gochujang or sambal oelek
 (Asian chilli/chile paste)
1 tablespoon fish sauce
4 garlic cloves, bashed
2 Serrano chillies/chiles,
 roughly chopped
2 teaspoons cracked
 rainbow peppercorns
½ teaspoon sea salt

SERVES 4-6

Lay the ribs in a single layer in a ceramic baking dish.

Put all the marinade ingredients in a blender and process until smooth. Pour over the ribs and sprinkle with the spring onions/scallions and sesame seeds. Cover and refrigerate for 6–24 hours.

Remove the ribs from the fridge and bring to room temperature.

Heat a grill/broiler or barbecue to a medium–high heat. Place the ribs on the rack and cook for 5 minutes, then turn over and cook for another 5 minutes. Transfer to a warm plate and tent with foil. Rest for 10 minutes.

Put the remaining marinade in a small saucepan and bring to the boil, then reduce the heat and simmer for 5 minutes. To serve, pour the marinade into a bowl and serve alongside the ribs.

TANDOORI-SPICED LAMB CHOPS

The marinade for these tandoori-spiced, charred and grilled/broiled chops works exceptionally well to enhance the natural meatiness of the dish. The blend of spices, mint, chilli/chile and lemon keeps the meat moist while also creating a wonderful harmony of flavours. Lamb chops don't tend to dry out too much because they are cooked on the bone and have a layer of fat.

2 teaspoons cumin seeds
4 tablespoons plain yogurt
1 teaspoon salt
5 garlic cloves
a 5-cm/2-inch piece fresh
    ginger
4 green chillies/chiles
1 red chilli/chile
1 teaspoon ground turmeric
1 teaspoon garam masala
5 fresh mint leaves,
    plus extra to garnish
freshly squeezed juice
    of ½ lemon
12 lamb chops
vegetable oil, for frying

SERVES 6-8

Toast the cumin seeds in a dry frying pan/skillet over low–medium heat until they become dark in colour and give off a fragrant aroma. Put all of the ingredients including the toasted cumin seeds (but not the lamb chops) in a food processor and blitz until everything comes together to form a coarse chunky paste.

Rub the paste all over the lamb chops, wearing gloves if needed. Allow the chops to marinate for 24 hours in the refrigerator if possible, or for at least 30 minutes at room temperature.

Preheat the grill/broiler to high.

Heat a little oil in a frying pan/skillet over medium heat and seal the chops on both sides for 1 minute. Transfer to a baking sheet and put under the preheated grill/boiler. Grill/broil the chops for 5 minutes on each side for medium-rare. If you want them more well-done, then leave them under the grill/broiler for a little longer.

Sprinkle the chops with mint leaves and serve straight away to prevent them from drying out.

ASIAN CARAMEL WINGS

Fried first and then tossed in a sweet yet savoury caramel sauce, these wings have the perfect balance of delicate Asian flavours and seasoning. They are tastier still when served with a green onion dipping sauce on the side.

200 g/1 cup brown sugar
120 ml/½ cup water
75 ml/⅓ cup fish sauce
75 ml/⅓ cup soy sauce
60 ml/¼ cup orange juice
60 ml/¼ cup freshly squeezed lime juice
vegetable oil, for frying
1.8 kg/4 lbs. chicken wings, halved at the joints, tips removed

GREEN ONION DIPPING SAUCE
250 ml/1 cup sour cream
225 g/1 cup mayonnaise
50 g/½ cup finely chopped spring onions/scallions
30 g/½ cup finely chopped fresh flat-leaf parsley
2 garlic cloves, finely chopped
1 teaspoon Dijon mustard

a deep fat fryer

SERVES 4–6

First, make the dipping sauce. Mix all the ingredients together in a blender until smooth. Cover and refrigerate until ready to serve.

Place the sugar in a medium saucepan with half of the water and bring to a boil. Continue to boil and swirl (don't stir) for 6–7 minutes so the sugar caramelizes evenly.

Combine the fish sauce, soy sauce, orange juice and lime juice with the remaining water in a small bowl. Once the caramel has turned a golden amber colour, slowly pour the fish sauce mixture into the pan and return to a boil. Continue to boil for 7 minutes until the sauce is well combined, then remove the sauce from the heat and keep warm.

Meanwhile, preheat the oil in the deep fat fryer to 180°C (350°F).

Fry the chicken wings in batches for about 10 minutes until cooked through and the juices run clear when the thickest part is pierced to the bone. Remove and drain on paper towels. Place in a large bowl, pour the caramel sauce over the wings and toss. Serve with the green onion dipping sauce on the side.

Serve these wings as they are for a bar bite but add rice and an Asian-style slaw to create a more substantial plateful.

THAI-STYLE FRIED CHICKEN WINGS

Let's be honest, for some fried chicken isn't so much of a craze as it is a way of life. This recipe is spicy, crispy and perfect for Friday night feasting.

vegetable or canola oil,
  for frying
9 garlic cloves
7.5-cm/3-inch piece of fresh
  ginger, peeled
6 tablespoons soy sauce
6 tablespoons curry paste
3 tablespoons rice vinegar
2 tablespoons coconut oil,
  melted
2 tablespoons runny honey
180 g/1⅓ cups plain/
  all-purpose flour
2 tablespoons cornflour/
  cornstarch
350 ml/1⅔ cups water
1.8 kg/4 lbs. chicken wings,
  halved at the joints, tips
  removed

**LEMONGRASS &
SOY DIPPING SAUCE**
3 stalks of lemongrass
2 spring onions/scallions,
  chopped
1 teaspoon finely chopped
  garlic
1 teaspoon brown sugar
1 tablespoon sriracha sauce
3 tablespoons freshly
  squeezed lime juice
1 tablespoon fish sauce
2 teaspoons soy sauce
1 tablespoon freshly chopped
  coriander/cilantro
1 tablespoon freshly chopped
  basil
3 tablespoons water

SERVES 4-6

First, make the dipping sauce. Trim the end of the lemongrass stalks and remove the outer layers, then finely chop. Place in a bowl with the other ingredients. Mix well, then cover and chill in the refrigerator until ready to serve.

Preheat the oil in the deep fat fryer to 180°C (350°F).

Chop the garlic and ginger by pulsing briefly in a food processor. Add the soy sauce, curry paste, vinegar, coconut oil and honey. Purée until smooth. Put the sauce into a bowl.

In a separate bowl, whisk the flour and cornflour/cornstarch with the water. Add the chicken and toss until well coated.

Fry the chicken in about three batches for 6–8 minutes until golden, then drain on paper towels.

Bring the oil back to 180°C (350°F) and fry the chicken for a further 6–8 minutes, until crisp and the juices run clear when the thickest part is pierced to the bone. Drain again, then toss the chicken in the sauce.

Serve with the lemongrass and soy dipping sauce.

SAKE WINGS

These oven-fried, Asian-inspired chicken wings are flavoured with reduced sake, teriyaki sauce, ginger and chilli flakes/hot red pepper flakes. A teri-sake infusion!

250 ml/1 cup soy sauce

120 ml/½ cup sake, dry sherry or dry white wine

3 tablespoons very finely chopped fresh ginger

1½ tablespoons finely chopped garlic

200 g/1 cup sugar

1½ teaspoons chilli flakes/hot red pepper flakes

100 g/1 cup thinly sliced spring onions/scallions, (white and green parts), plus extra for garnish

3½ tablespoons rice vinegar

3 tablespoons cornflour/cornstarch

2 tablespoons toasted sesame seeds

1.8 kg/4 lbs. chicken wings, halved at the joints, tips removed

SERVES 4-6

PLUM DIPPING SAUCE

1.3 kg/3 lbs. plums, pitted and chopped

4 garlic cloves, finely chopped

1 tablespoon finely chopped fresh ginger

1 small onion, finely chopped

200 g/1 cup brown sugar

2 tablespoons teriyaki sauce

1 teaspoon sesame oil

2 tablespoons soy sauce

½ teaspoon crushed dried chilli

freshly squeezed juice of 1 lemon

475 ml/2 cups water

2 tablespoons cornflour/cornstarch

First, make the plum dipping sauce. Place all the ingredients except the cornflour/cornstarch in a medium saucepan with the water. Bring to the boil, then reduce the heat and simmer for 30 minutes. Remove from the heat. Mix the cornflour/cornstarch with 1 tablespoon water, then pour into a blender with the plum mixture. Blend until combined. Pour back into the pan and cook on medium-low until the mixture thickens to the desired consistency. Set aside to cool, then refrigerate until needed.

In a small saucepan, whisk together the soy sauce, sake (or sherry or white wine), ginger, garlic, sugar, chilli flakes/hot red pepper flakes, spring onions/scallions, vinegar and cornflour/cornstarch with 3 tablespoons water. Set the pan over a medium heat and bring to the boil, whisking constantly (the mixture will be very thick). Let cool.

Preheat the oven to 190°C (375°F) Gas 5. Grease 2–3 baking sheets with cooking spray or vegetable oil.

Add the sauce mixture to a large bowl with the wings and mix well. Arrange the wings in a single layer on the baking sheets and pour over any leftover sauce. Bake in the preheated oven for 30 minutes. Stir and turn the wings over in the sauce, then bake for a further 20 minutes. Stir and turn the wings again and bake for a final 10 minutes, or until the chicken is tender and the juices run clear when the thickest part is pierced to the bone, and the sauce is thick and shiny. Transfer to a serving platter. Spoon some of the extra sauce over, then sprinkle with the sesame seeds and spring onions/scallions.

VIETNAMESE BBQ SPARERIBS

This mouthwatering fusion recipe has been adapted slightly to include English mustard as an ingredient. Your guests will be crazy in love for these succulent spareribs – they will polish off every last shred of meat. This marinade can also be used for chicken thighs, drumsticks and pork chops.

4 Asian shallots, finely chopped
1 large garlic clove, finely chopped
4 teaspoons English mustard
4 teaspoons soy sauce
6 tablespoons hoisin sauce
1 tablespoon Sriracha chilli sauce
1 teaspoon honey
800 g/1¾ lbs. pork spareribs (or chicken wings, thighs, drumsticks or chops)
1 teaspoon sesame seeds (optional)

SERVES 4-6

In a bowl, mix together all the ingredients (except the meat) to make a marinade. Add the meat and rub the marinade in well. Cover and refrigerate for at least 30 minutes.

Preheat the oven to 200°C (400°F) Gas 6.

Transfer the meat to a roasting pan and roast in the preheated oven for 45 minutes or until cooked through and the juices run clear when you stick a knife in. The meat can also be grilled on a barbecue, in which case times will vary, so check that it's cooked through before serving.

Scatter the sesame seeds over the top before serving, if using.

KUNG PAO WINGS

These hot and spicy Chinese chicken wings are sautéed in a pan for tender meat and a sweet and sticky sauce. Serve with other Chinese inspired bites such as Sweet & Sour Popcorn Tofu (see page 102).

120 ml/½ cup white wine
120 ml/½ cup soy sauce
4 tablespoons sesame oil,
50 g/½ cup cornflour/
   cornstarch, dissolved
   in 120 ml/½ cup water
1.8 kg/4 lbs. chicken wings,
   halved at the joints, tips
   removed
85 g/3 oz. hot chilli paste
1½ tablespoons distilled
   white vinegar
3 tablespoons brown sugar
4 spring onions/scallions,
   chopped, plus extra to
   garnish
4 garlic cloves, finely chopped
450-g/16-oz. can water
   chestnuts, drained and
   sliced
100 g/1 cup chopped peanuts
1 fresh red chilli/chile, sliced,
   to garnish

SERVES 4–6

Combine 4 tablespoons of the wine, 4 tablespoons of the soy sauce, 2 tablespoons of the sesame oil and 4 tablespoons of the cornflour/cornstarch mixture in a bowl and mix together. Place the wings in a large, resealable plastic bag. Add the marinade, seal the bag and toss to coat. Place in the refrigerator to marinate overnight, or for at least 4 hours.

In a small bowl combine the remaining wine, soy sauce, oil and cornflour/cornstarch mixture with the chilli paste, vinegar and sugar. Mix together and add the chopped onion, garlic, water chestnuts and peanuts. Transfer the mixture to a medium frying pan/skillet and heat the sauce slowly until aromatic.

Meanwhile, remove the chicken from the marinade and sauté in a second large frying pan/skillet until the meat is cooked through and the juices run clear when the thickest part is pierced to the bone. When the sauce is aromatic, add the sautéed chicken to it and let it simmer together until the sauce thickens, then serve immediately. Garnish with the sliced chilli/chile and spring onion/scallion.

THAI GREEN CURRY WINGS

Of all the curries, Thai green curry seems to have the most flavour and aroma. Here, chicken wings are baked with a spicy green curry sauce – they are perfect for a Thai tapas feast!

vegetable oil, for greasing
2 tablespoons plain/
    all-purpose flour
2 teaspoons salt
2 teaspoons ground coriander
1.8 kg/4 lbs. chicken wings,
    halved at the joints, tips
    removed
5 tablespoons green chilli
    sauce (either hot or mild,
    depending on your taste)
4 tablespoons unsalted butter,
    melted
1 tablespoon fish sauce
2 teaspoons Thai green curry
    paste
3 tablespoons freshly
    chopped coriander/cilantro,
    to garnish
1 red chilli/chile, sliced,
    to garnish

**COCONUT CREAM
DIPPING SAUCE**
400-g/16-oz. can of
    coconut milk
225 g/1 cup brown sugar

SERVES 4-6

First, make the dipping sauce. Combine the ingredients in a medium saucepan and bring to the boil over a medium-high heat. Reduce the heat to medium-low and cook, stirring, for about 20 minutes until the mixture is thick and the volume has reduced by about half. Set aside until needed.

Preheat the oven to 200°C (400°F) Gas 6. Line 2–3 baking sheets with foil and grease with cooking spray or vegetable oil.

In a bowl, mix the flour with the salt and ground coriander. Add the chicken and toss to coat. Spread the chicken on the baking sheets in a single layer and sprinkle with vegetable oil.

Roast the chicken in the preheated oven for 45 minutes, turning once or twice, until browned and crispy and the juices run clear when the thickest part is pierced to the bone.

In a bowl, whisk together the chilli sauce, butter, fish sauce and curry paste. Add the cooked chicken wings to the sauce and toss. Sprinkle with the chopped coriander/cilantro and sliced chilli/chile and serve with Coconut Cream Dipping Sauce on the side.

BBQ PORK-BELLY SKEWERS

All of Sài Gòn is perfumed with smoke from honey-grilled pork at lunchtime, and bún thịt nuóng (grilled/broiled meat on noodles) is a favourite. It is a great example of Vietnamese cuisine: juicy, sweet, savoury and succulent meat with vermicelli, sharp pickles and herbs create layers of flavours and textures.

1 lemongrass stalk, finely chopped

a 5-cm/2-inch piece galangal, finely chopped (optional)

2 shallots, finely chopped

4 garlic cloves, chopped

1 tablespoon honey

2 teaspoons fish sauce

2 tablespoons vegetable oil

1 tablespoon tapioca starch

½ teaspoon black pepper

1 tablespoon sugar

1 teaspoon shrimp paste

400 g/14 oz. pork belly, cut into bite-size pieces

DIPPING SAUCE

4 tablespoons cider vinegar

4 tablespoons sugar

4 tablespoons fish sauce

2 garlic cloves, finely chopped

2 Bird's Eye chillies, finely chopped

4 tablespoons of hot water

TO SERVE

lettuce leaves

4 tablespoons roasted salted peanuts, crushed

pickled carrots and rice noodle salad (optional)

10–12 bamboo skewers, soaked in cold water for 30 minutes

SERVES 4

First, make the dipping sauce, mix all the ingredients in a bowl. Cover and refrigerate until ready to serve.

Put the lemongrass, galangal, shallots, garlic, honey, fish sauce, oil, tapioca starch, pepper, sugar and shrimp paste in a bowl. Mix well, add the pork pieces and rub the mixture into the meat. Marinate in the fridge for 20 minutes.

Preheat the oven to 180°C (350°F) Gas 4, or preheat a grill/broiler to high.

Push 3–4 pork belly pieces onto each soaked skewer. Cook in the preheated oven for about 18 minutes, or under a preheated grill/broiler for 12–15 minutes, until well browned.

Serve with lettuce leaves, a sprinkling of crushed peanuts, pickled carrots and a rice noodle salad, if liked.

THAI PEANUT CHICKEN WINGS

These moreish chicken wings are grilled/broiled for extra crispness and served with a warm peanut satay-style sauce.

4 garlic cloves, finely chopped
225 g/1 cup smooth peanut butter
120 ml/½ cup freshly squeezed lemon juice
1 tablespoon crushed chilli flakes/hot red pepper flakes, plus extra for garnish
1½ tablespoons ground cumin
250 ml/1 cup warm water
1.8 kg/4 lbs. chicken wings, halved at the joints, tips removed
sea salt flakes, to taste
fresh flat-leaf parsley, chopped
cucumber wedges, to serve

SERVES 4-6

Whisk together the garlic, peanut butter, lemon juice, crushed chilli flakes/hot red pepper flakes and ground cumin with the warm water. Season with salt.

Toss the chicken wings with 225 g/1 cup of the sauce, cover and marinate in the refrigerator overnight or for at least 2 hours.

Preheat the grill/broiler to high. Grill/broil the chicken, for 20–25 minutes, turning occasionally, until cooked through, lightly charred and the juices run clear when the thickest part is pierced to the bone.

Serve the wings with the remaining peanut sauce, topped with chopped flat-leaf parsley and crushed chilli flakes/hot red pepper flakes, accompanied by chunky cucumber wedges to counteract the spicy heat.

STICKY TERIYAKI WINGS

These oven-baked teriyaki wings are marinated in a tangy pineapple-based teriyaki sauce. Serve with green onion–ranch dipping sauce.

350 ml/1½ cups soy sauce
300 g/1½ cups sugar
175 ml/¾ cup pineapple juice
120 ml/½ cup vegetable oil
2 garlic cloves, finely chopped
1½ tablespoons finely
    chopped fresh ginger
350 ml/1½ cups water
1.8 kg/4 lbs. chicken wings,
    halved at the joints, tips
    removed

**GREEN ONION–RANCH
DIPPING SAUCE**
225 ml/1 cup sour cream
225 g/1 cup mayonnaise
35 g/½ cup finely chopped
    spring onions/scallions
1 tablespoon finely chopped
    fresh flat-leaf parsley
1 garlic clove, finely chopped
1 teaspoon Dijon mustard

SERVES 4-6

First make the dipping sauce by combining all the ingredients in a blender and whizzing until smooth. Transfer to a small bowl, cover and refrigerate until ready to serve.

Combine the soy sauce, sugar, pineapple juice, vegetable oil, garlic and ginger in a large bowl with the water. Stir until the sugar has dissolved. Pour the marinade into a large resealable plastic bag. Add the wings to the bag and marinate in the refrigerator overnight or for at least 4 hours.

Preheat the oven to 180°C (350°F) Gas 5. Line 2–3 baking sheets with foil.

Remove the chicken from the marinade and arrange on the baking sheets. Brush with the remaining marinade. Bake in the preheated oven for about 1 hour, or until the juices run clear when the thickest part is pierced to the bone.

Serve these wings with the green onion-ranch dipping sauce for a bar bite but add cooked rice noodles and wilted Chinese cabbage/pak choi for a more substantial plateful.

CHARRED SHRIMP WITH NAM JIM

This is such a simple yet effective dish and is great for diving into and getting your hands dirty with a big group of friends. The Nam Jim is a wonderfully vibrant Thai sauce that makes these totally addictive. Make sure you use the roots of the coriander/cilantro and not the leaves, as this is where all the flavour is. Healthy coconut palm sugar is used here, it has been used for hundreds of years in Southeast Asian cooking. Don't confuse it with Thai palm sugar, which comes in white hard blobs.

roots of 1 bunch of fresh
   coriander/cilantro plus
   reserved leaves for garnish
2 garlic cloves
2.5-cm/1-inch piece fresh
   ginger
1 large red chilli/chile,
   deseeded, plus extra slices
   for garnish
1 tablespoon coconut palm
   sugar
sea salt
2 teaspoons fish sauce
freshly squeezed juice of
   1 lime
8 raw king prawns/jumbo
   shrimp, shell on

ridged stovetop griddle pan/
   grill pan

SERVES 3-4

Using a pestle and mortar, pound the coriander/cilantro roots, garlic, ginger and chilli/chile until you get a paste. This will take a few minutes of fairly aggressive pounding! The skin of the chilli/chile will also come loose so when that happens, you should pick it out and discard it.

Add the sugar and pound, then add a little salt, the fish sauce and lime juice. Mix together and taste. Adjust it ever so slightly until you get the right balance.

Heat a stovetop griddle pan/grill pan over a high heat. Cut the prawns/shrimp lengthways down the middle of the belly, so you have long halves. Place them, flesh-side down, on the dry pan, cook for 2 minutes, then flip them over and cook for another 2 minutes.

Once cooked, arrange the prawns/shrimp together on a plate scattered with the reserved coriander/cilantro leaves and extra chilli/chile slices. Drizzle with Nam Jim and serve.

SPICY PORK SATAY SKEWERS
with peanut sauce

These spicy pork skewers dipped in peanut sauce are heaven on a stick. They are great for weekend get-togethers, when you want to make delicious, easy food with minimum kitchen time. You can also pop these on a barbecue and forgo the hob.

450 g/1 lb. pork tenderloin
coriander/cilantro leaves and lime wedges, to garnish

SPICY MARINADE
2 tablespoons rice wine vinegar
2 green chillies/ chiles, chopped
1 tablespoon soy sauce
1 large garlic clove, finely chopped
1 tablespoon toasted sesame oil
2 tablespoons fish sauce
2 tablespoons peanut/groundnut oil
2 tablespoons freshly chopped coriander/ cilantro leaves
1 tablespoon grated fresh ginger

PEANUT SAUCE
1 tablespoon peanut/ groundnut oil
1 garlic clove, finely chopped

2 red Thai chillies/ chiles, finely chopped
4 kaffir lime leaves
1 stalk lemongrass, cut into 4
1 teaspoon garam masala or curry powder
2 tablespoons dark brown sugar
225 g/1 cup peanut butter
250 ml/generous 1 cup coconut milk
30 g/⅓ cup unsweetened coconut flakes
finely grated zest and freshly squeezed juice of 1 lime
2 tablespoons fish sauce

18–20 short metal skewers

ridged stovetop griddle pan/grill pan

MAKES 18–20 SKEWERS

Slice the pork into ½-cm/1/4-inch thick pieces and put in a bowl. Mix together all the Spicy Marinade ingredients and pour over the pork. Cover and put in the refrigerator for 30 minutes.

To make the peanut sauce, heat the peanut oil in a saucepan over medium heat. Sauté the garlic, chillies/ chiles, kaffir lime leaves, lemongrass and garam masala for 2 minutes. Add the sugar and stir. Now add the peanut butter, coconut milk and coconut flakes, along with the lime zest and juice. Cook for 15 minutes. Take off the heat and stir in the fish sauce. Pour the mixture into a bowl and set aside.

Remove the pork from the refrigerator and thread onto the skewers.

Heat the griddle pan/grill pan over high heat until nearly smoking. Grill the pork skewers for 3–4 minutes each side until brown and caramelized.

Garnish the pork skewers with coriander/cilantro leaves and serve with lime wedges and the peanut sauce on the side.

YAKITORI-GLAZED MUSHROOM & CHICKEN SKEWERS

These salty-sweet glazed chicken skewers go down well with all the family! Fresh shiitake mushrooms, with their distinctive flavour, are a pleasing element in the dish.

16 white/cup mushrooms, stalks trimmed off
250 g/8 oz. boneless chicken breast, cut into short, thin strips
16 fresh shiitake mushrooms, halved, stalks trimmed off
½ green (bell) pepper, deseeded and cut into 2-cm/1-inch squares
2 spring onions/scallions, cut into 2-cm/¾-inch lengths
finely sliced red chilli/chile, to garnish (optional)

YAKITORI GLAZE
50 ml/3 tablespoons rice wine or Amontillado sherry
50 ml/3 tablespoons mirin
50 ml/3 tablespoons light soy sauce
1 tablespoon white granulated sugar
¼ teaspoon salt

8 long metal skewers

SERVES 4-6

Make the yakitori glaze by placing the rice wine or sherry, mirin, soy sauce, sugar and salt in a small saucepan. Bring to the boil and boil for 1 minute until melted together into a syrupy glaze. Turn off the heat.

Thread the white/cup mushrooms, chicken, shiitake mushrooms, green (bell) pepper and spring onions/scallions onto the skewers.

Preheat the grill/broiler to high. Brush the prepared skewers generously with the yakitori glaze. Grill/broil the skewers for 8–10 minutes, until the chicken is cooked through, brushing repeatedly with the glaze and turning the skewers over halfway through.

Sprinkle with some finely sliced chilli/chile if liked and serve at once.

INDEX

RECIPE CREDITS

Valerie Aikman-Smith
Korean sticky ribs
Salt and pepper squid
Spicy pork satay skewers

Caroline Artiss
Vietnamese chicken and quinoa
  bites

Jordan Bourke
Charred shrimp with nam jim
Courgette/zucchini onion bhajis
Japanese okonomiyaki pancakes
Smoked mackerel sushi rolls
Tempura vegetables and shrimp
Vietnamese shrimp-stuffed

Dunja Gulin
Vegan maki and California rolls
Vegan temaki rolls with seed pâté

Tori Haschka
Sashimi and cucumber bites

Carol Hilker
Asian caramel wings
Chinese egg rolls
Kung pao wings
Sake wings
Sticky teriyaki wings
Thai green curry wings

Thai peanut chicken wings
Thai-style fried chicken wings
Vietnamese summer rolls

Vicky Jones
Indian lentil and rice dosas
Korean moong pancakes

Jackie Kearney
Cauliflower and kale pakoras
Oothapam
Sweet 'n' sour popcorn tofu

Jenny Linford
Crispy chicken wontons
Korean kimchi pancake
Mushroom pakoras
Mushroom-filled lettuce cups
Steamed Asian black garlic scallops
Taiwanese-style garlic pork bao
Yakitori-glazed mushroom and
  chicken skewers

Loretta Liu
Barbecue pork puffs
Beef bulgogi puffs
Chinese turnip cake
Chinese vegetable clamshell buns
Fried shrimp and scallop bao
Golden pumpkin and leek dumplings
Hoisin duck puffs

Lotus leaf rice dumplings
Mushroom puff pastry dumplings
Pork and cabbage shumai
Pork and leek jiaozi
Red Thai curry and lentil bao
Salmon and mushroom dumplings
Scallop and crab dumplings
Shrimp and mango wontons
Spicy chicken and shrimp
  dumplings
Traditional shrimp dumplings

Uyen Luu
BBQ pork-belly skewers
Rice rolls with pork and shrimp
Smoked duck summer rolls
Vietnamese BBQ spareribs
Vietnamese pork-stuffed crêpes

Dan May
Green chilli/chile bhajis

Nitisha Patel
Amritsari fish pakoras
Tandoori-spiced lamb chops

Louise Pickford
Beef bulgogi and rice noodle wraps

Milli Taylor
Chinese duck breast pancakes

PHOTOGRAPHY CREDITS

Ed Anderson 87

Peter Cassidy 13, 51, 70, 82, 83

Helen Cathcart 73

Tara Fisher 1, 53–57, 79, 118

Jonathan Gregson 139

Louise Hagger 2, 6, 10, 16–45, 49,
  58, 59

Erin Kunkel 78, 115

William Reavell 66–69, 98, 107

Toby Scott 92, 119, 120, 123, 127,
  128, 132, 135

Ian Wallace 4, 7, 50, 88, 104, 105,
  110–112

Kate Whitaker 95, 100, 121, 133,
  136, 137

Isobel Wield 96

Clare Winfield 3, 5, 11, 14, 46, 47,
  61–65, 74–77, 80, 81, 84, 85, 91,
  99, 102, 103, 108, 109, 116, 117,
  124, 131, 140, endpapers